ADVANCE PRAISE FOR
THE FINAL FIGHT FOR FREEDOM

"A chilling warning of where America could be headed if we do not change course. In the best tradition of Winston Churchill writing about the dire threats facing England in the 1930s, the Stewarts layout with sobering clarity why America must prevail in the technology race with China and Russia. Unlike those who merely shine a light on our problems, the Stewarts offer solutions for our nation at this critical time. Everyone interested in America's national security should read this book."

—**Robert C. O'Brien**, Former Trump National Security Advisor
Ambassador (ret.)

"Vividly portrays the great arch of freedom at the brink of peril. The intentional abuse by big tech/big media for political gain has shaken our frontier. Through courageous American tales juxtapositioned against real world costs of a bankrupt media and corrupt government agencies, we are starkly shown why the cost of freedom is so high, and why the final fight can and will be won. America is ready to be America again, we need only be brave enough to follow this riveting journey this book takes us on."

—**Kash Patel,** Former Deputy Assistant to the President for Counterterrorism;
Former Principal Deputy to the Acting DNI; Former Chief of Staff for the Department of
Defense

The Final Fight for Freedom:

HOW TO SAVE OUR COUNTRY FROM CHAOS AND WAR

POST HILL PRESS

By Congressman Chris Stewart & Dane Stewart

A POST HILL PRESS BOOK
ISBN: 978-1-63758-214-5
ISBN (eBook): 978-1-63758-215-2

The Final Fight for Freedom:
How to Save Our Country from Chaos and War
© 2021 by Congressman Chris Stewart & Dane Stewart
All Rights Reserved

Post Hill Press
New York • Nashville
posthillpress.com

Published in the United States of America
1 2 3 4 5 6 7 8 9 10

To all those who are willing to stand up for freedom.
— Chris Stewart

For Cass. It's all for you.
— Dane Stewart

TABLE OF CONTENTS

A NOTE FROM THE AUTHORS

A few notes on the content and structure of this book.

First, the threats outlined here are both realistic and imminent. They spring from our own internal chaos, the growing hatred and distrust of each other, the technological threats we face, some of which didn't exist even a few years ago, and the malicious intentions of foreign actors. We lay out these threats as clearly as we can.

Everything written here is based on open-source US and foreign intelligence, trends in recent history, public reporting, and the actions of real people. The technologies, tactics, threats, information, and foreign efforts against this nation are as accurate as we can portray them without revealing highly sensitive or classified information.

Second, though this is a book of nonfiction, very often ideas can best be illustrated through fictionalized first-person accounts and personal points of view. You will see these types of narratives throughout this work, all of which are based on real-world events. Hopefully, these first-person accounts make the arguments both more interesting and powerful.

The theme of this book is this: Two wars are coming. The first will be internal. Indeed, we are forming the battle lines for that war now. Then, once we have weakened ourselves to the point of fracturing our nation, our enemies will pounce, bringing a catastrophic technological storm upon a weakened nation.

Everything is on the line now.

PROLOGUE

WASHINGTON, DC

December, near future

The situation certainly was a bitter irony, if nothing else.

Darren Hardy had spent the better part of a decade vehemently opposing the private ownership of handguns and vilifying anyone who thought differently. Now, surrounded by the dead and dying, the violence and fear, he would literally give his left arm for a Glock and a dozen rounds.

Like most of his media colleagues, he'd spent much of his time over the past few years dieting to cut the fat from his body and carving his physique to meet the high standards required of his profession. Now, he hadn't had a single scrap to eat in two days. And just a few meager meals in the past week. He'd kill for a bowl of rice. At least he thought he would. He hadn't yet had a chance to test the proposition. But he knew that time was coming...

As the nation's most recognizable television journalist, Darren Hardy had spent his career warning about global warming and the "coming extinction." Socially conscious, he'd played his part in getting people to accept the proposition that they were facing an environmental disaster, one with inevitable and monumental consequences. He'd always wondered what that "extinction-level event" would be like.

Now he knew. But he never guessed it would have come from this!

"Do we have anything to eat today, Daddy?"

Darren looked up to see his daughter emerge from her bedroom and plod down the stairs. Dark-haired and dark-eyed, she had always been all smiles and energy and giggles. But over the past few weeks, her body had taken on a painfully different appearance. Her face was hollow now, gaunt and angular, her eyes deep in their sockets, her mouth stretched across her jaw. She was feeling a little better, but the hunger and stomach pain had wreaked havoc on her small frame, stretching her thin, so much so that he hardly recognized her. He knew she was starving.

"Not yet," he told her. "Soon, I promise."

She frowned briefly, then sat down on the bottom stair and leaned her head against the wall. "Let's get you warm," Darren whispered as he laid a blanket across her shoulders.

He knew she was confused and terrified. And she desperately missed her mom. She used to ask him why. What had happened? How long were they going to stay locked behind their front door? As their hunger grew, she started telling him they should leave, get out of the house, see what was out there. He had tried to reassure her, telling her things about FEMA and the police and the National Guard, telling her things about the government and how they would certainly send people who would help them, that everything would be better soon and that they just needed a little bit of faith in the system.

But he knew she didn't believe him any longer. He could tell she also knew that she was dying.

And that her dad was too afraid to leave the house.

She stared at him for several long seconds then closed her eyes and seemed to drift away. He wasn't sure if she was sleeping. It seemed like that was all she did now. Sleep. And ask for food.

He'd give anything if they could all go back to how life used to be, back to the time when he could feed his own child. His heart would have broken a little more if it were capable of such a thing. But he'd been through too much, seen too much violence, endured too much horror in recent weeks to suffer any more heartbreak. Darren's feelings had narrowed down now to only two things. Hunger and shame. Being a typical American, sheltered and naïve, he'd failed miserably to protect his family.

His thoughts drifted to Irene, the mother of his child, and a familiar ache returned to his throat. She had been so good, an honest-to-goodness angel. And though they had separated, he had always loved her. Just not as much, it turned out, as he had loved his work.

But now she was gone.

Because he couldn't take care of his family....

Darren shook his head and blinked away the tears. Tears wouldn't help him now. Neither would his phony friends at the FBI. And they certainly wouldn't help his daughter. He had to focus on how he was going to keep her alive.

He stood and moved to the window. He felt a cool draft and smelled the smoke in the air from random fires and the few wood-burning fireplaces that still worked in some of the old homes that filled this part of the city. He pulled the blinds back and looked through the shattered pane. Despair settled around him like the ash that had settled on the city.

Over the past twelve months, Darren had watched as the United States of America had committed suicide.

How did it happen?

It had started with another tight and outrageously emotional election, then quickly descended from there. A frozen Congress, impotent to fix it. A Supreme Court too terrified to step into the political mess. An incompetent president trying to govern a nation where more than half the states had rejected his authority.

Then stepped in the shadow government, those deeply entrenched bureaucrats who actually made the government work. But they simply were not up to it either.

Everything started to fail.

First came a wave of rising prices that, over the course of a year, mounted to a level of inflation that had never been seen before. Then came crushing job reports. More and more money created out of thin air. Shortages. Spiking interest rates. Waiting in lines for gas. Jokes about the US becoming Venezuela. But behind the acid humor was real fear. Thinking the time of crisis was the time to go big—as if the years before had not been big enough—the president enacted an agenda that was beyond radical.

Throughout it all, Darren and the rest of the supporting media had done a remarkable job of manipulating the minds of the people. Teaming with Big Tech, and using suppression technologies made available by none other than the Chinese Communist Party, they eliminated any voice not consistent with their own values and program, destroying any who tried to resist.

But it could not hold. They went too far. They went too fast. The people were not ready for the crisis or the controls. Too many of them were terrified. Too many of them were angry.

Too many of them were armed....

Riots and violence intensified with each new disaster, making the summer of 2020 look like a party in the streets.

Then came the failure of the banking system. At least that's what they had said it was. Some thought it was something else, some kind of cyber attack upon the financial system from overseas. Either way, in an instant more than half of the nation's bank accounts disappeared into the electronic void. More riots. Growing violence. From coast to coast, fires burned in all the major cities. When the violence expanded to the rural states and small towns, many members of the incompetent Congress—paralyzed and unable to pass any meaningful legislation other than to spend more money, which at this point was fairly pointless—abandoned their efforts and went home to protect their families from the growing chaos.

Seeing federal leadership abandon their own people, the nation seemed to explode. More riots. More rage. Unfathomable hunger. States threatening to secede, some of them actually leaving, though the legality of that was as contested as the election. The National Guard was called out, but to little avail; the situation simply overwhelmed them. Everyone soon learned that when people are scared and hungry, the rules suddenly change. The loss of faith and compassion made them vicious.

Another event, this one based in Russia—or perhaps it was China, or North Korea, who really knew?—but wherever it began, someone introduced a deadly virus that quickly spread. At that point, most of the police refused to report to work. They had their own families to find a way to feed and protect.

With the nation already on its knees, the final blow was served when most of the electrical grid went down. Some said the Chinese were responsible, but again, no one really knew. Regardless, the chaos was complete. No food. No medicine. No gas. Starvation from coast to coast. Hospitals were overrun. The president finally ordered the army to the streets, a move that was as efficacious as slapping a bandage on a patient with stage four cancer. Besides, it turned out no one had ever suggested that it might be a good idea for the nation to store some food, not even enough to feed its own army. So, most of the soldiers spent more time looting than protecting anyone around them, some of them even turning their weapons upon their fellow citizens.

In less than a year, the nation was in ruin, the survivors left fighting for dirty coats and scraps of food. All that remained was truly brutal violence. That was the thing that really shocked him, how quickly and completely it took hold. Ammunition became the only currency that mattered, guns more valuable than gold.

Yeah, looking back at the beginning, Darren realized he might have added a little to the anger and uncertainty. Sure, he had been a critic of the country. He'd preached against whiteness, railed against the capitalistic system, the economic injustice, the plight of the undocumented workers, the opposing party in DC. And yeah, he'd occasionally complained with a voice that had been a bit shrill.

But he hadn't intended this! He certainly wasn't in any way responsible. Not him. He was a man of peace. It had been the others, the mob, who'd done what two hundred years of foreign enemies had not been able to do: bring the greatest nation the world had ever seen to its knees.

No, he and his progressive colleagues had meant well. It wasn't supposed to be like this.

He looked out on the city. DC was barely a city anymore, torn apart by the riots, violence, and the rage of starving mobs. Rubble and ruin were everywhere. It was practically a ghost town. No, not a ghost town. Something worse. In a ghost town, all you had to worry about were the ghosts. There were many more things to worry about now.

Another draft blew through the broken window. He smelled the rank odor of smoke and excrement and dead bodies. He didn't think he'd ever get used to the stench of rot and decay.

But at that moment it wasn't the appearance or smell of his new world that bothered him most. It wasn't the sound of gunfire in the distance, nor the smoke and orange glow that revealed that somewhere in the distance the city was on fire again.

No, it was the setting sun that terrified him most—for then would come the darkness.

He felt a chill run down his spine.

Darren had spent his life laboring under the assumption that people weren't animals, that most people were compassionate and willing to lend a hand. Utter nonsense—he knew that now. Civilization was the only thing that had kept the worst of human nature in check, and it had proven to be no more solid than a wafer-thin sheet of ice, cracking in an instant and letting them all fall.

Which is why, like his ancient ancestors, he had relearned to fear the dark.

In these moments, when he was honest with himself, he would admit that the fear was what had kept him from leaving the city. That, and the irrational hope that help was on its way.

His daughter made a soft sound, and he turned and looked at her thin frame. She was having another bad dream, sitting there, her head against the wall at the bottom of the stairs.

He knew if they were going to live, he had to make a decision.

He took a deep breath and reviewed his options, which were precious few and equally terrible.

He'd heard that one of his colleagues had sold his wife to one of the gangs. But he knew he'd never do anything like that. He'd never sell his daughter. He still understood that some things were worse than death.

He could steal. But he didn't have any weapons. And he was not a strong man. He had no training or experience to make him believe he could ever win a physical confrontation with most of the people left on the streets; the weaker ones were already gone. But if he planned it right, there was a chance—

although a small one—that he could steal a meal or two for himself and his daughter.

But even if he were successful, he'd only get enough food to last them a few days. And if he was unsuccessful, then he'd be dead, and his daughter would be alone.

The last option: He could start walking. It was exactly what his daughter had been pushing him to do. But fear had held him back. Fear of leaving his house. Fear of what he'd find. Fear of what the world had become.

He'd heard the crazy rumors. Baltimore was just as bad. Philadelphia was worse. Rumors that the Black Plague had come back. The Russians were occupying some of the cities.

The stench of death and anarchy everywhere.

But glancing at his daughter, the only family he had left, he knew that whatever was out there couldn't possibly be worse than their present fate. He had waited long enough, perhaps too long. He didn't know how far he'd make it, especially if in his weakened state he had to carry his little girl; but he knew if they stayed, they were going to die here, hungry and alone.

Without another thought, he drank what was left of the water he had stored, grabbed what few supplies he had, picked up his sleeping daughter, stepped out the front door, and started walking.

Like millions of others in his country, Darren Hardy was now an American refugee.

Book One

NATIONAL SUICIDE

If destruction be our lot, we must ourselves be its
author and finisher. As a nation of freemen, we must
live through all time, or die by suicide.

— Abraham Lincoln

Abraham Lincoln understood the only real threat our nation has ever faced, the only thing that could actually destroy us, was the reality that we might destroy ourselves. And that hasn't changed over time. What he said was true when he said it and it's still true today.

The United States of America is the wealthiest, most generous, energetic, creative, and powerful nation on Earth. We have the strongest military the world has ever seen, and our adversaries know this. No other nation can destroy us.

But we can destroy ourselves.

Like many great nations that have come and gone before us, including some even in our time, we can commit national suicide. Indeed, it is apparent that we are deep into the process of doing that.

We know…we know…that sounds crazy! *The suicide of our nation!* Not here! Not now! Not after all that we've been through, not after all that we've accomplished. *We are the United-Freakin'-States! No way that's going to happen!*

Until it does.

Because if we don't change our present trajectory, it's not just a possibility, it's a nearly inevitable fact.

But could it *really* come to what we just described? Americans dying on the streets. The federal government collapsing. Local governments proving incapable of providing any services. Police protection disappearing like fog in the dark night. A financial collapse. Then, seeing our nation falter, our enemies attack with cyber warfare or a bio attack. Could any one of us actually become an American refugee? Is it realistic to think that things could spiral out of control to the point that we, citizens of the greatest nation on Earth, could be incapable of defending ourselves?

Surely that couldn't happen!

A friend in Israel once told us a phrase that we have often thought about. *Just because something's never happened, doesn't mean it never will.* The citizens of Israel may say this because they understand—far better than any other nation—that it's better to consider the impossible possibility, the idea that seems preposterous, the thing that only *crazy* people have considered, than to find yourself unprepared.

Okay, some may say, "So maybe it *could* happen…hypothetically—not that it will—but sure, maybe someday…when our grandchildren or maybe their children are old. But it *couldn't* happen now. We are generations away from such a horrible event."

But the fact is, no, it won't take years to get to the tipping point. We are at the tipping point now. The inflection point is here. And once we walk off that cliff, it won't take long to reach the hard rock of reality at the bottom. The collapse could come in a few years or months, maybe even weeks.

Once we have divided ourselves to the point that the only adversary we are interested in fighting is ourselves, once we have come to the point where we hate each other more than we hate any of our adversaries, once we have reached the point where the only battle we think worth fighting isn't with Russian or Chinese aggressors, but with the idiot next door (the guy *who voted for him!*), once we no longer take notice of the world, nor challenge our adversaries, nor care about what is going on in the world's hotspots— that is when our enemies will strike.

Which will bring us to the second battle we'll have to fight. Because if 1859 was the last time that our nation was so divided, then 1939 was the last time we faced an adversary so committed to removing us from our place as the leader of the free world.

A HOUSE DIVIDED

If you think such talk is crazy, remember that wise men, including more than just Lincoln, have seen this possibility from the very beginning. When asked what sort of government the Constitutional Convention delegates had created, Benjamin Franklin famously quipped, "A republic, if you can keep it."

He knew how difficult it would be. He knew the long-term viability of the infant nation was not certain. Indeed, quite the opposite: he knew what they had created chafed against the very nature of man, the nature of societies, the nature and history of every nation that had ever come before. The fall of man into a fallen world had surely proven that.

Such a sentiment was more recently expressed by Ronald Reagan when he said, "We didn't pass [freedom] to our children in the bloodstream. It must be fought for, protected, and handed on for them to do the same, or one day we will spend our sunset years telling our children and our children's children what it was once like in the United States where men were free."

It's hard to imagine, isn't it, that one day we might sit with our children and remind them that we once used to be free!

Or, as Reagan said more succinctly, "Freedom is never more than one generation away from extinction."

The reality is that one generation is all it takes to lose it. And we are in the closing moments of that generation, leaving our nation standing on the edge of a cliff.

When we read quotations like this from Reagan, most of us think he was talking about losing our freedom to some foreign threat. And he probably was. But that isn't the greatest threat we face now, or at least it's not the *first* threat we face. Clearly, the first battle for our survival will be fought from within, the battle lines growing clear. We see the division. The constant talk of civil war. The lack of truth. The hatred far too many Americans feel toward each other. The dividing not into teams, but into *tribes*, entities that seem to exist for assault and division. The silencing of views. Shunning. Shaming. Ostracizing those who don't think the right way. In the current environment, we're taking our fellow Americans, those who don't think exactly as we do, and reducing them to outcasts. They are imbeciles, evil and selfish and thuggish fools. We want to silence them. Fire them. Cast them from among us. Poison a neighbor's dog because they are on the wrong side of the aisle. Make them beg for forgiveness, which will never be granted, and then cast them out.

Perhaps Alexis de Tocqueville said it best:

> Tyranny in democratic republics does not proceed in the
> same way, however. It ignores the body and goes straight
> for the soul. The master no longer says: You will think
> as I do or die. He says: You are free not to think as I do.

You may keep your life, your property, and everything else. But from this day forth you shall be as a stranger among us. You will retain your civic privileges, but they will be of no use to you. For if you seek the votes of your fellow citizens, they will withhold them, and if you seek only their esteem, they will feign to refuse even that. You will remain among men, but you will forfeit your rights to humanity. When you approach your fellow creatures, they will shun you as one who is impure. And even those who believe in your innocence will abandon you, lest they, too, be shunned in turn. Go in peace, I will not take your life, but the life I leave you with is worse than death.

With our "woke" and "cancel culture," that is exactly where we are today. *I will not take your life, but the life I leave you with is worse than death.*

And it should terrify every one of us.

Because the fight before us goes as deep as our national soul. This isn't about politics or ideas out of DC. We are well past the time of arguing over policies and economics. Should the corporate tax rate be 21 percent or 27 percent? What is the right number of people we will allow to immigrate to this country? Is the government better able to provide health care than the private sector? Such questions, important as they are, are not the issues that will condemn or save our nation. The questions we are grappling with, the things we actually don't know and we have to figure out, cut to the very core of our nation and the very definition of our future:

Is America sustainable? Is it worth defending? Is it good? Is it time to tear it down and start over? What does it mean to be an American? What does our history teach us about ourselves?

CLOUDS ON THE HORIZON

We believe there are meaningful landmarks along the road that can tell us where we are headed, warning signs to alert us of what lies ahead. Surely these are a few of the many warning signs around us:

Privatization of Election Process

The 2020 federal election was, to a disconcerting degree, privatized when Facebook's Mark Zuckerberg and other tech titans donated more than half a billion dollars to state election management processes. (Amazingly, this is more money than was appropriated by the federal government, $400 million, in the CARES Act to fund the election security during the pandemic.) Zuckerberg alone donated nearly $420 million to various nonprofit organizations, with $350 million going to the *Safe Elections Project*, which essentially created a two-tier election system favoring swing Democratic cities, counties, and states.

But it's okay, nothing to worry about here, because, thankfully, Mr. Zuckerberg and other tech giants have assured us they have no political bias, nor particularly any bias against conservatives or former president Trump.

Whew. That's a relief!

Federal Reserve Bank Props

The last few years have normalized what used to be considered fringe in the financial world, tearing the mask from the fallacy that our financial institutions are capable of any introspection regarding the impacts of their actions. No better example exists than the Federal Reserve Bank's frantic effort to prop up the economy beyond any common sense.

As an example, for more than thirty years the Federal Reserve's policy has been to maintain a constant and stable M1 money supply, the primary measure of liquid assets within our economy. After a full generation of stability, 2020 saw M1 money supply explode on a percentage basis by more than 65 percent.

65 percent! In a single year!

Another astounding example: *The Wall Street Journal* (April 20, 2021) reported on the frightening spectacle of an economy awash in free money:

> "A cryptocurrency that was created as a joke exploded into plain view on Wall Street on Monday, with a surge in dogecoin sending its 2021 return above 8,100%— more than double the gains on the S&P 500, including dividends, since 1988.

> "Dogecoin's rise from a quirky meme into a widely traded asset worth about $50 billion—more than Marriott International Inc. or Ford Motor Co.—is the latest act of financial alchemy by rapidly moving individual investors who have used access to no-fee trading platforms and a wave of government stimulus money to transform markets over the past year."

And if that's not entertaining enough, the report continued:

> "Someone pointed us to Hometown International (HWIN), which owns a single deli in rural New Jersey. The deli had $21,772 in sales in 2019 and only $13,976 in 2020, as it was closed due to COVID from March to September. HWIN reached a market cap of $113 million on February 8.

> "The largest shareholder is also the CEO/CFO/Treasurer and a Director, who also happens to be the wrestling coach of the high school next door to the deli."

Soaring National Debt

During a year when our tax base was decimated by the forced destruction of a significant percentage of our small- and medium-sized businesses, the backbone of our economy, the 2020 annual federal deficit surged to $3.3 trillion.

Gone are the days when the Tea Party rebelled because President Obama spent $800 billion during the Great Recession; 2020 saw the federal government spend more than three trillion in economic stimulus.

This massive gush of spending pushed our total debt to 98 percent of our national GDP, a tipping point we have been warned about for years. And the debt in 2021 and beyond is predicted to be much worse.

Perhaps we should remember what Hemingway said in *The Sun Also Rises*.

> "How did you go bankrupt?"

> "Two ways. Gradually, then suddenly."

Modern Monetary Theory (MMT)

Any good socialist loves this, which explains why it's being embraced by so many Democrats in Washington. In its simplest form, MMT states that you can print all of the money you want, so long as you have a corresponding increase in demand. Print money. Have the government spend it. Then do it all again.

So long as a sovereign nation is able to control its own money supply, the national debt doesn't matter—or so the MMT theory goes.

But it doesn't take a PhD in economics to see the long-term viability of such an economic theory is zero. Yet a group of elite PhDs have convinced many of our elected officials of the merits of MMT. Free healthcare for everyone! *Sweet!* Ninety-three trillion dollars to implement the Green New Deal. *We can do that!* A couple trillion to buy electric cars for everyone. *What could go wrong?* Ten or twenty trillion for roads and bridges. Free college for everyone. *Sure!* (Except, of course, for the tradesmen, electricians, and builders. No free college for them! Not when there are important studies that need to be performed in gender theory and global warming.)

It's stunning that not just a few, but now *most* Democrats in Washington support these policies, leaving average Americans to shake their heads in wonder.

Shattered Faith in Elections

Soon after the 2020 election, nearly half the nation believed the election was rigged. Remarkably, even 30 percent of Democrats believed it was likely the election results were fraudulent.

But how can that be surprising, after an election process that looked more likely to have taken place in Columbia or Venezuela than in the US? Absentee voting that extended for weeks, much of it done by mail-in ballots, millions of them sent whether the voter requested them or not. Unmonitored drop boxes stuffed with ballots that had nothing close to normally accepted chain-of-custody standards. States that took days to count their votes instead of hours. Late night shutdown of the counting. Hundreds of sworn affidavits, under threat of criminal perjury, testifying of potential fraud and irregularities. Statistical experts claiming nearly impossible results.

The list of concerns is credible and long.

In addition, we know that China worked to influence the election and our own intelligence organizations sought to suppress this information. We also know that several tech billionaires spent tens of millions of dollars (while using shell organizations to hide their efforts) to influence US elections. Their efforts include creating thousands of fake Russian accounts to target Republican candidates, publishing false Facebook ads from fake accounts to stifle turnout in special elections, publishing misleading news stories, and donating millions of dollars to cover the legal defense of those involved in the illegal targeting of certain candidates.

No republic can survive such a breakdown of faith in the basic institution of the electoral process.

China without a Fight

Recent revelations have shown that tens of thousands of Chinese Communist Party members have been infiltrated into high positions in Western governments and businesses. And it's important to remember this: the CCP is not just another political party. A member of the CCP isn't the equivalent of a Democrat or Republican being placed in a position of power. The CCP is something much more. Something very different.

It is a very competitive process to become a member of Chinese Communist Party. In fact, it's about as competitive as it is to be admitted into an Ivy League university, with only about 5 percent of Chinese citizens making the cut. And consider the solemn oath that each Party member must swear upon admittance. *"It is my will to join the Communist Party of China, uphold the Party's program, observe the provisions of the Party Constitution, fulfill a Party member's duties, carry out the Party's decisions, strictly observe Party discipline, guard Party secrets, be loyal to the Party, work hard, fight for communism throughout my life, be ready at all times to sacrifice my all for the Party and the people, and never betray the Party."*

Consider a few lines from the oath again: *Guard Party secrets. Be loyal to the Party. Fight for communism throughout my life. Be ready at all times to sacrifice my all for the Party.*

Is it possible that, after taking such an oath, these CCP members who have been placed in Western embassies, agencies, universities, and industries are not working to advance the interest of the CCP?

China has stolen hundreds of billions of dollars of Western technology, manipulated markets, recruited hundreds of Western spies, forced millions of ethnic Uighurs into concentration camps, built an entire city dedicated to bio research, including research on humans, created a thriving market in human organ harvesting from political prisoners and Falun Gong, suppressed and persecuted millions of Tibetans, built a modern military to intimidate and threaten their neighbors...

Nearly all of this goes unchallenged by the US media, universities, Hollywood, or businesses.

Political Ethics of Death

Prominent US medical "ethicists" have suggested that, in order to "level the playing field," COVID-19 vaccinations should have been prioritized to individuals not based on risk, age, and underlying health concerns, but upon race—placing us in the untenable position of immunizing the young and healthy over the aged and infirm who are of the wrong color or ethnicity.

No nation can survive policies which literally place virtue-signaling above life and death.

Embracing Violence

In a recent Cato poll, more than a third of young Americans said that violence against their fellow Americans was justified.

A prominent progressive author recently wrote that the burning and destruction in Minneapolis after the death of George Floyd, including the burning and destruction of the Third Precinct police headquarters, evoked feelings of "undiluted elation," "beauty," and a "triumph of hope."

How does one speak to such a person—and there are millions just like him—who see violence and destruction as justified in advancing their political goals?

Fighting the Rule of Law

What we are witnessing is not just a cultural war, but an assault on the very rule of law. The Justice Brett Kavanaugh confirmation hearings were a good example of the effort to rescind legal principles and precedents that go back more than eight hundred years, even to the Magna Carta. The presumption of innocence until proven guilty. The right to face your accuser. Rules of evidence. All of these are under assault in a massive and well-coordinated drive to weaken our judicial system.

Corruption of Law Enforcement

During the closing months of the Obama administration, the FBI and DOJ opened multiple investigations into Trump associates, all of whom were private US citizens, which had the effect of smearing and destroying the lives of innocent people, all to achieve a political objective. The predicate for opening these investigations was not based upon *mere flimsy* evidence, it was based upon *no* evidence, and worse: at times, it was based upon *manufactured* evidence.

Reading the Warning Signs

The affronts to our society could fill a landfill. Taken together, they leave Americans feeling we live in a world that's been turned on its head. Nothing makes sense anymore. And it's not just that everything is changing, it's that it is changing *so fast*. Things we thought we might see at some point in our lifetimes we now see by the end of the week. We just can't keep up. The end result is half of Americans think they live in a nation where their countrymen have lost their minds. And they know, deep inside, that the other half think the same thing about them!

More worrisome is the fact that far too many believe those who disagree with them aren't just wrong, but that they are evil. For example, in a recent poll, 82 percent of Democrats said Trump supporters were the number one threat facing our nation. Imagine that! The number one issue facing our country isn't the pandemic or China or Russia or the cost of healthcare or the economy or protecting the Bill of Rights. No, 82 percent of Democrats feel the number one threat to our country is the fact that half of their neighbors voted differently than they did. White nationalists (which in the progressive mind is just another word for Trump supporters) came in as the number two threat. Racism (which in the progressive mind is just another word for Trump supporters) came in at number three. Why? Because our culture has convinced many Democrats that Republicans are evil, that they are a threat to democracy and their future. Which is why they don't just hate former president Trump; they also hate those who voted for him.

Are we any longer "one nation, under God," or are there now two nations existing within the same borders?

And how did we get here? What has brought us to the point where our future is actually in peril?

And what will happen to us, and to the rest of the world, if we stumble or fall? Will China, our primary adversary, move against us once we have weakened ourselves to the point of vulnerability? What are they likely to do? What weapons will they bring against us?

We need to understand the answers to those questions. And to really understand them, we have to look at how deep the problems really are.

ALONG THE TEXAS-MEXICO BORDER

February

The pair of soldiers who crossed over the American border on foot couldn't have stood in starker contrast to each other. Standing 6'6" and with a muscled frame to match his height, Peter Hardy looked like the TV version of a warrior. Carlos Ramirez, on the other hand, was 5'8", of average build, tough as nails, and ethnically ambiguous—a true representative of the American melting pot. Dressed in civilian clothes and with backpacks, they looked out of place in the desert. But that was okay. They only had to walk a mile. And it was dark.

The soldiers made their way through the desert. They'd spent the last week in Mexico working undercover ops, meeting with the few Mexican officials who still had the guts to work against the narco-terrorists. Once finished, the easiest way home wasn't to cross at a border checkpoint and be questioned, especially since they were military, but like a hundred thousand others every month, just to walk. So, they'd been dropped off a few kilometers behind them and arranged a ride to pick them up once they made it across the border.

Dark clouds covered what little light could have been thrown by the moon and stars, and the smell of coming rain filled the air. The border was unmarked, but Peter figured the next few steps would take them across the latitudinal line that defined the United States of America.

Carlos looked at the GPS, the dim light of the display gleaming in the darkness. Peter looked away, not wanting to spoil his night vision.

"Three…two…one…welcome home," Carlos said.

Peter exhaled deeply. Always in the past, whenever he had placed his boots on American soil, he felt instantly safe and at home. But no longer.

His home had changed.

Sometimes being home now just felt…he didn't know…wrong. And he knew that being on American soil didn't mean that he was among friends.

The transformation of his home into something he no longer recognized had started out with a handful of distresses: political dysfunction, growing hatred, more political dysfunction, more violence and division.…

With each event, people got angrier. And Washington got more powerful. And more brazen in their interactions with the people.

For a while, Peter had considered these events as nothing more than anomalies that would disappear with time. But with each passing year, the weird and the wild seemed only to multiply until he was suspicious of virtually every piece of information, every organization, every proclaimed lie or truth he was told, leading to the point that he even questioned his superior officers.

As he and Carlos continued through the Texas desert, his mind drifted to a conversation he'd had with a fellow soldier several months before.

"Mark my words: if the government can send the CIA against US citizens, they can also send the military," the colonel had said.

"No way," Peter had replied.

But now he wondered…

Peter knew they were getting near the rendezvous site, and the muscles in his body coiled tight. If he had concerns, he needed to voice them now. "Do you trust the drop?" he quietly asked his partner.

Carlos snorted. "What do you mean?"

Peter didn't answer. Carlos waited a minute and then said, "Don't be absurd." He sounded a little too convinced.

Peter couldn't help noticing his friend hadn't actually answered his question. "Do you trust the drop?" he asked a second time.

This time Ramirez thought before he answered. "Yes. I think we can trust the drop."

"Even with the flash drive?" Peter asked. Underneath his breath, he cursed. Why had they given it to them? Why did they have to know?

Ramirez didn't answer.

Peter grunted and swept his eyes across the barren terrain.

They were supposed to be met at the border by Hammond, their direct superior, but they had received a new message on their sat phone not more than six hours before. The plan had changed. They were given a pair of coordinates and instructions to travel on foot to a new meet-up location.

The deep rumble of distant thunder shuddered across the desert. They kept the same pace as they made their way toward the drop. A hundred yards and closing. They moved in silence. And then Carlos said something that Peter didn't expect.

"The moment we start second-guessing our superiors, the very second we begin questioning our orders, we are done. The reason the military has remained isolated from all the chaos in our country is because we stay out of politics. We are soldiers. We're not spies, not law enforcement officers, not FBI agents. We are soldiers. We stay out of the domestic crap. End of story, okay?"

Peter cleared his throat. "Got it. Agree. No freakin' doubt about it. Now, do you trust the drop?"

Flashes of brilliant lightning blazed across the sky. In the flash of electrical light Peter could see the black sedans waiting for them fifty yards in the distance. Thunder immediately followed and a sheet of rain collapsed from the sky, drenching them within moments.

Peter looked to his old friend expectantly.

"I'm not sure," Carlos finally answered, his voice drowned out by the sound of rain beating into pools upon the desert.

The knot in Peter's stomach turned cold. He said nothing as they marched through the desert that was turning to mud beneath their feet.

THE ATTEMPTED COUP

Some things are simply true. The media might ignore or lie about it. Some Americans may not care. One political party may deny it, the truth obscured by political smoke. But some things still are just true. And the following is a fact.

Starting six months before the 2016 presidential election, senior members of the FBI, Department of Justice, and CIA worked with select members of the Obama administration, along with a willing and hyper-partisan press, to lie to the American people for the purpose of destroying the candidacy of Donald J. Trump. Failing to do that, they then set out to destroy his ability to fulfill his duties as president.

The fraud and subsequent cover-up of their malicious actions include:

- Using opposition research (the Steele Dossier) that was initiated and paid for by Hillary Clinton and the Democratic National Committee, and which had zero credibility, to launch an investigation into Trump's team. This information was provided by a discredited former British spy who had no current ties to Russia, having not been in the country for more than a decade, and who, in his desperate search for derogatory information on Trump, ended up being fed misinformation by Russian agents.

- Sending multiple HUMINT assets (human intelligence assets, more commonly known as spies) against members of the Trump campaign. Many of these US agents were wearing secret recording devices.

- Providing spiteful and misleading leaks to a complicit media that carried forward the false accusations of Russian-Trump collusion. These malicious leaks continued for more than three years.

- Deliberately presenting false evidence before the United States Foreign Intelligence Surveillance Court (FISC), the highly classified federal court that is specifically and solely authorized to issue surveillance warrants against foreign spies operating inside the United States.

- Framing former national security advisor Michael Flynn as well as withholding exculpatory information that would have proven his innocence.

- Apparently attempting to frame other associates of President Trump.

- Appointing a highly partisan special prosecutor team, many of whom had voiced fierce opposition to Trump and who were clearly determined to charge the president with a crime, despite the lack of evidence.

The story of this frame-up is long and complicated, the details far more tangled and complex than can be shown here. But the essence of their malfeasance can be conveyed fairly efficiently through this simple timeline.

2016

February: Michael Flynn, the former director of the Defense Intelligence Agency, joins the Trump campaign.

March 6: George Papadopoulos joins the Trump campaign.

March 14: In what now appears to be the first step in a process for entrapment, Joseph Mifsud, who would later be identified as having ties to US intelligence, meets George Papadopoulos in Italy and tells him the Russians have "dirt" on Hillary Clinton. (Later, in an effort to give credibility to the narrative that Trump associates were colluding with the Russians, the Mueller report will make it appear that Mifsud was a Russian agent, something they certainly knew was not true.)

March 21: Carter Page joins the Trump campaign.

April 1: Lacking any justification other than he had a vague association with the Trump campaign, the FBI initiates an investigation into Carter Page, a private US citizen who had served honorably in the military and as an asset to help the CIA in previous investigations. The purpose of opening this investigation into Page is now clear: to use him as a conduit to initiate further surveillance on Trump and other members of his team.

Their investigation would claim that Page was a foreign agent working against the US. But their work would quickly show that Page had no association with Trump, and in fact had never met or communicated with him in any way. It also would quickly show that he had no foreign contacts and that the entire basis for their investigation was utterly unfounded.

Despite the lack of any evidence, FISA surveillance on Carter Page would be renewed multiple times.

April: The Clinton campaign pays the law firm of Perkins Coie $5.1 million. Perkins Coie then hires opposition research firm Fusion GPS to conduct research on candidate Trump. Fusion GPS then hires former British intelligence agent Christopher Steele to conduct the opposition research. Steele would later acknowledge that he is "desperate that Donald Trump not get elected."

May 2: In the final report on the Clinton email investigation, senior FBI agent Peter Strzok changes the description of Clinton's actions from being "grossly negligent" to only "extremely careless," the less severe language allowing the FBI to avoid filing charges against her.

May 10: During a meeting in London, George Papadopoulos tells Australian diplomat Alexander Downer that Mifsud had told him that the Russians have "dirt" on Clinton. At no time does Papadopoulos ever mention or indicate any knowledge of stolen DNC emails.

May 11: Australian officials send a message to the US State Department notifying them of the meeting with Papadopoulos.

May 23–25: Democratic National Committee emails are hacked.

June 8: Glenn Simpson, CEO of Fusion GPS (the opposition firm hired by the Clinton campaign), meets with Russian lawyer Natalia Veselnitskaya in New York City. Veselnitskaya has set up what would become the infamous Trump Tower meeting for the following day.

June 9: Donald Trump Jr. hosts a meeting with Natalia Veselnitskaya. The meeting was short and focused on foreign child adoptions and US sanctions against Russia. A translator at the meeting would later testify to the FBI that "there was no discussion of the 2016 United States presidential election or collusion between the Russian government and the Trump campaign." The translator also would testify before the House Permanent Select Committee on Intelligence that there was no talk of elections during the Trump Tower meeting.

The day after the Trump Tower meeting, Natalia Veselnitskaya had dinner once again with Glenn Simpson.

Robert Mueller omits both of these meetings between Veselnitskaya and Simpson from his report.

June 14: *The Washington Post* publishes a story headlined, "Russian government hackers penetrated DNC." That it was actually the Russians who hacked the Democratic National Committee (DNC) has, even to this day, never been proven. Indeed, neither the FBI nor any US law enforcement entity has ever been granted access to DNC servers. Instead, the DNC hired a Democrat-associated company called CrowdStrike to investigate the allegations of Russian hacking. CrowdStrike's CEO later testified before the House Intelligence Committee that the company could not determine if any data had ever been extracted from the DNC servers.

July 5: During a widely viewed press conference, FBI director James Comey announces Hillary Clinton acted in an "extremely careless" rather than a "grossly negligent" manner regarding her email server and declines to prosecute her.

July 19: Steele provides his first memo to Fusion GPS, which claims that Carter Page was promised a *multi-billion*-dollar stake in a Russian energy company called Rosneft in exchange for convincing Trump to lift sanctions if he were elected president. Subsequent investigations make clear that no such discussion ever took place. Indeed, most US officials (except those in charge of the Trump collusion investigation) considered this Steele accusation as having no credibility. Page clearly had no access to Trump and no ability to persuade him on any policy. More, the promise of such a ridiculously large sum of money to a minor political figure was obviously absurd.

July 22: WikiLeaks dumps the DNC emails. Soon after, Clinton's campaign manager tells the media that Russians stole the DNC emails to help Trump.

July: Steele authors another report alleging a well-developed conspiracy, in which Russia would dump the DNC emails if Trump agreed not to make an issue out of Russia's military activities in Ukraine. No evidence of this claim has ever been produced by the Mueller report or by any other investigation.

July 28: CIA director John Brennan briefs President Obama on a plan by candidate Clinton to accuse Trump of Russian collusion. Brennan later claims that he instead briefed Obama that Russian president Vladimir Putin had "authorized his intelligence services to carry out activities to hurt Democratic candidate Hillary Clinton and boost the election prospects of Donald Trump." No evidence has ever been produced that backs up this accusation.

July 31: FBI opens investigation into Trump-Russia collusion, code named Crossfire Hurricane.

August 8: FBI lawyer Lisa Page texts her FBI coworker and romantic partner Peter Strzok, "Trump's not ever going to become president, right? Right?!"

Strzok replies, "No. No he's not. We'll stop it."

August 10: FBI opens counterintelligence investigations into three former Trump advisors: Carter Page, Paul Manafort, and George Papadopoulos. When unable to open an investigation on Michael Flynn due to the lack of evidence, Steele miraculously provides the FBI with another report—the same day!—that supposedly ties Flynn to the other targets, providing the needed predicate to investigate him as well. FBI agents would later testify how they "couldn't believe their luck" to be provided this remarkable information that suddenly tied the defendants together.

August: The Office of Legal Counsel denies the first attempt to get FISA surveillance on Page, remaining unconvinced he was a foreign agent who had committed a crime.

August 15: Strzok texts to Lisa Page, "I want to believe the path you threw out for consideration in Andy's [FBI deputy director Andrew McCabe's] office—that there's no way he gets elected—but I'm afraid we can't take the risk. It's like an insurance policy in the unlikely event you die before 40."

August 16: Crossfire Hurricane team opens an investigation into Michael Flynn based on the fact he was a Trump advisor and that he had traveled to Russia.

August 17: The CIA sends the FBI a memo which states that, contrary to their accusation, Carter Page was not a Russian agent, but instead he had been working with the CIA to counter Russian interests. This exculpatory information is deceptively altered to indicate just the opposite, leaving Page open to further investigation.

August 19: Manafort resigns from Trump team.

August 20: The FBI sends Stefan Halper, who was secretly wearing a recording device, to meet with Carter Page. One of the purposes of this meeting was to tie the supposed conspirators together. Page tells Halper he has "literally never met" Manafort. This exculpatory information is not included in the FISA application. A few weeks later, the FBI sends another wired spy to meet with Papadopoulos.

September 7: The Intelligence Community forwards to FBI Director Comey a referral to look into Hillary Clinton's plan to accuse Trump of colluding with Russia. When questioned, Comey denies receiving this referral. Instead, the FBI continues to investigate the Trump campaign.

September 15: Once again, Stefan Halper meets with George Papadopoulos. Once again, he is secretly wearing a wire. Once again, Papadopoulos indicates he has no ties to Russia, nor to any of the other individuals under investigation. Once again, none of this exculpatory information is included in the FISA application.

September 23: Steele leaks information from his dossier to investigative journalist Michael Isikoff. Isikoff then writes a news story about the Steele Dossier. The FBI then uses this media report—about a report that they already had—as evidence to justify FISA surveillance.

September 30: Suspicions arise at the Pentagon regarding hundreds of thousands of dollars for "research" being paid to a mysterious individual named Mifsud. No one can identify who he is nor any research he has submitted.

October 3: Steele admits to the FBI that one of his sources may not be trustworthy.

October 13: The FBI is told that Steele's client wants to see his opposition research come to light before the November election.

October 21: First FISA application on Carter Page is marked as verified. This allows the government "two hops" of surveillance on Page, meaning they can monitor everyone he communicates with, and everyone those people communicate with as well.

The file for this FISA application eventually will go missing.

October 31: Another wired spy meets with Papadopoulos. More exculpatory information is not included in FISA application.

October 31: Christopher Steele leaks more information on his reports to other members of the media.

November 1: The FBI terminates their relationship with Steele for leaking to the press. Despite the fact he was fired from the FBI, and that he had been found to be untrustworthy, senior DOJ official Bruce Ohr—whose wife, remarkably, works for Fusion GPS—continues to serve as a back channel to pass information from Steele to the FBI.

November 18: Trump names Flynn as National Security Advisor.

December: Multiple Obama officials request to unmask Flynn's identity from classified national security reports. His identity is then leaked to the press.

2017

January 4: The FBI clears Flynn of any wrongdoing and attempts to close their investigation into him. Strzok overrides this decision and keeps the Flynn investigation open.

January 5: Steele deletes all data regarding Fusion GPS from his firm's computer systems.

January 6: FBI director Comey and Director of National Intelligence James Clapper brief President-elect Trump on the Steele Dossier, including the infamous "golden shower" accusation. Comey then writes a memo regarding his meeting with Trump, which he subsequently leaks to the press, giving the media the credibility they need to report on the dossier.

January 10: CNN and BuzzFeed report on Steele Dossier. Christopher Steele goes into hiding.

January 12: Comey sends the director of national intelligence an email in which he admits, "We are not able to sufficiently corroborate the reporting" in the Steele Dossier.

Despite this fact, Comey signs the FISA surveillance warrant application that stated the Steele Dossier had been "verified."

> **Winter:** To minimize their criminal exposure, multiple members of the Russian collusion investigation team purchase professional liability insurance.

> **Mid-July:** In an obvious attempt at setting a perjury trap, and against multiple DOJ and FBI procedures, Comey decides to send two FBI agents over to the White House to interview the new national security advisor, Michael Flynn. This was done without prior coordination with the Department of Justice and left acting attorney general Sally Yates "flabbergasted" and "dumbfounded." Other senior DOJ officials also "hit the roof" when they learned what Comey had done.

Comey later explained that he thought he could catch Flynn off guard and susceptible to FBI questioning.

FBI agents Joe Pientka and Peter Strzok are instructed to "casually" interview Mike Flynn without a lawyer present or letting him know he was under investigation. To help ensure this would happen, McCabe and other FBI officials had "decided the agents would not warn Flynn that it was a crime to lie."

> **January 23:** FBI senior agent Bill Priestap writes a personal note regarding the upcoming Flynn interview: "What's our goal? Truth/Admission or to get him to lie, so we can prosecute him or get him fired?"

One day prior to questioning Flynn, FBI investigators leak to the *Washington Post* that "Flynn himself is not the active target of an investigation." The clear intent of this leak is to give Flynn a sense of false security and to make him less careful when they interview him.

> **January 24:** Flynn interview takes place. As Mueller would later report, Strzok believed that Flynn appeared to answer their questions truthfully.

The original notes from the Flynn interview are now missing.

> **January 24–26:** Crossfire Hurricane team interviews Steele's primary sub-source and determines the dossier

is likely unreliable. Still, they report to the FISA court that "the FBI found the Russian-based sub-source to be truthful and cooperative."

Early February: After one of Flynn's first meetings with his National Security staff, Obama holdover Eric Ciaramella comments to another NSC staffer, Sean Misko, "We need to take him out."

"Yeah, we need to do everything we can to take out the president," Misko replied.

Sean Misko would later join Democratic Chairman Adam Schiff's staff on the House Intelligence Committee.

Eric Ciaramella has been identified in multiple media outlets as the whistleblower who initiated the Trump impeachment investigation.

February 11: FBI interviews Mifsud. Later, the Mueller report would reveal that Mifsud "falsely stated" and "omitted" information. Mueller does not charge Mifsud for making false statements. Mueller's team does charge George Papadopoulos, Michael Flynn, Rick Gates, Michael Cohen, and Paul Manafort for making false statements.

When questioned during congressional testimony why they charged the Trump officials but not Mifsud, Mueller only states that he "can't get into it."

February 11: Joseph Mifsud goes into hiding in Europe.

February 13: Flynn resigns.

April 7: Comey signs off on another Carter Page FISA renewal.

June 8: In yet another—and brazen—attempt at criminal entrapment, while traveling overseas, George Papadopoulos is given $10,000 cash by Charles Tawil. Papadopoulos surrenders the money to attorneys before returning to the US.

July 27: Papadopoulos flies back to the US and is arrested upon landing in Washington, DC. FBI agents search for the $10,000 cash but don't find it. The only thing the FBI can charge him with is making a false statement.

June–July: In a flagrant attempt at intimidation, Special Counsel Mueller begins prosecuting Michael Flynn's son.

October 26: Former director of national intelligence James Clapper goes on CNN and claims they have corroborated all of the information in the Steele Dossier, something which he had to know was untrue. (The Steele accusations were not corroborated at the time and have not been corroborated since.)

December 1: Hoping to save his son from Mueller prosecution, Flynn pleads guilty to making false statements to the FBI. Legal costs have left him nearly bankrupt.

December 18: Continuing his media misinformation campaign, James Clapper tells the always-pliable CNN that Putin is a great case officer and that he knows what he's doing with President Trump.

2018

February 2: The Republican-led House Intelligence Committee releases the Nunes memo, which shows that the FBI and DOJ had deceived the FISA courts and withheld critical information from FISA judges.

February 20: Faced with evidence of prosecutorial abuse, Judge Emmet Sullivan demands Mueller prosecutors provide all exculpatory evidence to Flynn's attorneys. Mueller's team ignore this order and continue to withhold substantial evidence favorable to Flynn.

February 24: Ranking House Intelligence Committee member Adam Schiff releases a Democrat memo contradicting the Nunes memo. Later, the inspector general's report would utterly destroy the credibility of the Schiff memo.

March 16: Andrew McCabe is fired from the FBI.

March 21: Continuing his media misinformation campaign to his willing media partners, former CIA director John Brennan claims that Putin has enough information on Trump to blackmail him.

May 4: Lisa Page resigns from the FBI before she could be fired. Mysteriously, her official phone is factory reset.

July 16: Still continuing his media misinformation campaign to his willing media partners, former CIA director Brennan claims that Trump's statements after his meeting with Putin in Helsinki are "nothing short of treasonous."

August 10: FBI fires agent Peter Strzok. Mysteriously, his phone is also factory reset.

September 7: Papadopoulos is sentenced to prison for fourteen days.

2019

February 19: Continuing his own media misinformation campaign to his willing media partners, Andrew McCabe tells CNN that he believes it is possible that Trump is a Russian asset.

April 18: The Mueller report is finally released. To the dismay of Trump's opponents, it clearly states that the Mueller team could not establish any coordination or conspiracy between any US persons and the Russian government.

Mid-2019: Joe Pientka, one of the key FBI investigators responsible for FISA abuse, is promoted.

July 16: A classified FBI spreadsheet comes to light, showing none of the accusations in the Steele Dossier had ever been confirmed by the FBI or were believed to be true.

July 24: In a stunningly inept display, Special Counsel Robert Mueller testifies before Congress, admitting he is unfamiliar with significant parts of his own report, that he is unable "get into" fundamental issues, and that many of the most basic questions asked of him were "beyond his purview."

December 9: Inspector General Michael Horowitz releases his report on FISA abuse, citing multiple failures of the DOJ and FBI, including:

- fifty-one violations of Woods Procedures

- seventeen significant errors or omissions which misled the FISA court

- that the FBI provided false information to the National Security Division

- that, against multiple denials by senior FBI officials, the discredited Steele Dossier was central to the FISA application of Carter Page.

December 17: FISA court judge Rosemary Collyer issues a severe rebuke to the FBI.

2020

January 14: Flynn withdraws his guilty plea.

May 7: Adam Schiff, now Chairman of the House Permanent Select Committee on Intelligence, is forced to release all fifty-three transcripts regarding the Trump-Russia investigation. These transcripts unquestionably prove that Schiff's claim of having "ample evidence" of collusion is untrue. Senior Obama officials are shown to have testified under oath that they had seen no evidence of collusion or conspiracy, despite the fact that they made such claims repeatedly to the press.

May 7: The Department of Justice files a motion to dismiss the case against Flynn.

August 19: Former FBI lawyer Kevin Clinesmith pleads guilty to altering the email from the CIA that showed Carter Page was a previous CIA asset.

September 10: The Justice Department is forced to admit that thirty-three phones of key Mueller investigators were wiped clean and reset to factory settings before they could be examined by the inspector general. Chief Prosecutor Andrew Weissmann wiped his phone multiple times before turning it over to the IG investigators.

BROKEN TRUST

One cannot read this timeline of abuse and not realize that this was an orchestrated attempt by the very most senior people within the Department of Justice, the FBI, and even the CIA, to override the will of the American people—a conspiracy from a group of elitist bureaucrats who essentially said, "We don't care who the voters want to be president. We don't care that we had a legitimate election. The American people are obviously too stupid to be trusted. This man should not be—this man *cannot* be—our president, and we are going to stop him."

The malicious intent they displayed toward the bedrock of our democracy—free, unfettered, and unmanipulated elections—is stunningly dangerous to our future and our freedom.

For more than three years we were told that President Trump had committed treason by conspiring with the Russians to steal the election and put himself in office. *And none of it was real.*

Yet none of the senior leaders involved in the campaign to sabotage the presidency have ever been held accountable. No one in the press has ever recognized their deceit. None of the members of Congress who knowingly lied to the American people have faced any consequences. Not legally. Not ethically. Not professionally. Not financially.

Yes, it really is like that.

And this wasn't the first time this sort of thing has happened. Think of Senator Ted Stevens (R-AK), who was driven from office by a false, malicious, and politically motivated prosecution that destroyed his reputation. Think of Lois Lerner and her cohorts who abused their positions at the IRS to target conservative groups. Think of the political groups who are targeted every day now by the FBI or DHS.

When we remember these other examples, we may realize that what happened to President Trump is not all that remarkable. In fact, it has happened many times before.

Among every challenge we could write about, nothing is more destructive for our nation than the realization that there are now two systems of justice: one for people like us, and another for the elites. One for those who head the most powerful agencies in our nation, and one for those against whom that power is used.

Is it any wonder people say, "I don't know who to trust anymore!"

Putting aside the lives that were destroyed in this effort, the greater concern is the damage to our democracy, which is hard to imagine.

To test how this has impacted your trust, ask yourself this: If an FBI agent wanted to talk to you for any reason, would you refuse to talk to them without a lawyer present?

Interestingly, when we asked this question to different groups of Republicans, the vast majority of them say they would refuse an FBI interview without their lawyer present. Democrats don't seem to have the same reservations; most of them say they would agree to such an interview, showing us that these agencies have come to be viewed as political tools of one party, not fair and non-political arbiters of truth.

Which then begs the question: How far will it go? When will the breakdown in trust end? And where will it leave our nation? What will it be like to live in a country with a government so hungry for power and so corrupted by the elites that it that considers itself beyond the reach of its own laws?

ALONG THE BORDER

February

Watching the extraction site, Peter Hardy could feel the adrenaline course through his body.

Eight men exited their vehicles as Peter and Carlos approached the sedans. As the group moved to something of a semicircle around them, a thousand alarm bells began shrieking in Peter's head. One of the men moved to the front of the pack—dark-skinned, cold eyes, a thick beard that went six inches below his chin. He was obviously an operator. A man used to Special Forces combat. A specialist in foreign operations. Probably CIA.

Peter swallowed hard.

He really hated spies.

It wasn't right. The CIA was not supposed to be here. And that wasn't the only thing that bothered him. There was the change of instructions. Meeting here this way. The darkness. The isolation. Everything about this was wrong, and his instincts tied his gut into a knot. Glancing at Carlos, he saw the hard look in his eye.

"You were supposed to be unarmed," the man said with a nod toward the pistol on Peter's hip.

Neither of the soldiers answered.

"Do you have it?" the CIA agent asked.

"No," Peter answered quickly.

The dark-skinned man frowned and narrowed his eyes. "We were told you would have a flash drive," he said as he turned to Carlos for confirmation.

"We have it," Carlos said as he frowned at Peter with gentle reproof. "But we're not going to give it up to anyone but our team."

Two soldiers took a few steps to their right and Peter shifted his weight in response. No way he was going to let the men surround them. He stepped back, his hand moving to his handgun underneath his leather jacket. "Actually, with all due respect, Carlos, we don't have the drive," he offered frankly. "I hid it on the south side of the border."

The CIA agent snorted. It was clear he didn't believe him.

Peter had seen the information on the drive. He knew how dangerous it was. And his heart sank as he stared at the men.

The bearded man moved forward, staring at Peter through the darkness and heavy rain. "I know you," he started, almost talking to himself. "I know you. You're the guy…your old man…" He stopped and grunted angrily.

Peter knew that for the operator, this made everything so much more difficult.

The man hesitated and swore. "No worries," he finally said. "We'll figure it out back at the Farm. Everyone back in the cars." But none of his men moved toward the vehicles. In fact, two of them moved to complete the circle around the soldiers.

Lightning flashed and the rain continued to pour from the sky in heavy sheets. In the quick strobe of light, Peter recognized for the first time that the other men weren't carrying rifles, but stun guns and tranquilizers.

This wasn't an exfiltration. This was something else.

The CIA and FBI were running ops against the military!

He tried again to swallow. "Here's what's going to happen," he started to say, forcing his voice to be calm. "You're going to give me the keys to the lead sedan. Then you're going to—"

The lightning flashed again, the men all rushed in together, and Peter felt the biting needle of the tranquilizer hitting the carotid artery his neck. He started to lift his pistol but was unconscious before he could move his hand toward the trigger.

THE DEATH OF TRUTH

The politicization of the DOJ and FBI against a political party is a re-markable milestone in our nation's history. How can any nation survive an attack upon its core foundations? How can any democracy survive if the most senior members of the most powerful agencies within the government are able to break laws, violate constitutional privacy, lie to the federal courts, frame innocent people, use government human intelligence assets to spy on US citizens, then lie to Congress and the American people with no consequences?

And perhaps the most important question: How can so many of our own citizens, even when confronted with the evidence, seem not to care?

The answer is pretty simple.

Because no one knows what is true anymore.

And why do they not know the truth?

Because the elites have a powerful partner who is willing to lie to deceive us.

WASHINGTON, DC

Two Years Before

Time would come when Darren Hardy would find himself wandering the streets of Washington scavenging for food. But that day was in the future. And the thought that he would ever be really hungry had never yet entered his mind.

He was a media rock star, a legend, a dude at the top of his game. Darren Hardy didn't want for anything. He had everything he could ask for.

His fresh combination of wit and a charming smile, his keen intellect and a hyper-tuned sense of how to rev up fear and emotion, had rocketed Darren Hardy to the highest peaks of journalistic stardom. And he was only thirty-one. In less than two years he had gone from a social media influencer to a podcaster with thirty million subscribers, his ratings so impressive that he had just signed a contract with the largest cable news network, making him the youngest anchor in news history.

Quite an accomplishment. But one not explained by just his great wit and smile.

There were lots of guys with bright teeth who didn't host network news, lots of guys with keen intellect and wit. And there were plenty of other journalists who shared his flexible relationship with the truth.

But there weren't a lot of guys who had a billionaire father. There weren't a lot of guys with his father's friends. And there weren't a lot of guys who had the backing of the people who really mattered.

People like the gentlemen in this room.

Glancing at their faces, Darren felt his chest tighten up. He knew that in the game of life, there were wolves and there were sheep. He knew which one he was. Despite his money, despite his father, his fame, and everything that came with it, he felt as wooly as his suit.

He desperately wanted that to change.

This meeting would determine if it would.

The director of the FBI sat across from the other lawyer—General Counsel, Department of Justice—both of them sipping dark spirits from shot glasses. It was late at night, the bar nearly deserted, and they were down on the waterfront, popular with tourists, tech snobs, and drunken college kids, making it unlikely they would be recognized by anyone who mattered. But to be sure, the booth at the back of the narrow bar had its lighting turned down, and a six-foot removable wood barrier separated them from the rest of the bar.

The DOJ attorney, one of the most senior lawyers in the United States, smiled weakly at the reporter and poured him a glass of Irish whiskey. He was a bald man, mid-sixties, with pale skin, a stubble beard, and no chin.

Darren took his glass, then glanced at the bottle the lawyer still held in his hand. He knew the kind of money the men made—even as senior government employees, neither of them made even two hundred grand a year—and wondered how they could afford such fine liquor.

He calculated very quickly. Two hundred thousand. He made that in five days. Did that make him a wolf?

He knew it didn't. It wasn't that easy. The world was full of rich and bleating sheep.

"To fine whiskey," he said as he lifted his glass.

"And cheap beer," the FBI director answered with a smile.

"Funny," Darren said as he rolled the glass under his nose. "I spent four years at Harvard. The only thing I remember about the time I was there was sleeping in strange beds, drinking cheap beer, and getting chased by a wild turkey through the streets of Cambridge a couple days before Thanksgiving."

The lawyer smiled. It was a fake smile, sure, but even better than his real one, which hadn't appeared in years.

"I'm not sure I believe you, Mr. Hardy," the FBI director said.

"True story. The turkeys used to come out with the first snow—"

The director waved his hand. "Oh, I believe you about the turkey. What I don't believe is that you ever drank cheap beer." He poured another shot of whiskey. "I know your father," he said.

Darren lifted his glass again. "To fathers," he said.

The FBI director took a serious tone and leaned forward. "Mr. Hardy, there's a reason we invited you here. A reason we need someone of your exceptional talents."

Darren forced back the smile and waited without answering. Because wolves were not anxious. They let the game come to them.

"We think we can help you," the general counsel said.

"Help me?" Darren wondered. "I think, gentlemen, there is very little I need help with."

The FBI director sat back. His face was calm. Completely assured. As if he knew his target had it wrong. And Darren himself knew the truth. Everyone needed help with something. No one was ever completely satisfied. The drive…the lust…the ambition within the human soul was never fulfilled. Maybe for a short time. A moment. An hour. A week. But it was always there, always growing hungry, always needing more.

A million dollars was never enough. Neither was a billion. A beautiful woman. There was always someone better, someone who weighed two pounds less or had better hair. And power! Come on! That was like eating cotton candy, a hunger that was never satisfied.

"We think we can help you," the FBI director repeated, as if there was no reason to say more.

Darren stared at him a long moment. He shifted his weight and waited longer.

It was true. He wanted more. A lot more. More viewers. More money. More influence. More power. There were fifty million people out there who still didn't know his name. And more space from his old man. More that he could prove to him. Make the old man shut up.…

The FBI director watched him as if he could see his mind work, and he nodded to his friend. The lawyer poured another drink. "We realize the power you have," the director said. "We also recognize that your influence will only grow with time. We like you. We think that we can trust you."

Darren sipped again. These were the guys who had purged the deplorables from the agency. So yeah, he already trusted them.

"If you let us, we can increase the volume of your microphone. We can do it by an order of magnitude."

"And why would you be willing to do that?"

"Because there are some things we want people to know. But we want them to know it in such a way, and at such a time, so that it is beneficial."

"Beneficial?" Darren wondered.

"Beneficial to society. Beneficial to good order. Beneficial to social justice and the goals that we all have."

Beneficial to yourselves, Darren interpreted in his mind. Then he decided to let his wolf out. "I think I'm doing pretty well already," he said. "I've got an entire organization supporting me. We do very good reporting. Why should I need—"

"Very good reporting," the director said, his voice thick with sarcasm. "Let's talk about that for a moment. Reporting. Informing. Telling the truth. Here's the world as I see it, and you know that I am right.

"The truth is dead! The truth doesn't matter anymore. There's more life in a bucket of rocks than truth in this world. You and your colleagues—many of whom, by the way, we work with as well—can make our fellow Americans believe virtually anything you want."

Darren nodded slowly. He might as well argue that the sun doesn't rise as to try to prove them wrong about that. "But we pride ourselves—"

"Of course, you do!" the director said quickly, clearly showing he had no interest in debating the obvious. "Whatever you are going to say, it's all good. But we don't need to hear it. You don't need to say it. We understand each other. Let's just leave it at that."

The general counsel snorted, his eyes cold and angry. He had that dismissive look that Darren had grown to hate. Wolf eyes. Wolf smile. Darren turned away, his gaze resting on his own face in the mirrored wall. "Neither of you are in media or journalism," Darren offered in a voice that he realized sounded defensive. "I know exactly what I'm doing. I'm on a good path."

The director's voice was soft now, cool and manipulating. "All we need is a man that we can trust. We'll feed you information. Good stuff. Important stuff. Stuff you're going to want to get on the air. We're talking Emmy Award for journalism stuff. Pulitzer-winning stuff. The kind of stuff that changes history."

In the mirror, Darren saw his eyes shoot up, his perfectly waxed eyebrows arching. And he knew they noticed. That was it. They knew they had him. Still, he tried to recover the advantage. "I've already got good sources. Other friends. I have an entire—"

The lawyer cut him off. "There's nothing we don't know. Nothing. No one. Nowhere. We are the all-seeing-freaking-eye." He leaned forward, his voice as hard and cold as ice. "We…know…it…all," he said.

The director smiled. "We know who is doing what to whom. Who is where and why and when. Who is doing illegal stuff. Who is straight and can't be touched without planting a few inconvenient pieces of evidence in their path. Sure, we don't act on everything we see or hear. In fact, we act on very little. But that doesn't change the fact that we could act if it were necessary."

Darren tried to seem unimpressed. "But still—"

"Let me illustrate," the FBI director cut him off again. "Right now, sitting here, you think your neighbor is having an affair with the babysitter you both use. Yeah. He is. And yes, the fact we know that is only marginally impressive. But the fact we know that you were wondering about it, should scare the hell out of you! Have you ever mentioned it to anybody? Ever talked about your suspicions with your wife? Your boss…anyone at all? Yet we know what you were wondering." He paused, his voice hanging in the air.

Darren's mind was racing as he went through every conversation…every text…every phone call and email…. When had he said something? How did they know?

Suddenly, he was angry. "You make me sick. Spying on me, just to set me up. I'm a United States citizen. You have no right—"

"Of course, we don't," the FBI man said. "But sometimes we do it anyway. And then we know."

"You're going to get nailed for it," Darren said. "Someone, maybe me, they're going to report your abuse."

"To whom?" The DOJ lawyer took a deep breath and closed his eyes for a solid count of three. "Think about it, Darren," he said. "In the last ten years, think about all we've done. We've spied on Americans. We've lied to the courts. We've buried a thousand inconvenient stories for the guys who are on our team. We've colluded with foreign governments. We've destroyed sitting representatives for nothing more than the fact that they had the gall to fight us. For crying out loud, we ran an operation against a sitting president! Think about that, and then tell me there isn't anything in the world that we can't do."

Darren lowered his gaze and sipped his whiskey as he thought.

"You know what I have really grown to appreciate?" the lawyer went on after wiping his lips against his napkin. He was talking to his friend the director, now, and not to Darren. "The thing that really stuns me? Even now, after all of the chaos the nation has been through, it's the one thing that still drops me to the floor."

"Tell me," the director said.

"Even when we get caught, no one cares."

The director smiled as he nodded. Darren glared at them.

"Sure, some care." The lawyer emphasized the word "some" and waved dismissively in some far-off direction. "The crazies. The Walmart shoppers. But no one who really matters. And the few who do, can't do anything about it.

"We—the FBI and Department of Justice—we have enormous power," the director interjected. "We can spy on people, listen to their phone calls, read their emails and texts. We know what they ask Alexa. We know the things they search for. We can go through someone's garbage. Talk to their neighbors, their boss, their old girlfriends, the choir boy at church. We can monitor everything they look at on the web. And if we get a little out of hand, absolute worst case, some judge might order an investigation. But whatever becomes of that? Even with the Stevens case, against a sitting US senator, no one was fired! A couple low-level prosecutors are suspended for a few weeks, but that was it."

"One of them took his own life," Darren added tartly.

"Which was a tragedy, of course," the DOJ lawyer answered. The sadness in his eyes was as fake as his smile. "But think about it, Mr. Hardy. The FBI director who oversaw the malicious Stevens case was untouched, his pristine reputation for leadership and ethics intact. He left without a scratch. The attorney general who oversaw the case, which ultimately had every single charge dismissed, never paid a price, either. Amazing, but it's true. We have this unrivaled power, and no one to hold us accountable.

"And do you want to know the thing that really makes me smile? It's the unspoken golden parachute. Everyone knows it's there. Think of our guys who got taken down in the Russian probe. Former deputy assistant, DOJ, he's making what? A couple million a year for doing nothing. Sure, he had to resign, but someone always comes along and picks 'em up. He's given money and enough status to keep his ego in check. And the lovely miss—what's her name?—the one who was married and loved texting late at night. She gets a sweet gig with cable news.

"The list goes on, but I think you see my point. If some of our guys take a hit, our team will always take care of them. So yeah, sure, sometimes the little guys get whacked. But the directors, the guys like us, we walk away without a scratch."

Another sip.

"It's pretty nice," the lawyer concluded as he stared at Darren.

OUR KIM JONG-UN PRESS

The question is frequently asked, "What is the greatest threat facing our country?" Most people expect a response like China, Russia, or North Korea, or maybe socialism.

But the answer is none of these. The greatest threat facing our nation: *no one knows what is true anymore.*

No free nation can survive in a world where no one knows what is real. No nation can survive when its citizens no longer know what to believe or whom to trust. Broken trust weakens our nation in unimaginable ways, and every time we learn that we've been duped, our distrust grows.

But we want to be clear on two things. First, our concerns are far greater than just the behavior of our press. It's also the politicization and manipulations of respected institutions: the FBI, CIA, DOJ, and other agencies critical to a trusted government.

Second, we adamantly support and defend a free and unfettered press. But like every foundational organization upon which our democracy depends, they have to be accountable. Not only are they not exempt from criticism if they fail in their responsibilities, but they should be held to a higher standard.

In our modern world, our quest for truth requires constant work. Content is hurled at us like water through a firehose, leaving us pinned against a wall of doubt, to the point that sifting through what is biased and what is objective information has become nearly impossible. Many people tell us they have given up on network news, major newspapers, and especially the internet. Social media is great for keeping in touch with your kids, but not for getting the facts, and many Americans are beginning to understand this.

Google is designed now to control what you see when you search, a fact that is easy to demonstrate for yourself. Compare the search results you get with Google with any other search engine. If the subject is political or controversial in nature, you will get a notably different result from Google than from other search engines. Simply put, Google will not show you what you're looking for, but what they want you to see.

Media have gone from bias to propaganda to open deception and suppression. And yes, it is suppression when Big Tech/Big Media not only ignore facts, but actively suppress things they don't want you to know, making it impossible for you to share information they don't agree with, or destroying the media platforms they don't want you to have access to.

There are several possible explanations for this lack of truth. For one, the immediacy of content has created an urgent race to be the first to reach our eyes. Big Tech/Big Media also have learned that anger is a powerful motivator to hold customer attention; thus, distorting stories to generate a fire of addictive rage can pay off. Fact-checking has become increasingly tedious too—rarely more accurate or unbiased than those they are supposedly "fact-checking."

But the core reason for the lack of truth is really fairly simple. And also frightening.

Those who control the media see our nation, our culture, and our future in a very different way than most other Americans do. They think our nation is so deeply flawed, so racist, so unfair and arrogant that it needs to be fundamentally rebuilt. They think that half of Americans are rubes: backward, racist, homophobic, sexist, anti-science, closed-minded religious zealots who are too dumb to know what's good for them. So, they have to tell us what is true and good. No, not just tell us; they have to jam it down our throats until we join them or cry for mercy.

And truth dies in the process of forcing us to convert to their vision of America.

This list of such distortions is far beyond what can be adequately addressed here. There are tens of thousands of examples. And they're not just honest mistakes. We readily accept that mistakes are bound to happen. What we are talking about are deliberate, thoughtful, calculated lies and manipulations intended to deceive the American people.

To illustrate, we will mention just a few examples of media lies and distortions:

- In what would prove to be a great irony, Politifact (who, being fact-checkers, are the ultimate arbiters of truth, because you know fact-checkers are never wrong) awarded President Trump their "2017 Lie of the Year" for claiming that "Russian Collusion" was a "made-up story." Of course, the Trump collusion story was shown to be bunk. But so far as we know, Politifact has not pulled back the Lie of the Year Award from President Trump and re-awarded it to themselves.

- In an oldie-but-goodie example, in 2005 the Associated Press ran a news story about a US soldier who had been captured and was being held hostage in Iraq. The article—which had an accompanying photo of the supposed hostage, an assault rifle being held to his head—ran at a time when the American people were becoming war-weary and resentful. A barrage of reporting sought to gin up more anger to support the anti-war effort, and the "fact" that an American soldier had been taken captive would surely add fuel to the fire. As it turned out, the story was not true. No American soldier had been taken captive. There was no hostage. In a stunning example of botched reporting, the photo of the supposed hostage was actually *a military action-figure doll.* The gun to his head was a plastic toy. (Surely, somewhere in Iraq, a terrorist propagandist was given the employee of the month award and an extra day of vacation for this astounding dupe.)

- Multiple news outlets reported that, upon entering office, President Trump had removed the bust of Martin Luther King from the Oval Office because, you know, Trump is a racist. Yet pictures of the media event from which the story was reported clearly show the bust was in its honored position.

- In 2018, the *New York Times* reported a story from Smith College in which a black student claimed she had been racially profiled and threatened. "All I did was be Black," she posted on Facebook. "It's outrageous that some people question my being at Smith College, and my existence overall as a woman of color."

The incident became a national story. The janitor who had questioned the student was forced to take leave. Another employee, who had nothing at all to do with the incident, was harassed at home, accused of being a racist.

The only problem? None of the accusations were true.

But none of the news organizations who reported on the story bothered to gather the facts. All of them got it wrong. Innocent people were targeted. Yet in trying to justify its original (and botched) reporting, the *Times* wrote, "The story highlights the tensions between a student's deeply felt sense of personal truth and facts that are at odds with it."

There you have it. A "personal truth" is the same as the facts. Better, even. Because in the world of modern media, lies are often better than facts.

- During the summer of 2020, as the presidential campaign was heating up, the *New York Times* (of course) reported that a special unit of the Russian GRU, the military intelligence arm of the Russian government, was paying bounties to Taliban forces for the deaths of US soldiers in Afghanistan. Despite the fact that the marine corps general in command of operations in Afghanistan said there was no evidence the accusations were true, and despite the fact that the story provided no evidence besides anonymous sources, papers throughout the nation repeated the accusations, giving life to the story for many weeks. Candidate Biden accused the president of ignoring Russian aggression and suggested it provided evidence that President Trump was protecting Russia and ignoring the deaths of US troops. Months later, the media were forced to admit the story was not true.

- There is a multitude of examples where media outlets rigged results of supposed "tests" in order to deceive. From rigging transmissions in automobiles that had supposed uncontrollable acceleration, to packing automobiles with explosives in order to guarantee a dramatic explosion, to filming themselves violating food safety standards to prove claims of unsafe food, they have proven again and again that they are willing to actively deceive.

- Recent examples of NBC, ABC, PBS, and other national news organizations editing out images of knifes or other weapons in the hands of those who have been shot by police, or deceptively editing 911 calls, are yet more instances of obvious deceptions.

- CNN reported they had proof that Donald Trump Jr. had advance knowledge that WikiLeaks was going to release stolen emails from the DNC, until their own memo showed they had misrepresented the date, shattering their own story.

- On January 19, 2021, NPR ran an article headlined, *"As Death Rate Accelerates, U.S. Records 400,000 Lives Lost to the Coronavirus."* Amazingly, just two days later—and surely only coincidentally after the inauguration of President Biden—the tide had turned, and they reported, *"Current, Deadly U.S. Coronavirus Surge has Peaked, Researchers Say."* From *accelerating* to *peaked*, in just two days. Amazing what a new Democratic president can do.

- Multiple studies show that 92 percent of media coverage of Trump was negative, 4–5 percent was neutral, and only 2–3 percent was positive. This, for someone whom half of the American people supported.

- *The Washington Post* claimed to have "verified" from anonymous sources that on December 23, 2020, President Trump called an official working in the Georgia Secretary of State's office to demand that they "find the fraud," and said that they would be a national hero if they did. Months later, in correcting the story, the *Post* claimed they had "misquoted" the president. Of course, they did not misquote him. They fabricated a quotation out of thin air, deceiving the American people with a blatant lie.

Many other media companies also claimed to have independently "verified" the story, including NBC News, ABC News, *USA Today*, PBS News-

Hour, and CNN. Of course, none of them could have "verified" the story, for the story was not true, making it pretty clear that an "anonymous" source is another word for a source that most likely doesn't exist.

- After the January 6, 2021, riot at the US Capitol, the *New York Times* reported that a Capitol police officer had been murdered when Trump supporters beat him in the head with a fire extinguisher. Over the next few months, the story was repeated hundreds of times in other news sources. Problem is, there was never any evidence the story was true other than— wait for it—an anonymous source.

Months later, it was finally admitted that the police officer died from natural causes the day after the Capitol Hill riots.

This list goes on and on…. *Russians hacked into and took over C-SPAN.* Wrong. *Russia hacked into Vermont power grid.* Wrong. *Trump created secret server to covertly communicate with Russian bank.* Wrong. *CNN claims Lanny Davis as its source.* Not just wrong, a flagrant lie. (And this to protect the sourcing of a story that was also false.)

The list of botched stories is thousands of examples long. Yet, as troubling as these examples of a corrupted press may be, the far more dangerous reporting takes place in such a way as to make it difficult to challenge or to be proven wrong: little jabs of untruths that are presented as facts, the framing of arguments in a manipulative way, dishonest headlines or deceptions presented in such a way as to obscure the lie behind the facts.

For example, after the fiasco of the 2020 election, many Republican state legislators initiated efforts to improve confidence in election integrity. CNN distorted these efforts to read, "…*Republicans in statehouses around the country work to advance voter suppression legislation, including a bill in Georgia that voting rights groups say targets Black voters.*" This isn't just a reporter's view on a complicated piece of legislation, their best efforts to explain a difficult story. It's pure nonsense. And the reporters surely know that. They work in the political world. We're (relatively) sure they aren't so unintelligent or uniformed as to actually believe that dozens of statehouses around the country have set out to create voter suppression legislation specifically targeting minorities. This was a purposeful distortion of facts.

Becket Adams wrote in the *Washington Times* about "recent examples of media organizations inserting straight-up falsehoods into their news coverage…. These are not misleading statements. These are not poorly chosen words. These are not inaccuracies published in the fog of a breaking news event. These are falsehoods written by reporters, approved by editors, and published despite the availability of contradictory data and facts."

Such distortions happen every day. Which leaves us living in two different worlds, separated by an endless list of distortions that cause us to wonder of each other, *"How can you believe that?"*

It leaves Democrats actually believing that Republicans hate minorities. That we put children in cages on the border. That we don't want minority citizens to vote and are passing legislation to stop them. That we hate clean air and water, want more violence, support mass shootings, want women to be seen but not heard, support the rise of white supremacists, are okay with our daughters being paid less than our sons, are okay if people die because they can't afford insurance, want to keep our employees in poverty, and want people to die from COVID.

These are the kinds of things many Americas actually believe about their neighbors. And the only way they could believe such things is because the press is willing to lie to them a thousand times a day.

It's also important to remember that many of these false narratives, indeed, perhaps all of them, have a real human cost.

Early in 2019, a four-minute video clip of high school junior Nick Sandmann went viral. Sandmann, wearing a MAGA hat while attending the March for Life, was a poster boy for the backwards America the media love to hate. The video showed Sandmann smiling while a Native American beat a drum near his face. Media outlets lashed out, calling Sandmann a racist and a kid with a "punchable face," all of which destroyed the privacy and normality of his teenage life. Virtually overnight, Sandmann became the most hated person in America. In the words of Sandmann himself, "The mainstream media revved up into attack mode. They did so without researching the full video of the incident, without...ever asking me for my side of the story. And do you know why? Because the truth was not important."

When the longer video was finally examined, it showed a very different story. But once again, Americans had already been deceived. (Sandmann filed lawsuits for damages against major media outlets, and received financial settlements from CNN and the *Washington Post.*)

More recently, Americans have been forced to examine the chasm between election polling and what turned out to be the truth. In the 2020 election, nearly every national poll predicted a blue tidal wave, followed by down-ballot Democrat party wins across the nation. But when American finally had a chance to vote, none of it proved true. At the time of the election, twenty-seven House races were considered too close to call. Republicans won every single one. Seven were considered "lean Democrat." Republicans won all of these as well, proving that the polls were fabulously wrong... again, for the same thing had happened in 2016.

Which begs a simple question. If polling just gets it wrong, why do they *always* get it wrong against the same side? A simple explanation is that they are just incompetent. And yes, perhaps they're just terrible at their jobs. But we don't think so. We think a more plausible explanation is they didn't want you to know the truth. Most of these polls are paid for or published by the same organizations that manipulate information every day. They understand the power of suppressing the vote. They understand that it can have an impact if they can convince a group of people not to vote, that their candidate is going to lose, their vote doesn't matter, or the outcome is assured.

This is nothing but a subtle and yet legal form of voter manipulation. And once again, we are left to wonder what is real.

The current state of media and the lack of credibility of our institutions is simply unsustainable. No nation can survive when its citizens no longer know what is true. And yes, we understand the press will never be perfect. There will be mistakes. But what we are seeing isn't an occasional slip-up or even a brief foray of incompetence. It's a deliberate, calculated, and pervasive attempt at dishonesty and malice. It's a culture where lies are encouraged and rewarded if they attack the right side.

Multiple polls demonstrate how little trust the American people now have in Big Media. For example, a recent survey from Edelman shows trust in Big Media had fallen to an all-time low. According to this poll:

- 56 percent of Americans agree with the statement that "journalists and reporters are purposely trying to mislead people by saying things they know are false or gross exaggerations."

- 58 percent think that "most news organizations are more concerned with supporting an ideology or political position than with informing the public."

Think about this: Americans no longer believe the press just innocently makes mistakes. The majority think that the media are actively trying to mislead people.

And botching stories can have tragic consequences. How many times have we had reporting on police shootings that led to riots, death, and millions of dollars in property damage, only to find out the media missed the facts?

But as chilling as the death of truth is, and as terrifying as the thought of how this impacts what our democracy should be, there is something that is more frightening than all of this. And it leaves us to the question:

Just what, exactly, are they trying to achieve?

WASHINGTON, DC

Two Years Before

The DOJ attorney wiped his hands across his eyes and rubbed them. He was getting tired. He glanced at his watch and cleared his throat. "So no, we're not too worried about the consequences of our actions," he concluded.

Beaten, Darren nodded in agreement. Then neither was he.

"So, this is where it leaves us," the attorney said. "We help you. You help us. It's like a fifth-grade art competition; everyone's a winner. We all end up better off."

The FBI director pushed back from the table. It was clear that he was done. "We're building something important, Mr. Hardy," he said abruptly. "Something delicate and new. A new nation. New rules. A great new order. But we need your help to do that.

"There are particular stories that are critical to be told. Other times, we need to ensure others are buried or kept secret. Sometimes, we need you simply to destroy those enemies who oppose our vision—if necessary, their reputations, their livelihoods, even their families.

"So, we're going to share some information with you from time to time. But Mr. Hardy, we have to know that you'll report it. And report it the way we frame it. Report it when and how we want it. It's not a lot to ask in order to help us make a more socially just country."

Darren nodded slowly. "I can do that," he said.

DEATH OF THE
BILL OF RIGHTS

E arl Warren, one of the most well-known justices ever to serve on the Supreme Court, once famously said, "It is doubtful that Congress would pass the Bill of Rights if it were introduced today."

Kind of shocking, isn't it? The very thing our Founding Fathers fought, bled, and sacrificed for might be something we wouldn't be willing to pass through Congress any longer.

But how could anyone argue with that observation when we see the constant attacks on the Bill of Rights by members of Congress, members of the executive, including sometimes even our president? These leaders don't see the Bill of Rights as a valued feature of our government, but as an obstacle that has to be overcome, something they constantly have to find a way around in their relentless reach for power.

Put each one of the Bill of Rights to a vote before a Democratic Congress, and most of them would fail.

And when you remember that the entire purpose of the Bill of Rights is to guarantee individual freedoms from an oppressive and overly powerful government, it's easy to see which side values individual liberty and which side values something else.

When the first Congress convened in 1789, their first order of business was to fulfill a promise they had made to the thirteen states (especially powerful states such as Massachusetts, Virginia, and New York): that in return for their support in ratifying the Constitution, Congress would quickly pass a set of explicit amendments guaranteeing individual rights. (Ironic, isn't it, that states such as New York and Massachusetts now have leaders who seem intent on dismantling the Bill of Rights?)

James Madison, the youngest member of Congress, took on the responsibility of writing the proposed amendments. Taking ideas from other members of Congress, as well as from various state constitutions, he initially recommended nineteen possible amendments, ten of which were ratified in 1791. Becoming known as the Bill of Rights, they stand today as a final guard against aggressive federal overreach, enshrining the ideals of American liberty—a model and example to the rest of the world.

But the final guard is in its death throes, bleeding from a thousand cuts.

The Bill of Rights includes these ten amendments:

Amendment	Rights and Protections
First	Freedom of speech, press, religion, assembly, and the right to petition the government
Second	Right to bear arms
Third	Protection against being forced to house soldiers
Fourth	Protection against unreasonable search and seizure and the issuing of warrants without probable cause
Fifth	Protection against trial without indictment, double jeopardy, self-incrimination, and the seizure of property
Sixth	Right to a speedy trial, to be informed of charges, to be confronted by witnesses, to call witnesses, and to a legal counsel
Seventh	Right to trial by jury
Eighth	Protection against excessive bail, fines, and cruel and unusual punishment

Ninth	Rights enshrined in the Constitution will not infringe on other rights
Tenth	Powers not granted to the Federal Government in the Constitution reside solely in the states or the people

Reading this list of protected rights, one would wonder what is contained there that is so troubling to progressives? Why have they fomented so many attacks upon them?

When we consider the current attacks upon the Bill of Rights, we should start by considering those targeting the First Amendment—the First Freedom—which is in many ways the foundation of all other constitutionally protected rights.

RELIGIOUS FREEDOM

Though attacks on the freedom of religion certainly predated COVID-19 restrictions, since the pandemic began they have become particularly noxious, proving that the government and our society are growing overtly hostile toward religion.

The liberal theory of *never let a crisis go to waste* has never been so brilliantly implemented.

Multiple state governors have ruled that home improvement stores, skating rinks, drug stores, grocery stores, liquor stores, and bars may remain open during the global pandemic—but that church services must end, or at least limit their services so as to make it impossible for members to meaningfully participate. One state governor even threatened to arrest parishioners for attending church—while remaining in their cars, listening to the service on their phones, their cars socially distanced in the parking lot, and their windows were rolled up!

The liberal position on the First Amendment: *Yes, on going to the liquor store. No, on attending church.*

Another example. Little Sisters of the Poor, an organization run by Catholic nuns dedicated to serving the sick and elderly, were forced to engage in a decade-long battle against the Obama administration when it sought to force the Little Sisters to provide health insurance that included various forms of contraception, some of which the FDA has ruled could cause an early abortion, and which the Catholic nuns opposed based on moral and religious teachings.

Perhaps the best way to illustrate the war on religious freedom is to quantify the legal assaults against it. The numbers don't lie, facts being stubborn things, and they paint a frightening picture.

It took more than a hundred years for the Supreme Court to take up and decide just three cases regarding religious liberty. The principle was just not commonly challenged in the courts. More than forty years then passed before it took up another case. But starting in 1940, litigation against religious liberty exploded to more than seventy-five cases, as parties hostile to religious liberty began to understand that the courts could be an avenue to restrict it. Prayer in schools, prayer in government meetings, wearing religious clothing, distributing religious literature, religious use of land, the ability to religiously assemble...the list of cases before the Court has grown long, leaving no doubt there is a legal, political, and cultural battle against religious freedom.

FREEDOM OF SPEECH

In China, there is no freedom of speech. Instead, every tweet, public statement, and action is observed, recorded, and judged. Everything from what you read on the internet to what you say to your neighbor across the hall is put into a "social score." This score is orders of magnitude more meaningful than a credit score, as the communist system will determine virtually every reward and punishment imaginable to incentivize "proper" Chinese behavior. The results of low social scores include loss of utilities (from slowed Wi-Fi to actual loss of power and water), lack of access to loans or the banking system, expulsion from schools, professional demerits, demotions, loss of income or jobs, travel and flight bans, displays of your mug shot on pubic screens where you commonly walk...in China there is no limit to the punishments one can receive for being guilty of wrongspeak.

And while it once seemed like such a dystopian hell could never come to America, it's very clear it is here. Conservative voices, opinions, podcasts, and social media influencers are disappearing from the internet. People across the nation have been fired for voicing support for local police departments or for simply having a Parler account. Democrat members of Congress are currently drafting legislation to "regulate" talk radio and the internet. COVID commentators—including supremely qualified physicians and other medical professionals—have lost income, reputation, and even their jobs simply for questioning the accepted narrative. A sitting US president was muzzled on social media. And even that wasn't enough for Twitter CEO Jack Dorsey, who then threatened, "We are focused on one account [@realDonaldTrump] right now, but this is going to be much bigger than just one account, and it's going to go on for much longer than just this day, this week, and the next few weeks, and go on beyond the inauguration."

Perhaps there is no better example than a recent *New York Times* editorial that proclaimed: "Free speech is killing us. Hate speech leads to violence. Free speech will lead to totalitarianism and even genocide!" The suggested answer: "rethinking" the First Amendment, to allow both the government and private companies to limit speech.

From Vladimir Lenin to Vladimir Putin, from the CCP in China to tech oligarchs in Silicon Valley, from Hollywood (yes, the same Hollywood that selects some actors because they have lighter skin in order to satisfy racist Beijing's demands) to the mainstream media and our universities, the left has shown again and again that they hate hearing anything they don't agree with.

But why do they hate free speech? If their ideas are more moral, superior, and fair, why would they not be eager to defend them? If conservatives' ideas are so inferior, then they should be easy to refute. Indeed, it seems they should *demand* to debate their ideas against the broken and failed conservative ideas of the past.

If what you are saying is true, you don't have to crush dissent. If what you are saying is true, you don't have to lie, exaggerate, misinform, indoctrinate, or seek to silence those who disagree with you. But if you know what you are selling is vapidity and hate, well…then maybe you're not so hot on debate.

If there is debate, their ideas will be examined. If their ideas are examined, they will lose the argument. If they lose the argument, they have no power.

And *that* is why the left hates free speech. It all comes down to one thing: *Power.*

Benjamin Franklin once presciently stated, "Those who would give up essential liberty, to purchase a little temporary safety, deserve neither liberty nor safety."

The left knows they must convince the American people they will be "safer" if they will but surrender their rights of free speech. January 2021 gave them the opportunity to do that.

The logic is pretty simple: "hate speech" leads to violence. "Hate speech" is the offspring of the right. The riots in Washington, DC, were nothing less than a violent insurrection intended to overthrow the US government. It could happen again. Indeed, one demonstration or Parler post is all it would take to wipe all of our freedoms away. Therefore, for the good of us all, and in order to protect our country, we must shut down this toxic speech.

Europe has already attempted this very thing, as "hate speech" was recently criminalized. Not surprisingly, these laws have utterly failed. In spite of them, anti-Semitic hate crimes (actual crimes of violence against a person, not a violation of a speech code) are thirteen times more frequent in the U.K. than in the US, and four times more likely in France. It seems the only thing European hate speech laws have done is to empower bureaucratic bullies with oppressive tools by which to enforce their agendas. The failure of hate speech laws has become so obvious that even the ultra-progressive Human Rights Watch has concluded that "...there is little connection in practice between draconian hate speech laws and the lessening of ethnic and racial violence or tension."

Another way the left hopes to convince Americans to trade away their right to free speech is to redefine it to a mere "value," not a constitutionally protected right. Rights do not change. Rights are inherent in the life of every human. But values come and go. Values change with public opinion, with the news of the day, with changes in attitudes, or in competition with other "values."

If free speech is not a right, if it is redefined to be just a value—well, that opens up all sorts of possibilities. The selective suppression of speech. The redefining of conservative speech as "hate speech." The de-platforming of conservative voices on social media. It opens up the possibility of commercial banks and credit card companies refusing to provide financial services to conservative media platforms or even private American citizens, as recently happened when Chase Bank began closing the personal banking accounts of right-wing personalities without explanation.

More recently, the six largest banks in the United States pledged to align their activities to support the goals of the Paris Climate Agreement, and they said they would use the agreement to guide their operations. Several of the largest banks have also cast their lots with the ESG (environmental, social, governance) movement, saying they will use various matrixes to measure customers' impacts on the environment, social justice, and other progressive goals. All of this casts doubt on whether someone who didn't agree with these goals could receive comprehensive financial services. Surely many customers will remain silent on such political issues rather than risk losing access to banking services without which no business or person can survive in the modern world.

Several years ago, fifty-four Democrat senators voted for a constitutional amendment that would put restrictions on the First Amendment right of free speech. They seemed not to understand that if you don't support free speech for those you disagree with, then you don't believe in free speech, period.

After this atrocious vote, none of the Democrat senators was rebuked for this "atrocious proposal." Indeed, as it turns out, they were simply ahead of their time.

WASHINGTON, DC

February

Darren Hardy glanced at his phone, saw the name on the screen, and exhaled a slow breath. Not the person he wanted to talk to, at least not right now. But frankly, it wasn't the person he ever wanted to talk to. Never was a good time to talk to his brother. So much had passed between them now. Time. Emotion. A lot of anger. A growing chasm. Fewer and fewer words.

One of them had betrayed his family, and one of them had not. One of them had seemingly lost his mind, all of his potential wasted in the military; one of them was growing into one of the most influential people in the country. They weren't living in different worlds; they were living in different universes now.

Still, he picked up the phone and tapped the green button to take the call. "Peter, how you doing?" he asked his brother.

Peter Hardy—Special Forces soldier, Scout Sniper qualified, able to live in the desert for weeks without resupply, son of a billionaire father whom he hadn't spoken to in years, brother to a man who couldn't change the roll of toilet paper hanging on his bathroom wall if his life depended on it—answered quickly.

"Darren, I need your help."

Darren sat up. Not because he was concerned but because he was surprised. Those were words he had never heard before, not from Peter, and ones he'd thought he never would.

"What's up?" he asked, already enjoying the moment. Big Brother Peter had finally come to his senses. Big Brother finally regretted what he'd done. Big Brother wanted back into the family, back into his father's graces, back into the money.

This was going to be fun.

"I need your help." Peter repeated.

"Alright," Darren said, the most noncommittal response that he could think of.

"I've got a problem. No, I take that back. All of us have a problem. I don't know what to do. But I think that you can help me…us…help us get the word out."

"Us? Who is us?"

"Me. My team. A couple of the guys I work with."

Darren was suddenly less interested. "You're okay? You're not in trouble?"

"No. This is something else."

A mix of emotions settled over Darren. A little disappointed that his brother wasn't in real trouble, something that would force him to his senses. But he was also curious. Help us get the word out? What was he talking about?

"Where are you?" Darren pressed.

"Down at the Farm." The CIA training compound, two hours from DC.

"I thought you were overseas?"

"I was reassigned another mission."

"You're not shot or blown up or anything?"

"Obviously not."

"You do something wrong?" His voice sounded almost hopeful.

"Really, Darren?" Peter answered.

"Hey, we haven't talked in a couple years. I don't know—"

"I have something. It's important. And I don't know what to do with it."

"Tell me," Darren said.

"I'm not sure we can talk on the phone."

Darren was silent. His communications were certainly being monitored. No way his friends trusted him with some of the secrets he kept, not without a little babysitting. So yeah, not a good idea to talk on the phone. "Do you want to get together? I could open up some time next week," he offered.

Peter took a breath again. There were about a hundred reasons that was not going to happen. And though he knew they would be listening, he decided he didn't care. Everything he was about to say, they knew already anyway.

"I was doing some work south of here," he started. "We were collecting on some of our neighbors. I was given something by our friends in the Centro Nacional de Inteligencia, the CNI—you know, the Mexican CIA."

"I know what the CNI is," Darren lied.

"They gave us a flash drive. Surveillance from the Mexican government. A recording of the president, our president, talking to the Mexican leader, last year. Felix was telling POTUS that the Mexican police had intercepted some targets on their side of the border. Eight women. Syrians. He wanted to know if POTUS wanted his government to hold them. The president ripped into him. Told him he was a racist and a xenophobe. Said the US welcomed refugees. She told Felix that was exactly the kind of sexist attitude she was trying to snuff out here in America. So fine, President Felix says. And he let them go."

Darren started fearing where this was heading. "These were the people responsible for the National Cathedral bombing?" he asked.

"Yep. The same. Darren...think of that. More than four hundred people killed. A couple senators. Half a dozen congressman."

Darren swallowed hard. "That's going to be a problem for the president."

"Yeah. And it's worse than you can imagine. When you listen to the recording, when you hear the things she says, it's pretty shocking. Then to know these women hooked up with the others and immediately went to Washington and killed four hundred people. Yeah, I'd say it's going to be a problem for the president."

"Have you told anyone else about this? Anyone in the press?"

His brother hesitated a few seconds. "A few."

"You've already gone to someone else!" Darren shouted. "You didn't come to me!"

"I didn't...I didn't know if you'd be...you know...interested."

Darren stewed as he translated in his mind. "Interested." Another way of saying "on my team." And actually, that was smart of him, because he was defiantly dressed in blue and not red.

Yeah, smart for his brother not to trust him. But that was going to be a problem, because now it wasn't a matter of just spiking his own story; they would have to find a way to kill the other sources.

Difficult, but not impossible. Not in this day and time. Freedom of speech... with the partners he had with him...such a quaint little thing.

"You say that you have evidence of this conversation between the two presidents?" Darren asked.

"I did."

"You did. But now you don't?"

"We were intercepted. The drive was taken. It is gone."

Darren felt his chest relax, the task of suppression suddenly much less of a challenge.

"Our own guys took it," Peter said.

"Our own guys?"

"I'll fill in the details later. But I need to know you'll help me. The American people deserve to know their president was culpable in the deaths of hundreds of our people, including senators and congressmen. She's lying about it now. She's covering everything up. You are one of the most powerful journalists in America. You need to get this out."

Darren shook his head. No way that was going to happen. He didn't spend a single brain cell wondering about that.

The only thing he was considering was what was going to happen to his brother. Could he protect him? Did he even want to? Was the chasm between them now too great?

Because Darren knew one thing: if he had to choose, and heaven help them if he had to, he knew which side he was on.

The moment he hung up the phone, he reached out to his contacts. Within the hour, every reporter to whom Peter had spoken was told either to drop the issue, or to be let go from their respective news organization. By the end of the day, the various social media companies had de-platformed anyone even discussing the topic. Peter's cousin, a relatively minor social media influencer and semiprofessional blogger, had his servers deleted and was disappeared from the internet. By the end of the week, fabricated evidence began making its way across the globe that the Mexican government was responsible for the bombing.

Darren couldn't help a smug feeling, knowing the amount of power he held. The teams had been established. There were no trades and no going back.

* * * * *

The Second Amendment: In 2016, House Democrats conducted a "sit-in" on the House floor to force a vote on legislation that would prohibit anyone on the government No Fly List from purchasing a firearm. The No Fly List is the blacklisting system for what the government calls "known or suspected terrorists." What a great idea, the media cried. "Of course, we shouldn't allow suspected terrorists to buy firearms," the *Los Angeles Times* was quick to say.

Problem was, it wasn't that simple. Hundreds of thousands of law-abiding Americans are on the No Fly List, many of them even without their knowledge. How many Americans are on the list? No one knows. The list is so sloppy and disorganized, it's impossible to tell. But one thing we do know: the majority of the Americans on the No Fly List have never been convicted of a crime. Never accused of a crime. Never even suspected of a crime.

Even the liberal ACLU opposed the idea, stating,

> Our nation's watchlisting system is error-prone and unreliable because it uses vague and overbroad criteria and secret evidence to place individuals on blacklists without a meaningful process to correct government error and clear their names.

> The government contends that it can place Americans on the No Fly List who have never been charged, let alone convicted of a crime, on the basis of prediction that

they, nevertheless, pose a threat (which is undefined) of conduct that the government concedes "may or may not occur." The overly broad criteria result in a high risk of error and it is imperative that the watchlisting system include due process safeguards—which it does not. In the context of the No Fly List, for example, the government refuses to provide even Americans who know they are on the list with the full reasons for the placement, the basis for those reasons, and a hearing before a neutral decision-maker.

Yes, even the ACLU realized that using such a system to preclude any citizen, including perhaps millions who have never even been accused of a crime, from purchasing a firearm is clearly unconstitutional.

On President Biden's website, he has laid out his war plans for destroying the Second Amendment. His tactics include, but are not limited to, repealing the Protection of Lawful Commerce in Arms Act, the law that prevents manufacturers being held liable for their products. What this means is that you can't sue Chevrolet when one of their vehicles is involved in an automobile accident, but very soon you may be able to sue Winchester when one of their rifles is used in a crime. The left also plans to ban the manufacture and sale of any weapon or magazine that holds more than three rounds (and then, absurdly, justifies this action by saying we "protect" *ducks* by limiting hunting to three shells in a shotgun—a comparison so inept it begs the question, has *anyone* on the left *ever* been hunting?).

The left will then proceed to "buy back the assault weapons and high-capacity magazines already in our communities," and restrict the number of firearms an individual may purchase over a span of time. Background checks will be required for all gun sales, which will result in person-to-person sales, exchanges, or even family gifts becoming a federal crime. The online sale of guns and ammunition will be criminalized. If the Biden administration has their way, they will even require the Social Security Administration to send to the background check system "records that it holds...because they have been adjudicated by the SSA." They also plan to "put Americans on the path to ensuring that 100% of firearms sold in America are smart guns" that "allow only authorized users to fire a gun."

And they won't stop there. Indeed, like all power-hungry regimes, there can be little doubt they will not stop until *all* private gun ownership has been criminalized. Perhaps the most concerning proposal of them all is when

President Biden promises to enact other "common sense" reforms limiting Second Amendment rights. Who knows what these additional "common sense" ideas might be? But one thing we know for sure: it will *never* be enough. The cycle is predictable. Implement policies that strip away some gun rights. Gun violence is not abated. Obviously, we need more gun control. Strip away more Second Amendment rights. Another mass shooting takes place. Obviously, we need more gun control. Strip away more rights. The cycle will go on.

And do you notice something familiar in Biden's language? He describes the "scourge of violence" and the "gun-violence epidemic," language designed to generate fear. Just as with "hate speech," the left wants to convince Americans that guns are a real and imminent threat to our very survival as a nation, thus justifying any action they take in order to protect us from the abyss.

WASHINGTON, DC

April

After another tragic shooting left more than a dozen students dead in a small town in Texas, the president declared a national emergency and invoked emergency powers. When the last of the gun confiscation executive orders had been signed, the cascading events that followed could only be described as a monumental cluster.

Take every single privately owned weapon in the entire country! No way that was going to happen.

Within minutes of the final order being signed, eighteen states sued the federal government. But the feds made it clear they intended to enforce the new orders. Dozens of cities around the country said they would ignore the new laws. Several governors then designated these cities "rogue governments" and tried to send state troopers in, heavily armed to defend themselves and with the supposed purpose of "retraining" the sheriffs.

Wyoming proved to be a very difficult case. Several local law enforcement officers denied state troopers entrance into their cities and threatened to arrest any who came. More than half of the state troopers openly defied the governor and sided with local law enforcement. The governor was furious. He petitioned the feds for support—which he received—and they threatened maximum penalty for any of the local law enforcement they arrested, and lethal force for those who resisted. An unknown number of deputies then defied the sheriffs, turned in their badges, and crossed to the other side.

To call it a crisis was a generous understatement, and one with no solution in sight. But with each passing hour it became clear the federal government was intent on winning the standoff. The US attorney general designated Wyoming a rogue state, and the feds were assembled at various locations, intent on making a point, and making it severely.

But there was another motivation for the federal government to press the crisis in Wyoming, unrelated but important to a few very powerful men in DC.

He had made it personal. He had made them angry.

And there was a relationship they could use to punish him. Kill a couple birds with one stone.

Back in DC at the federal command center, the question was asked of the FBI director: where to start?

With many of the rural states, and much of the West, in open rebellion against the federal mandates, it was a target-rich environment. The director could have thrown a dart at the map to choose a place to send in the feds. But he didn't. He had something more in mind.

He glanced at his general counsel. "Are we in agreement here?" he asked.

The counsel nodded. "You might as well start there, sir. It's as good as anywhere. Broadly, it will allow us to send a message to the nation. To our other needs, it will keep Peter in his place."

"He's going to know we did it? I mean, specifically. To him."

"We'll make sure he does, sir."

The director thought and then nodded.

SHERIDAN, WYOMING

April

As a general rule, Jesse Hardy kept to himself. He hadn't traveled outside of Sheridan since his wife had died nearly two years before, and he only left his ranch when he needed something from town or when a neighbor needed help. He was old. Happy. Content, and without a dog in any fight.

But in a twist of bad fate, Jesse Hardy was about to become famous. And were it not for his grandson, none of it would have happened.

Cody Williams, the local sheriff, knocked on Jesse's door and waited patiently. Though it was early, he knew the old cowboy would be awake. The sun had crested the horizon just a few hours before, the air was still cool, and the young sheriff blew into his fisted hands to warm them.

The door pulled open. Cody looked anxiously at his old friend. Despite the early hour, no bathrobe or sweatpants for him. Jeans. Old boots. White mustache. Blue eyes. Deep crevices on a tan face.

Cody followed Jesse inside and sat down across from him at the modest kitchen table and took the offered cup of coffee, knowing it would be black. "Would it kill you to sweeten it?" the sheriff asked as he poured some sugar into his cup.

"You're up kind of early," the cowboy said.

Cody laughed softly. It was a strange sound, laughter at a time like this. "I'm not up early, I stayed up late."

Jesse nodded and sipped his coffee.

"How's Peter?" Cody asked as he stirred the sugar into his cup.

Jesse face remained firm, but his eyes were still proud. "Doing good."

"Where is he now?"

"Not sure. He doesn't tell us much."

"But he's healthy and okay."

"Far as we know. I guess the army would tell us if it was otherwise."

"He's a good kid." A pause. "And your other grandson? Darren?"

"He's okay. Way too much like his old man. I don't hear much from either one of them. Money. It kills families." His voice trailed off.

Cody nodded and looked around at the old ranch home. Jesse's son had made billions in tech and then the market, but he never came home. To him that said a lot. "I see Darren all over the news," he said. "I'm sure you're proud."

"Don't care much for his politics, but to each his own. So far as I know, nothing he's done has driven down the price of beef, so I'm okay with it all."

They both fell silent. It was time to face the obvious.

Cody felt the strain flow through his body. He hadn't slept in two days. He hadn't eaten in nearly as much time. Things were changing so fast. There was so much on the line, the stakes so high. "You know why I'm here, don't you Jesse?"

"Tell me," Jesse answered.

The sheriff studied the old rancher for a moment then nodded toward the front door. "You can't do it, Jesse. You can't defy them like this."

"Why are they here? Why me? What did I do?"

"Nothing really, Jesse, but that's not the point. You were given an order. You've got to comply."

"I've had some of those guns for more than sixty years. Ain't been no problem until now."

"What about the assault rifles?"

"Everyone has them!"

"The ones that Peter gave you—"

"Every one of them is legal. Legal, you hear me, Sheriff. Ain't no laws broken here. Not so much as a jaywalk. And Peter didn't give them to me, anyway. I only store them for him while he's overseas. He comes out to the ranch to go hunting.

"And tell me something, Sheriff. How did they even know I had them? How'd they know I had any weapons at all?"

The sheriff didn't answer.

"No laws have been broken here, Sheriff," the old man said again.

Cody swallowed. "They've surrounded the house, Jesse."

"I know that," Jesse said as he stood. He moved to the nearest window and drew back the blinds, throwing shafts of morning sunlight into the room. The black metal of a dozen federal vehicles shone in the Western morning sun, with dozens of paramilitary federal cops spread behind them.

"So, what are you going to do?" Jesse asked, turning from the window to study his young friend.

"I'm going to follow the law, Jesse. I'm the sheriff. The laws of the land aren't like a buffet. We can't just pick the ones we will follow and ignore the rest."

"You here for my guns, then?" Jesse asked.

"No, Jesse, I'm not here to take your guns. I think…I think the law is wrong. But I also think it's crazy to talk about killing each other over something like this!"

"So, whatever the government tells you to do, you'll do it then?"

The sheriff only sipped his coffee.

"Kind of like the Germans did to the Jews in Germany," Jesse said.

The sheriff scowled. "I'm going to ignore the fact you said that. Come on, Jesse. Let's do the right thing. The smart thing. Let's not pick a fight you can't win. Let's give them what they want and let the courts figure it out."

"You think the courts will get it right?" Jesse asked. It was clear he didn't.

"I know that this isn't worth dying over," the sheriff said. "I'm just trying to do my job."

"Just following orders," Jesse said.

Cody's eyes drifted downward. For nearly a minute the silence dragged on, Jesse staring at the sheriff, the sheriff staring at the floor. It was Jesse who broke the silence. "It's okay, Cody. My days aren't much longer for this earth."

Cody huffed in anger. It wasn't going to come to that! "Let me talk to them," he said as he stood. "Sit here, Jesse. Don't move. Don't do anything. Just sit here while I go talk to them."

The walk from Jesse's front porch to the black SUVs was as long as any the sheriff had ever taken. There were at least a dozen federal troopers there.

Black fatigues. Body armor. Heavily armed. Faces hidden behind black masks. They looked like they were about to storm Osama bin Laden's lair, not an old rancher's farmhouse.

Two people removed themselves from the group and met him in front of their vehicle, both of them women in black business suits and dark glasses. Neither looked in the mood for anything other than a fight.

Cody held his palms out as he closed the final yards between them. "I think it would be best if everyone remained calm," he said. "I don't want a fight. Jesse certainly doesn't want one, either."

"And I think it would be best if you surrendered your weapon," a dark-haired woman answered. Even behind her sunglasses he could see that she was glaring. Cody felt a twinge of defiance run through him, but he kept the emotion from his face.

"Easy, ma'am. I'm on your side," he said. "Let's just take a deep breath here."

"It's not ma'am," she spat back. "It's Agent Jackson. And I have neither the time nor patience for a deep breath, Sheriff. So, I will say it again. Surrender your weapon, or we take it. And anyone who tries to stop us will find out the hard way that we have been authorized to use lethal force."

Cody felt his body tensed and his temper flared in rage. Why was she so defiant? She was itching for a fight!

His thoughts flashed to the conversation he'd had the night before. His wife had wanted him to stand up to the feds. To Cody, it seemed myopic. Dangerous. He had told her that the federal government was misguided, but they weren't their enemy. They weren't dangerous. Things would work themselves out.

But standing here, staring down dozens of federal agents threatening force... against an old man who was only protecting his rights... he had to wonder.

"Look," he said in exasperation. "I'm not defying you or anyone else here. And I'm certainly not here to fight you. I'm just trying to talk some sense into an old friend. I don't want any trouble. Believe me when I say that."

"The problem, Sheriff," she snapped, "is I don't believe you. Frankly, I haven't believed a word anyone in this God-forsaken state has told me. And there are a couple of things you need to understand. The president has designated Wyoming a rogue entity. We aren't playing by the normal rules now. We're federal agents dealing with state terrorists. Miranda rights don't apply to terrorists. And I'm only going to say this one more time: surrender your weapon or we'll bring you to your knees."

Cody felt his world spin around him. It seemed as if time slowed down. He froze, staring, his eyes focused on the dark glasses reflecting back the morning sun. For a painful moment, he didn't know what to do. Fear. Rage. Doubt. His *head spun. He felt instantly sick. Half a dozen times he had faced armed men. He'd been shot at a thousand times in Iraq. But he'd never faced...what? Whatever this was he was facing now. He felt his stomach churn, his mind spinning in confusion.*

Then he knew what he had to do. It was clear. He had no choice.

And for the first time in weeks, he felt the discontent that had dominated him evaporate.

He touched the brim of his cowboy hat, turned around, and began to walk back to Jesse's house.

The gun shot rang out.

It would be debated for years who fired the first shot.

History would never be satisfied; proof would never be definitive. The bodycam footage could never convince anyone. Deep fakes multiplied across social media too quickly for them to be pulled down. Forensics teams were sent to examine the scene and interview the feds, but it was clear that the evidence had been altered and the testimony was inconsistent.

There were only two facts about the standoff that were beyond debate.

First, the sheriff and the rancher were dead, a federal officer wounded.

Second, the standoff in the middle of nowhere Wyoming had started a confrontation from which they would never recover.

When Peter Hardy found out what had happened, he immediately understood it was retaliation against him by the president of the United States.

DEATH OF PRIVACY

The Fourth Amendment guarantees "protection against unreasonable search and seizure and the issuing of warrants without probable cause." The point being that the government cannot violate your privacy without a justifiable reason to do so.

Surely, this includes protections of our privacy against private sector intrusion as well as the growing and extremely troubling alliance between government and Big Tech.

The titans of tech make no bones about the fact they seek to know us better than we know ourselves. They make trillions of dollars by selling your curiosity, the things you know, the things you want, fear, lust for, and hate. And with the dawn of 5G and the Internet of Things, there is virtually nothing about you that will not be known. Everything about your family. What's in your fridge? How hot do you like your shower? Are there traces of blood or alcohol in your urine?

All of that information is going to be bought and sold.

To make things worse, we now have a loathsome alliance growing between Big Tech and government spy and law enforcement agencies. It has even gone so far as for the Biden administration to propose they use the private sector to spy on US citizens in ways that they, as government officials, are not authorized to do. *Can't get a warrant to surveil a US citizen? No problem. Contract Big Tech to do it for you.*

And when you bring in the power of the media, it creates an environment that will suffocate the soul.

Award-winning journalist Glenn Greenwald has written on this alliance:

> A new and rapidly growing journalistic "beat" has arisen over the last several years that can best be described as an unholy mix of junior high hall-monitor tattling and Stasi-like citizen surveillance. It is half adolescent and half malevolent. Its primary objectives are control, censorship, and the destruction of reputations for fun and power. Though its epicenter is the largest corporate media outlets, it is the very antithesis of journalism.

After the 2020 elections, we saw a frightening shift in security priorities as the new administration directed intelligence agencies to change their focus to what they claimed was a new threat. It used to be they were focused on threats from abroad: ISIS, Kim Jong-un, narco-terrorism, and such. Now they want us to believe the greatest threat to our national security comes from within. Happily, the government is ready to protect us from these emerging threats. As an example, John Brennan, CIA director under President Obama, assured us that American intelligence agencies "are moving in laser-like fashion to try to uncover as much as they can about what looks very similar to insurgency movements that we've seen overseas." He goes on to describe these domestic insurgents as "an unholy alliance frequently of religious extremists, authoritarians, fascists, bigots, racists, nativists, even libertarians."

Brennan's words make it very clear that the power elites in DC are seeking to criminalize any opposition to the ruling class. To do this, they will define the "insurgency" as anyone who isn't willing to bow to the power of the elites.

But US intelligence agencies have no legal authority—none—to turn their power on any US citizen, be they libertarians, religious extremists, or any other such group. The awesome powers of the NSA should *never* be used against American citizens. Neither the CIA nor any of the other seventeen intelligence agencies should *ever* be focused on our nation's own people. The wall between US intelligence agencies and law enforcement should *never* be violated.

The former director of the CIA, John Brennan, knows this. But apparently, he doesn't care.

And do you notice anything missing from Brennan's list? Notice there was no mention of the thugs of Antifa, the most savage anti-American organization that we've seen in years. No mention of the threat from the months of violent riots, with more than a billion dollars of property damage and dozens of people killed. No mention of political leaders such as Representative Maxine Waters calling for protesters to "get more confrontational." No mention of rising socialist leaders and their threats against democracy, demanding to "burn it all down."

Imagine giving a political operative such as John Brennan and his fellow elites the power to define who fits in the category of "extremists." Then imagine giving them the power to decide what to do with you once they have identified you as a threat. But we don't have to wonder about that. At the same time Brennan was describing US intelligence as being focused laser-like on our fellow citizens, his colleague was demanding that Republicans must be forced to offer "the truth" before they're "allowed" to speak on anything else. Another senior former Obama national security official was demanding that Republicans should be subject to a detox of their bad ideas, this detox to take place under the supervision of benevolent national security officials such as…you know, himself.

Some have even called for protecting children from their parents, who might be creating future conservative insurgents.

Representative Adam Schiff (D-CA), chairman of the powerful House Permanent Select Committee on Intelligence, has introduced a bill that would take the existing language from legislation authorizing the global war on terror and amend it so that now they could use those powers within the United States.

The Fourth Amendment is being decimated. And it should scare every one of us.

If we allow federal leaders to describe any citizen with whom they have political disagreement as an "extremist" or "potential terrorist," in order to justify turning the powers of the government upon them, how long will it be before this unholy alliance between Big Tech, media, and government agencies creates conditions that are Orwellian to the core?

The answer is pretty simple. Like…you know, by the end of the week.

And when the claim for absolute power over our lives is complete, will any of us object? Or will we be like Winston Smith, the victim of totalitarianism Orwell described? *"But it was all right, everything was all right, the struggle was finished. He had won the victory over himself. He loved Big Brother."*

*   *   *   *   *

There are countless examples we could give of the Bill of Rights being under attack. The rights to be informed of charges, confronted by your accuser, and the presumption of innocence were viciously attacked by Democrats during the Justice Kavanaugh confirmation hearings. College students charged with harassment or assault are regularly denied due process: the right to face their accusers, cross-examine witnesses, or introduce evidence that might show their innocence. The right of protection of your property from rioters, arsonists, and vandals has certainly been challenged. The right to be free from violence for your political views was tested during the past few elections. The right to privacy is little more than a whimsical myth. The Patriot Act. Enhanced interrogation and indefinite detention. Red flag laws. Civil asset forfeiture. Judicial activism. Federal supremacy.

All of which makes one thing very clear: the Bill of Rights is being murdered before our very eyes. And if we lose the Bill of Rights, we lose our nation.

THE RE-EDUCATION OF AMERICA

Who controls the past, controls the future.
Who controls the present, controls the past.

— George Orwell, *1984*

It is in the interest of tyrants to reduce the people to
ignorance and vice. For they cannot live in any country
where virtue and knowledge prevail.

— Samuel Adams

We can't examine the suicide of our nation without discussing the role that education has played in our demise.

A society that does not pass on its values to the next generation cannot sustain itself. An uneducated people are unable to govern themselves. Worse, an ignorant society, indoctrinated in things that are demonstrably untrue, not only can't be governed, but will actually assist in its own suicide.

One thing is clear: Social Justice ideology has seeped from academia into media, nonprofits, foundations, corporate boards, the military, human resource departments, entertainment, sports, Silicon Valley, and government bureaucracies. It has become as pervasive as the air we breathe. That being true, what we are witnessing today can come as no surprise. A purposefully miseducated people, indoctrinated to the point that they are no longer able, or willing, to recognize truth, condemns a nation to demise.

We are a systemically racist nation, corrupt to the very core.

Global warming is going to destroy mankind if we don't do something within the next nine years.

Capitalism has led to more poverty and despair than any other economic model in history.

The Founding Fathers were corrupt and bigoted simpletons. Nothing they produced is worth preserving.

Those who oppose the rise of progressive thought are not just uniformed, they are evil and must be silenced, shamed, and if necessary, destroyed.

Such are the ideas that are taught to our youth today.

For multiple generations, a corrupt and dishonest education system, one that began at the university level but then seeped down to the K through 12 levels (as those university students became the educators of our children) has left our nation with an ignorant populace. Unaware of the most obvious facts of history, economics, or the realities of the world in which we live, they are unprepared to defend the ideas of a free republic.

As an example, in a recent poll nearly 40 percent of young people disagreed with the statement that the United States "has a history we should be proud of." This is stunning. In all of our history, there is *nothing* to be proud of? Could anything be any further from the truth! Worse, it shows the equally stunning success of educational indoctrination.

Multiple polls also show that between 35 and 40 percent of millennials believe our nation is "among the most unequal societies in the world." Not Iran. Not China, with millions of ethnic Uighurs in re-education camps. Not Russia, controlled by an ex-KGB thug and brutal oligarchs. Not the dozens and dozens of failed socialist states. Not Pakistan or Afghanistan, with their repression of minorities and women.

For anyone to believe that the United States is among the most unequal societies in the world shows a breathtaking lack of knowledge—a generation that has not been taught or read about, observed or traveled to any place beyond our own borders—other than, perhaps, to some of the beaches in Mexico on spring break.

But it also proves an important point. Parents can't rely on schools to teach the most basic facts. Some of this has to be taught around the dinner table, or our children will never know the truth.

When considering how our nation arrived at this point, it's clear that the effort to revise our history was an effort to destroy faith in the Founders, as well as the inspired documents that they produced and the system of government they created. The reason for this revision is very simple, coming down to two polarized frames of thought that are now in conflict.

> *Frame One:* The Founding Fathers, despite being imperfect and fallible men, were able to produce a revolutionary form of government that became enshrined in the Declaration of Independence, the Constitution, and the Bill of Rights, and this nation has created the greatest opportunity for individual freedom ever known to man. Because this new system of government is, as Abraham Lincoln said, *the last best hope on earth*, it needs to be defended.

> *Frame Two:* The Founding Fathers were racist, selfish, dishonest, sexist, uneducated, and immoral men. The very conception of the United States was based on slavery and continued oppression. Free-market capitalism did not lift billions of people out of poverty, but instead it is a racist tool of white oppression. Indeed, any wealth the United States has created was built upon the backs of slaves, the economic oppression continuing even to this day. This being true, not only is it appropriate to tear it down and start over, it's also a moral necessity. Anyone who would defend the indefensible must be ignored or silenced.

It's clear which of these opposing views has won the day within our education system.

Many historians use revisionist history for political purposes. Indeed, in this day we can safely say that *most* historians do this. To understand how they do it, it's helpful to look at the genesis of the revisionists' movement and a historian who had enormous impact on the teaching of history about our nation.

Charles Beard was a professor at Columbia University who wrote a book in 1913 titled *An Economic Interpretation of the Constitution of the United States.*

At that time, the history of the writing of the Constitution was in the genre of the "heroic" or "inspired." Almost all people within our nation, from vaunted professors in our elite universities to journalists, politicians, humble villagers, and uneducated farmers, accepted the view that our Founding Fathers were heroic, that they had sacrificed to accomplish something for the benefit of "the people."

But Beard wanted to change what he called the "stale" or "barren" view of the Constitution.

In essence, what Beard claimed is that those involved in creating the Constitution were motivated not by principles, ideals, or the general good of "We, the people," but rather by their own self-interest and how the new government could advance those selfish interests.

When Beard's book was published in 1913, there was an immediate negative reaction. But within a decade, his controversial thesis had become widely accepted. Soon, any dissenting voices were ridiculed or ignored, so much so that by 1935, of the forty-two new college textbooks in history that had been printed since 1913, thirty-seven of them had incorporated Beard's thesis of our Founders as selfish elites working to form a government to advance their own interests. Of nineteen older texts that had been revised and reissued during this same period, fourteen included Beard's theses.

Ironically, though Beard had once explained that he had wanted to publish his controversial work in order to generate debate, it had the opposite effect. During the 1930s and 1940s, his theory reached such a level of acceptance that no one dared to challenge it, his work becoming the orthodoxy of a new academic religion.

Multiple scholarly studies have examined the accuracy of Beard's work, most to devastating effect. Even Beard was critical of his own work, admitting that the historical evidence upon which he drew his conclusions was "fragmentary." Some academics have tried to justify Beard's fallacious conclusions by claiming he was only being a "devil's advocate." However, the lies simply cannot be justified. Beard clearly misrepresented history to undermine the Founders and the Constitution.

Still, as just one example for how Beard's thinking lives on, his work became a major inspiration for socialist writer Howard Zinn's *A People's History of the United States*, which has sold millions of copies and is taught in almost every university in the nation. The fact that Zinn's work is an extremely

critical and completely fraudulent history of our nation has not det
from its acceptance.

And this is just one example of history being weaponized. The
hundreds or thousands of others. By 1951, William F. Buckley note
our great universities, including specifically Yale, were no longer prod
students who believed in basic American values; yet most went on to
prominent positions in the private sector, education, and government.

The *New York Times*'s "1619 Project" is the most recent example o
rupt revisionist history. The major thesis of this work is that the real bi
the United States didn't take place in 1776 with the Declaration of Ind
dence but instead in 1619, with the arrival of the first slaves in Jamest
It goes on to claim that any economic success we have achieved as a n
is based on the advantage given to us by slavery, further claiming tha
Founding Fathers declared our independence from England not to cre
more perfect union" but to preserve slavery within the colonies.

Slavery was a horrible stain upon our nation, one that will in some
be impossible to be cleansed. But to claim that it was the foundational e
of all our history is to miss the mass of evidence of the good this na
has created.

The fact that much of the scholarly evidence of the 1619 Project
been debunked, that significant revisions have been issued to its major
sis, that more than fifty recognized scholars have refuted its integrity-
the point of demanding the Pulitzer committee rescind its award of the
litzer Prize to its chief author and the *New York Times*—has not stoppe
from being taught in elementary and high schools throughout our natio

Another part of the agenda of revisionist historians is to expunge
role of religion in the making of America, its struggle to survive, and its ev
tual growth into superpower status. A good example of this is found i
book by historian Doris Kearns Goodwin, *Team of Rivals*, in which Go
win details the events leading up to Lincoln's departure from his long-ti
home in Springfield, Illinois, following his election to the presidency. S
quotes Lincoln's farewell speech:

> My friends - No one, not in my situation, can appreciate
> my feeling of sadness at this parting. To this place and
> the kindness of these people, I owe everything. Here I
> have lived a quarter of a century and have passed from a
> young to an old man. Here my children have been born,
> and one is buried. I now leave, not knowing when, or

whether ever, I may return, with a task before me great-er than that which rested upon Washington... I hope in your prayers you will commend me, I bid you an affec-tionate farewell.

What did she leave out in the ellipses following "Washington"? Just this:

Without the assistance of that Divine Being who ever attended him, I cannot succeed. With that assistance, I cannot fail. Trusting in Him who can go with me, and remain with you, and be everywhere for good, let us confidently hope that all will yet be well. To His care commending you, as...

Such a convenient omission is consistent with much of Goodwin's writ-ing. She even goes so far as to assert later in the book, "While Lincoln rarely acknowledged the influence of faith or religious beliefs..."

This is an outright falsehood, as innumerable instances of Lincoln's reli-ance on God and religion are readily available to anyone who takes the op-portunity to look, despite the efforts of today's historians to conceal them.

Such is the essence of the re-education of America: *Our Founding Fathers were bad. Religion played no positive role in the development of our nation. Our country is steeped in racism, making all white Americans racist at their cores. We are one of the most unequal nations in the world. Free-market capitalism didn't create the economic miracle we have before us. America continues to exploit her minority population.*

All of which is simply not true.

An easy example of the continued corruption and simple foolishness in the education bureaucracy can be found in a statement by the Chicago Teachers Union. Regarding the reopening of schools that had been closed because of COVID-19, they declared that "the push to reopen schools is rooted in sexism, racism, and misogyny."

Such a claim is simply malicious. The data clearly show that minority children, especially blacks, have suffered far more detrimental effects from school shutdowns and distance learning than other racial or ethnic groups. A frightening 40 percent of all classroom grades in Minneapolis schools under lockdown are "Fs." And that's not counting the students who have aban-doned school altogether. As to the reference to sexism and misogyny, it seems simply inexplicable, a reflexive trope to leftist hearts.

If these teachers got their way, the fact that female and minority students would be hurt the most from continued school closings seems not to matter to them.

Another example: The Minnesota K-12 public schools recently went through a ten-year revision of accepted curriculum. Under their liberal governor, the State Board of Education recommended that their social studies curriculum no longer cover the American Revolution, Civil War, World War I or World War II, the Holocaust, or the rise and fall of Communism.

Which seems to beg the question: What exactly would they cover, then?

The answer should not come as a surprise. The recommended new curriculum focused on how racism was rooted in the founding of our nation and how whiteness, Christianity, and capitalism have failed our nation.

A final example of this madness: The Oregon Department of Education (ODE) recently sponsored a teacher training course that pushed *ethnomathematics*—the idea that white supremacy is expressed whenever students are encouraged to find the right answers, even in something so objective as math. The training course included a toolkit to help teachers "dismantle racism in mathematics," by understanding that white supremacy infiltrates math when it focuses on "getting the 'right' answer," or requires students to show their work. "The concept of mathematics being purely objective is unequivocally false, and teaching it is even much less so," the toolkit reads.

Yes, these are the teachers of our children...

"Upholding the idea that there are always right and wrong answers perpetuates objectivity as well as fear of open conflict," the workbook reads, while describing objectivity and neutrality as characteristic of white supremacy. Remarkably, one of the teacher guidelines prompts teachers to "identify and challenge the ways that math is used to uphold capitalist, imperialist, and racist views."

How can anyone read this nonsense and not fear for the next generation? That, and not immediately take their children out of any blue-state public school?

WHERE WE STAND (OR FALL)

The world feels like it's going stark raving mad. And it's not just a feeling among the right. It's common across the spectrum, from left to right, from activists to homemakers, from farmers in the heartland to investment bankers sitting in high-rise buildings in New York City.

And this feeling of madness and despair leads to doubt, uncertainty, and fear.

There are plenty of reasons to be frightened. COVID has taken hundreds of thousands of our countrymen. The rise of China. Russian aggression and interference throughout Eastern Europe. Riots that cast a dark shadow across our greatest cities, but also our small towns. The rewriting of history, leaving statues of Abraham Lincoln toppled for not being sufficiently supportive of the fight to end racism. The destruction of our founding principles by the destruction of the reputation of our Founding Fathers. Muzzling and ridicule for anyone who doesn't accept the groupthink. The silencing of opposition. Taking ideas that have been held for thousands of years and tossing them out in a week.

We have seen anxious times before, but we've never seen anything like this. And it leaves many people fearful for our future.

But among all this fear and confusion there are two things that are true.

> *Thing one*: This country has been the greatest force for good in the history of the world. Through the sacrifice of blood and treasure, we have freed hundreds of millions

of people while our model of free markets and liberal democracy have raised more people out of poverty than any other government, economic model, or philosophy in the history of man. We have normalized a standard of living that the richest of the pharaohs could not have dreamed of, creating wealth and leisure unmatched in human history. No other nation has done more to defend human dignity, devolve power to the people, fight against tyranny, birth creative genius, or give to the needy than has the United States. Any fair reading of history proves this is true.

And the thing that makes us exceptional isn't luck or people. It isn't natural resources, geography, or any other physical explanation. The thing that makes us exceptional is a set of *ideas*. The fact that the Declaration of Independence is the greatest statement on human rights that has ever been written. The fact that the Constitution is the greatest document ever written to govern a people; that the Bill of Rights is the strongest guarantor of liberty in the history of mankind.

And those things still stand.

Thing two: We are not perfect. Indeed, we never have been perfect. We have always been led by imperfect men and imperfect women. Some of them were good people who struggled and sometimes failed. Some of them were dreadful leaders—selfish, inept, or power-hungry. We are not always equal in our justice, and we don't always protect minorities, implement laws, divide responsibilities, guarantee religious freedom, or institute government policies in a perfect way.

But despite these imperfections, the United States is still good. And though still imperfect, we are better than we used to be. We have constantly tried to improve. We have struggled to see our own weaknesses and to address them. And by nearly every measure—racism, care for our environment, income distribution to the middle class, care for the poor, and so forth—we are better now than previous generations.

We are also a people who don't give up easily. We've been that way since our inception, even from that fateful day in Jamestown when a handful of desperate colonizers, having survived the Starving Time, had a chance to return to England but decided they would stay in Jamestown and try again.

That is one of reasons why we still believe in the future of our nation.

The past few years have fundamentally changed our country. They have fractured us, brought out the very worst in some of us, and left everyone on edge, tight as wire and seemingly ready for the draw. It's already led to violence and it will likely lead to more. With so much upheaval in our society, and with it happening so fast, many of us are left to wonder when will it end? How far will this go?

The answer is…all the way to the end.

The opposition will never be satisfied. They will never grow tired. And they will never give up until their goals are accomplished.

Which leaves us with a choice.

First, there is talk of a separation. You know, a gentle and amicable divorce. A friendly dividing of our nation into two respectful and orderly halves. Should be easy, right? Let's just come to an agreement to live and let live. You take the West Coast and the Northeast. We'll throw in Colorado and Nevada and then keep the rest.

And if a friendly dividing of our nation doesn't work, perhaps a talking unicorn might tell us what to do. Because if you're going to believe in fantasies, you might as well go all in. And the idea that we could easily divide our nation is a fantasy. It simply won't work. And it will almost certainly lead to violence in the end.

Do you really think conservatives in California—and there are about ten million of them—are going to want to divide the nation in such a way that leaves them isolated in the cold world of liberal domination? Do you think that even Texas—despite the fact that it is a state known for its fierce streak of independence, and one that already culturally identifies almost as a separate nation—would agree to leave the union? Would increasingly progressive cities like Dallas, Houston, and Austin just say, "Okay, that sounds swell, let's pull the plug on the United States and join the Republic of Guns and Religion?" Would millions of bricklayers and other blue-collar workers in Massachusetts want to join the liberal union, or high-tech workers in Nashville want to join the union of conservative states?

The reality is, offering such a proposition leaves tens of millions of Americans on the wrong side of the wall, forcing them to culturally barricade inside a new and hostile nation.

Putting the philosophical and political concerns aside, the practical applications of a divide are nearly impossible. Who is going to maintain our military? How do we divide the military bases in the different states? Who manages the CIA? What about Social Security? Who is going to pick up the cost of that? How do we divide the Social Security trust fund and all of the other funding intricacies that are necessary to ensure that senior Americans are not left destitute? Who controls the Fed? How do we assure the financial integrity and value of the dollar? What about Medicare and Medicaid? What about all of the other federal obligations we have made to each other? Trillions and trillions of dollars are at stake.

From trade to transportation, from access to river navigation and critical minerals to funding for the federal courts, from power generation to access to the seas, the list of issues we would have to navigate is nearly endless. And every one of them is incredibly complicated and controversial, every problem a potential powder keg. It would be like walking through a minefield, every issue having the potential to blow both new nations to bits. And if we live in a day when we can't find solutions even to relatively simple problems—like how to run an election, something that used to be easy—how could we come to agreement on all of these critical issues that far surpass in cost, urgency, and complication anything we are dealing with now?

Whether we like it or not, the people within the United States, left and right, are like conjoined twins. We share the same blood, the same heart, the same lungs and legs. We share the same history, the same soil and air. We share the same ancestry, the same future, the same dreams.

We simply cannot amicably separate. It would kill us both.

Which leads to the second option that many people are now talking about, at first in quiet whispers, but now out in the open,

Maybe it's time for civil war.

Which, to be clear, would be a catastrophe of unimaginable proportions. That reality should terrify us all. Death and destruction such as we can't even comprehend. Homelessness. Starvation. No doctors. Destroyed hospitals. A destroyed nation. A hopeless future. Sickness and pain. Nothing left to build on.

And all of this suffering might be for nothing. It wouldn't guarantee the freedoms that we hold dear. Instead, it would guarantee those freedoms would be put in constant and intense danger. It would weaken us beyond measure, taking us from the world's most powerful, generous, enlightened, and admired nation to the trash bin of failed states. It would kill the country and virtually everything we stand for. Family. Devotion. Pride in our nation. Pride in our past. Any hope or faith in our future.

At which point, our adversaries would act to finish off whatever was left.

WASHINGTON, DC

June

Darren sat in the back seat of the gray SUV and looked out on the massive crowd that was building in the streets, furious citizens drawn into the city like starving wolves to a kill.

Another day, another riot....

The drive down Constitution Avenue was agonizingly slow. Glancing impatiently at the driver in the front seat, he was about to shout instructions, but he bit his tongue. He was an expert at many things, but driving wasn't one of them. The truth was, he hadn't driven for many years. Not to work. Not to any social function. Not to the gym or the market or out with a few friends to get a beer. Driving was for the other guys, and he wasn't one of the other guys anymore. He had a wall of security around him, a pool of drivers and staff, all of whom had but one purpose, to make his life easy so that he could concentrate on the critical work of telling the American people the truth. Or some version of it. Or whatever it was he said...

The driver maneuvered through the mob and stalled traffic, cutting between cars and angry people. Another bodyguard sat beside the driver, a large man with a shaved head. Darren leaned forward and studied the crowd, growing anxious at the intensity of their anger, then turned to the bodyguard. "We doing okay here?" he asked.

"We're fine, sir."

Darren wasn't sure. He could smell smoke and there was black haze on the other side of the Mall. Fires were common in the city now. And the people were walking right beside the automobile, brushing up against it and slapping on the hood as they crossed in front.

"Sometimes these things can get away from us," he said.

"Understand, sir. But our scouts say the crowd thins out once we get past Eighteenth. Worst case, we could call for a police chopper out of Reagan. It would be here in minutes if we need it."

Darren watched through the windshield, then sat back and swore. He had to be in the studio by noon. No way he was going to make it. Okay. He could improvise. He'd just do some show prep while in makeup. No biggie. He could multitask.

Tucked inside his heavy automobile with its massive engine and full tank of gas, he tried to relax and ignore the mob on the other side of the tinted glass.

"The fight is here," kept rolling around in his head. "The fight is here." Where had he heard the phrase before?

Closing his eyes, he leaned against the headrest and thought of the conversation he'd had with the FBI director a couple months before, before the election and everyone turning into monsters....

They were at a party at the Hay-Adams, five hundred of DC's finest. With everything seemingly on the edge of a cliff, this group wasn't feeling any pain yet and was still up for some fun.

He stood next to the FBI director, both of them smoking thick cigars, the reason they had found themselves on the balcony of the hotel. Time and again, some of the partygoers approached them, but the FBI director had asked his security to keep them back, and the two men were left alone. The night air was wet and a heavy overcast obscured the moon and stars. The forecast called for rain, and it felt like the last warm breath before the coming storm.

They smoked quietly for a few minutes, two of the world's most powerful men standing side by side, satisfied to take in the husky smoke as they looked out on the White House that seemed close enough to touch.

The director pulled a drag on the Arturo Fuente and blew a thin smoke ring that whisked away in the breeze. The heavy smell drifted between them, filling the crisp air. "Democracy is completely broken," he said while motioning to the White House. "It simply doesn't work anymore."

Darren flicked a trace of ash from the tip of his cigar. The more he got to know the director, the less he liked him.

The FBI director had spent his college years as a yoga instructor and Peace Corp volunteer while dabbling in communism, the Eastern arts, and Zen. Joining the FBI at a time when the agency was definitely out of style, he'd risen through the ranks as a competent bureaucrat, his magnum opus being that he had the good fortune of making an early friendship with the man who would eventually become the president of the United States.

But that was enough to bind them. Their common lust for power.

Darren grunted in response and stared at the White House. Beyond that, the Washington Monument. Beyond that, the Chesapeake Bay. "Any other time, I would say you've lost all perspective," he said. "But indeed, it now seems obvious we're about to drive off a cliff."

"The Constitution is obsolete," the director continued in a voice so low it seemed he was talking to himself. "It has to be updated. It has to be fixed. The Founding Fathers never intended for it govern us without any changes until the end of all time. That couldn't have been their intention."

Darren pulled on his cigar, held the smoke then coughed it out. It was hard to argue with that.

The director sniffed hard, then spit over the edge of balcony. "The Constitution was written by a group of slave owners who didn't think women were smart enough to vote. Men who thought it was okay to let their daughters be raped by forcing them into marriage while still in their early teens. It was written in a day of oppression and bigotry. A day before they had the brains to invent toilet paper, for heaven's sake! And we're supposed to defer to their judgment on good government until the end of all time! No! I won't do that!" He stopped suddenly, sniffed and spit again.

Darren, son of a billionaire who hoarded money like a squirrel hoarded nuts, wearily rubbed his eyes. "Capitalism has failed us as well," he said. "The rich just get richer. Take a look at my old man. Look what he has! Free markets are obsolete. The American spirit has been shattered." A final pull on his cigar, the end glowing deep orange in the dim light.

"We've got to change it," the director said. "Before it's too late."

"I wonder…," Darren answered. He was yet unconvinced.

"Trust me," the director told him. "The fight isn't coming. The fight's already here."

The SUV came to a sudden stop. Darren opened his eyes. Shaken from his memories, he looked out on the crowd and wondered if this was what the director had been talking about?

The riots had started right after the tight election. Rumors once again of it being stolen. A Congress that was capable of holding hearings on funding for the arts, but not on the growing crisis before them. They were completely frozen now, worthless as a carcass in the snow. The Supreme Court had proven to have the courage of a mouse, way too terrified to step into the chaos. DC had tried to move forward, using bureaucrats and agency holdovers, but it only took a few months to prove that incompetence was the reason they had spent their lives in government.

Everything was failing. It simply couldn't hold. Far too many people. Too many of them terrified. Too many of them armed.

The riots had been going on for months now. Every city. Every town. Violence was growing, not getting better. No one was in control. Every drive to work, every trip to the supermarket, every walk down the block to take his daughter to the nanny, who no longer ventured out of her house, had turned into a trip of terror.

How long could this go on?

There was a literal gunfight out West, half the states in open rebellion. Who knew that such a thing could happen over something as idiotic as the right to keep their idiotic guns? Neanderthals. Simple idiots, fighting over something so meaningless! And the fact that it had started with his grandpa…well, that just made it worse.

Then the economy had tanked. Not tanked. It had swan-dived into the rocks. A 57 percent collapse in the market wasn't a "correction," it was a catastrophe. Interest rates at 17 percent and going up. Inflation was supposed to be in check, but he knew that was a lie. The administration had simply revised the formula they used to calculate inflation. No way they were going to tell the people how really bad it was. Not that Darren cared about that so much; it was pretty much assured he could always afford to buy some milk and cheese...but that was only true if there was any left to buy.

Which apparently there wasn't. The last two trips to the grocery had proved a bit discouraging. Maybe even a little scary.

The thought of going hungry had never in his life occurred to him. But now it did. And he hated it.

It wasn't supposed to be this way!

CRASH!

Darren felt the SUV lurch as a metal bat smashed through the passenger window, glass exploding across his face and eyes.

OUR ADVERSARIES ARE WATCHING

The well-being of our nation rests upon these few key factors that, if broken, jeopardize our future.

Respect for the rule of law. Having cities that aren't racked with violence and fires every night. The expectation that if you do something illegal, you will be arrested and prosecuted. Not having your legal standing dependent upon your political affiliation.

A stable dollar. Resisting the impulse to accept fantasy economic propositions that ignore the realities of debt and spending. Reasonable efforts to protect our economic future from an economic collapse.

An education system that doesn't indoctrinate our children to hate their history, their heritage, and even themselves.

Constitutional order that respects the precedents of more than two hundred years of history. Respect for the size and character of the Supreme Court. Resisting the temptation to pack it for political manipulation. Respecting the significance of adding another state. Not pursuing a new addition in a raw power grab. Respect for the necessity of the Electoral College. Recognizing the constitutional requirement that the individual states manage their own elections rather than federalizing elections in Washington, DC.

A military that is not politicized. Combat commanders focused on the foreign threats, not the political leanings of their troops. Intelligence and law enforcement agencies that don't turn their awesome powers on US citizens.

Basic institutions that don't treat half of all Americans as if they were the enemy. Businesses that don't politicize everything, from the sports teams we cheer for (or used to cheer for) to the razors we buy and shoes we wear.

The ability to conduct secure elections.

A public that knows the truth.

These things are required to secure the future of our nation. They are also the issues that tear us apart. Divide us. Drive us to the edge. Continual, emotional, divisive failures in these areas will weaken us to the point that our society will break.

Our enemies know this. They are watching. They see and listen. They monitor our internal dealings as closely as we do, in some cases even more. They measure our distractions and commitment to protect our own freedoms. Our emotional exhaustion. The things we are willing and not willing to fight for anymore. They will know when the time is right.

And when the time is right, they will move against us in ways that are difficult to imagine. Which is the most important point. We have to win the first war, the war within ourselves, or the second war is inevitable.

But if we win the internal conflict, if we find a way to keep our nation united and together, then the second war with China may not ever be fought.

Book Two

SILK SHEETS THAT STRANGLE

The first blow is half the battle.

— Chinese Proverb

As of the writing of this book, the United States of America is the strongest nation in the world. We have the greatest economy by an impressive margin and the most powerful and experienced military in every meaningful sense. Our extensive network of friends and allies, the result of a century's worth of goodwill overseas, our intelligence-gathering capabilities, as well as our diplomatic and other strategic assets entrenched in hundreds of vital locations around the globe, make us the only superpower in the world.

But if we are the lion on the world stage, it is worth noting that the analogy comes with a twist: we have been injured. We are wounded, and our enemies are hyenas hiding in the grass. The scent of blood is thick in the air, and it is driving them mad with desire. They see the limp in our step, they hear our labored breathing; and with every minute that passes, their hunger grows, muscles readying to pounce in our moment of weakness.

If America falters, the fallout that ensues will be devastating, reaching the farthest corners of the globe. Every nation, region, institution…indeed every *person* would be affected. If our enemies take advantage of our weakness and are able to dethrone us, a number of things could happen. And they could happen very quickly.

The mullahs at the helm of the Iranian government could be at war with Israel by the end of the hour. And since Israel would almost certainly defeat their neighbors in any sort of conventional confrontation, Iran would deploy every weapon in their arsenal: chemical, biological, and nuclear. On the very same day that Iran attacks, Russia could make their move as well. Vladimir Putin is fiercely intelligent and exceedingly ruthless, and he wants nothing more than to restore the glory, power, and leadership of the former USSR. He has already taken Crimea and Eastern Ukraine, and if we could not defend the Baltics, Poland, and other vulnerable nations in the region, he would do the same to them. Seeing the world descending into chaos, North Korea would see it as their opportunity to act, deploying the threat of nuclear weapons to bring the South under their monstrous regime. The faltering governments of Central and South America would crumble under the pressure of narco-terrorism and socialist oppression. The entire African continent could fall to the growing presence of ISIS, Al-Shabaab, and Boko Haram.

The list of catastrophic consequences that would result from the fall of the United States could not be counted in this chapter alone.

But more than any other, there is one entity that will truly benefit from the collapse of the United States of America—an entity that has been growing stronger as they watch our nation implode, a strategic player that has been waiting for their moment to ascend the ladder of global supremacy, a player that has been implementing strategies to bring about our demise, positioning their pieces in anticipation of this moment. If America falters, they will spread their way of life and impose their will on the peoples of the world. And make no mistake; their willingness to oppress their people and impose violence on those who oppose them, their long history of racism and oppression and civil rights abuse, indeed their entire life philosophy, could not possibly be more antithetical to American values and ideals.

If we fall, the Chinese Communist Party in China will rise.

NINOY AQUINO INTERNATIONAL AIRPORT, MANILA, THE PHILIPPINES

September

Marco huffed in frustration. Bodies bustled around him as he made his way to the front of the plane, some of the passengers mumbling in resentment and anger, others seemingly excited at the adventure. But he didn't much notice, preoccupied with his thoughts.

He hadn't seen his daughter in nearly two years and, as he waited impatiently to disembark, he could feel his heart race at the thought of their reunion. But his flight had been unexpectedly rerouted to the Philippines due to mechanical problems, and he would now have to take the layover to Melbourne, which meant another eight hours cramped in yet another space too small for his large frame. Still, he smiled at the thought of being with his daughter after so many years.

Victoria Rossi had inherited her grace from her mother, and, incredibly, was even more beautiful. She was smart and kind and remarkably capable, and for some reason had always taken a special interest in her father, seeming to look past his every flaw. A nationally ranked athlete, she was as smart as she was fast, and he was as proud of her as any father could be.

What was the big thing she wanted to tell him? She had sounded nervous on the phone. Maybe she'd gotten another promotion; maybe she'd finally met a man. The thought made his heart pump, his protective instincts kicking in.

As Marco exited the plane, he was greeted by a trio of unfortunate developments. The first was a slug of tropical heat that brought instant sweat. The second was the smell of ten million people living in too little space. The third was a handful of armed security personnel that started moving toward him.

"You, sir, come with us, please?" one of the guards said, his voice so thickly accented that Marco struggled to understand what he was saying. But the guard's hand gestures made it clear what he wanted, and Marco followed the airport personnel away from the other passengers and across the tarmac.

Marco's training and instinct kicked in. His work had compelled him to live a life with a lot of secrets, but certainly no crimes, and this was probably just some sort of mix-up. But the farther the security guards led him away from the other passengers, the less he worried about just missing his next flight and the more he worried about a problem of a more malicious nature. His concern deepened when he noticed how closely the guards watched him, and unless he was mistaken, they appeared to be nervous.

A cold fear began to gnaw in the back of his mind.

He was led through a back door labeled Authorized Personnel Only, through two security checkpoints, down another stale hallway, and into a small room with a dirty tile floor and a worn steel table with two chairs. One of the walls was a one-way mirror, and Marco immediately knew that he was in very serious trouble.

An interrogation room.
This was not going to be fun.

A Jealous Adversary

From the hellish ashes of the Second World War, the United States showed the world the way forward. Rather than exploit our enemies in the aftermath of the war, Americans charitably forgave our enemies and helped them to rebuild their nations. We taught them a better way to live. Enduring institutions such as NATO, the UN, USAID, and the WTO were created, institutions that have led the world like lights on a hill, and whose purpose was to demonstrate that shared prosperity is truly possible and a benefit to all. But far more impactful were the actual moral values we demonstrated: civil discourse, free press, free speech, the necessity of free elections, the imperative of religious freedom and equality, trial by jury, and more.

Over the ensuing decades, much of the world accepted the liberal democracy/constitutional republic model as the safest, most prosperous form of government, for despite its imperfections, it was orders of magnitude more successful than any of the other options available, options that were inherently prone to corruption, violence, and suppression. The areas of the world that chose not to accept liberal democracy were left behind. The USSR, North Korea, and much of Southeast Asia. Brutal dictatorships in South America and Africa. The list was extensive, the outcomes always the same: the fewer freedoms the people enjoyed, the sooner the country seemed to implode, showing that individual freedoms are not merely helpful in creating a prosperous nation, they are strictly necessary.

The ensuing decades were far from perfect, but the United States's model led the world to what is unquestionably the single most successful and prosperous era in the entire history of humanity. Across the globe, rates of poverty, disease, and child mortality plummeted. Civil rights, education, and wealth expanded at rates once thought impossible. For a time, it appeared that the world seemed to have saved itself from the calamity of its own self-destruction.

For many reasons, people now get a sense this might be ending.

It turns out that China is a jealous adversary.

REPRESENTATIVE DEMOCRACY VS. AUTHORITARIANISM

If you want to know the true aim of President Xi and the Chinese Communist Party, you don't have to look very hard for evidence of their long-term goals. They are hardly hidden. In fact, China has been shamelessly open about their aspirations.

Do they want total control over their hemisphere? Absolutely. Do they want to be a superpower? Unquestionably. Do they want to see the destruction of their enemy, the United States, with the resultant fall of American hegemony, leaving them as the world's only superpower? Of course, they do. Indeed, they see it as their destiny.

It's true that for the past two generations, China has needed the US as an important trading partner. They needed our technology, both that which has been shared and that which has been stolen, to lift a billion people out of abject poverty. They needed access to our education system to build a foundation of technically trained professionals. They needed access to our financial services, agricultural products, rare earth minerals...the list is long.

But the simple fact is, they no longer need us. They have come to the point technologically, militarily, educationally, and in almost every other sense, that they can now move forward on their own. Would they prefer to maintain access to US markets and technology? They would. Will they allow these considerations to hold them back from their ambitious goals? They will not.

And the Chinese are brazenly honest about their long-term goals.

Amazingly, the dystopian Chinese model of autocratic rule, mass surveillance, and total control by the ruling class is beginning to appeal to the world. Across the globe, democracies and individual rights are on the decline. The inherent flaws of democracy are being exploited by our enemies. Oppressive regimes are adopting the Chinese model and becoming more widespread, causing us to lose allies at an alarming rate. We couldn't stop many of our closest allies from joining Asia Bank. The 17+1 initiative, targeting the weakest and newest members of the EU, is a direct assault on the unity of the EU and aims to put the same number of European nations firmly in the pockets of the Chinese. It is no secret that by allowing Huawei to build most of the global telecom infrastructure, governments of the world have given the CCP carte blanche to spy on many of their most sensitive communications.

Which leaves us with a choice: confront the Chinese Communist Party now, or lose in ten years.

Some think that is hyperbole. The CCP says this is nothing more than Western propaganda designed to keep an adversary from growing to its full potential.

So, let's take a closer look....

MANILA, THE PHILIPPINES

September

What could they possibly want? Marco wondered, his heart pounding in his chest.

One of the security guards motioned to the table across from the one-way mirror. Heavy. Solid metal. A steel bar welded across the center. Marco obliged, and without being prompted held his hands out to the bar so that the guard could handcuff each wrist to the table. The guards cuffed him down and left the room.

Minutes passed. The room grew warm. Marco's throat grew dry. The door opened. A man walked in.

Immaculately groomed, with European boots that added two inches to his height and a long Asian face, he moved swiftly into the room. Taking the seat across from Marco, he stared at the New Yorker for a long moment. "I am Lee," he finally said.

"I'd shake, but..." Marco nodded to the handcuffs.

"Indeed," Lee said, lifting his hands in an exaggerated motion of shaking thin air. He laughed, but there was no joy in the sound.

"If you don't mind, I'd like a cigarette," Marco said, his voice barely managing more than a whisper. He was scared. He felt timid.

Amused, Lee raised a brow.

"Please," Marco said, "I can see the box in your breast pocket."

Americans! Lee thought. Arrogant fools. In all his years of interrogation, no prisoner had ever dared make such a request. He considered for a few seconds. What did the American really want? But if his underlings on the other side of the mirror thought he was afraid of the American, he would lose face. So, he acquiesced with a huff. Marco held out his right hand to be uncuffed, but Lee ignored the request and loosed the cuff around his left wrist instead. He then reached into the breast pocket of his tailored suit, handed Marco a cigarette, and lit it with a lighter painted communist red.

Lee tried his best to hide his disdain as he watched the American close his eyes and pull deep on his cigarette. No American deserved to feel so relaxed, so arro-

gant. Lee controlled this man's life. If he wanted him in prison, it would happen. If he wanted him dead, he would die.

Didn't he understand that?

Breathing more easily and now visibly relaxed, Marco blew a puff of smoke to the side. Lee mirrored the American and lit his own cigarette. "Do you know why you are here?" he asked.

"I know I haven't done anything wrong. My record is cleaner than your suit. Which means that you've made some kind of mistake. I don't think you have any idea who I am."

"Well, you're right about one thing, Mr. Rossi. I am well aware of the fact that your record is quite clean. Well, for a couple years at least. But I wouldn't be so sure that we don't know anything about you." He opened the file between them and leafed through the pages. "I know you like The Office, but you hate Friends. I know you have problems sleeping at night, but you refuse to take the Ambien your doctor prescribed. I know how much you owe on your mortgage and how much money you have in your different bank accounts, including the one you hid from your ex-wife. I know every late payment you've ever made. I know you allegedly gave up smoking for your daughter. I also know that she knows what you used to do. You see, Mr. Rossi, I know very much about you."

Marco stiffened at the mention of his daughter, but he shrugged his shoulder to make sure it didn't show. But it had. And he knew Lee had seen it.

"Not bad," Marco said as he forced a smile. "But do you have a pen? You forgot to mention anything about my online gambling habit. I can add that, if you want."

"Hmmm…," Lee responded with a bit of resignation before he forced another grin. "You left the Agency two years ago, Mr. Rossi."

Marco didn't respond.

Lee hunched his shoulders. "You wonder how we know that? I'll tell you. Twenty-two million government personnel records were hacked from the US Office of Personnel Management in 2013. It was a bit of a challenge to put all of the pieces together. It took us a couple years, and we really couldn't do it until we started applying artificial intelligence to the problem, but yes, we were pretty much able to identify every US spy from the stolen records, even those operating under deep cover. Digital pixie dust, you call it, and yes, it is real.

"But Mr. Rossi, no offense, but it's not you that we are interested in. Retired CIA officers are a dime a dozen. And most of you know so little about things that really matter. It's your daughter that we want to get to know."

Marco cleared his throat with a deep hack, leaned to the edge of the table, and spit on the floor—then turned back to Lee with a blank stare.

Lee shook his head. "I find yours a fascinating ilk, Mr. Rossi. You hide behind your New York bravado and fake Italian leather. But I know that you're no idiot. You know exactly what is going on here, don't you, Mr. Rossi? Just as you know how this is going to end. You surely have figured out that your plane wasn't diverted here because of engine problems. We forced it to reroute here. Think about that, Mr. Rossi. Think about the power it takes to reach out to your commercial aircraft, flying along at 38,000 feet, and have them bring you here, to a place where my power is a little more"—he paused, eyes rolling up as he searched for the correct word, and finally settled on—"absolute."

"You're Chinese?" Marco asked.

Lee smiled in affirmation.

"Well, I don't know what you want, but I can tell you that if it involves my daughter, I will never do anything to hurt her," Marco said firmly.

Lee stared at him before he smiled again. And this time it was genuine.

CHINA ROSE

For much of humanity's time on Earth, China viewed themselves as the center of the universe. And for more than a thousand years they were, proving to be a far more advanced culture than anything comparable in the West.

While all of Europe suffered during the oppression of the Dark Ages, Western intellectual and cultural progress stymied by fear and self-doubt, China had become the most advanced nation on Earth, the Middle Kingdom united in one of the world's most sophisticated empires. While the capitals of Europe built a few stone castles and modest cathedrals and called them masterpieces of architecture, China built the Forbidden City and the Great Wall of China, engineering marvels even to this day. While European scholars were still trying to figure out if the sun rotated around the earth, Chinese scholars were advancing scientific theories on sunspots, equatorial astronomical instruments, solar winds, novas, solar and lunar eclipses, and Halley's Comet. Using this information, they designed a calendar that was accurate to within twenty-six seconds a year. While the West was still copying a few books by hand, China had perfected paper and movable type. When the entire library of the King of England was a total of six handwritten books and scriptures, the Emperor of China commissioned two thousand scholars to produce a four-thousand-volume encyclopedia. While Europeans hunted whales to harvest their fat for oil lamps, China was exploring, exploiting, and burning natural gas. Millions died in Europe from smallpox. China developed a method to inoculate against it. Before Columbus set sail on three ships, each of which could fit in a space not much longer than half a basketball court, China had de-

veloped treasure ships that were four hundred feet long and one hundred sixty feet wide. Accompanied by their service vessels, these treasure fleets were capable of circumnavigating the globe.

Engineering, navigation, medicine, mathematics, warfare, transportation, sanitation, and research—China excelled in them all.

So, it should not be surprising that the Chinese leaders feel the last few centuries have robbed them of what is their birthright and destiny. In their minds, the last century, in particular, is little more than an anomaly in the greater history of mankind. They desire nothing more than to once again become the center of the universe—to remake the world as it was a thousand years ago, with China at the center and every other nation in their orbit, vassal states that pay tribute, monetary and otherwise, to their inherent superiority.

And if the last few decades are any indication, the rise of China may appear to be inevitable.

China's long-term goals are clearly manifest in their "Belt and Road Initiative." Though later rebranded, initially this policy was referred to as "One Belt, One Road *Strategy*," giving insight into the thinking and real purpose of the project: to rebuild the Silk Road. When one remembers that the Silk Road was a vast network of trade routes that connected China to the rest of the known world—reaching from Korea and Japan down through India, Iran, and Africa, before extending throughout most of Europe—one gets a sense of what the Chinese leaders have in mind.

Yearning for the days of past Chinese supremacy, the "One Belt, One Road Strategy" was unveiled by President Xi in 2013. It truly is his brainchild and represents his vision of the future. Consisting of a number of bold policies aimed at increasing infrastructure development and investments in sixty-eight countries in Asia, Africa, and Europe, the plan includes enormous transportation projects (railways, roads, and highways), the exploration and transportation of energy, creation of digital pathways, and the development of shared "super grids." In addition to these hard-asset goals, there also exists within Belt Road an aim to export so-called "soft infrastructure," such as trade agreements, cultural influence, legal agreements, and the expansion of international court systems to support trade between China and its "partners." Not surprisingly, this network of trade routes, "shared" infrastructure, and trade is—and will continue to be—Chinese-dominated. This has been demonstrated time and time again. The entire purpose of these agreements between China and her coerced allies is to strengthen and fortify China's position in the world, not to benefit

any of their partners. Ruthless, patient, and brilliantly executed, the Belt and Road Initiative is one of the greatest jewels in President Xi's crown of world dominance.

The Chinese government calls the initiative "a bid to enhance regional connectivity and embrace a brighter future." But you'd be hard pressed to find anyone educated on the topic who believes this initiative is anything other than a blueprint for China to become the world's only superpower. China doesn't even try to hide this fact. Xi has stated that his centennial goal in 2049, which will be the hundred-year anniversary of the creation of the Chinese Communist Party, is to reorganize the entire global economy, with China at the helm.

THE SOCIAL CONTRACT

Despite the profound implications such a shift in world power would hold for everyone, the average American knows little about the true nature of the Chinese Communist Party, or CCP.

But it isn't very difficult to understand.

The Chinese culture has only one central belief: the social contract. It is their governing principle, their proverbial Bill of Rights, their religion, their central creed. It is the single truth of governance upon which all others are predicated.

Following Mao's disastrous Great Leap Forward—a human travesty that resulted in the death of more than fifty million people by starvation, and millions of others who were massacred through violence by the government—the Chinese people were desperate for something, anything, that would not expose them to mass starvation, deprivation, and violence from their leaders. Realizing they were in danger of a billion people rising up against them, Chinese leadership was equally desperate to find a way to placate their people while still maintaining control.

Thus was born the Chinese Social Contract.

Through the Social Contract, the CCP promised one simple thing: economic growth. Food. Jobs and opportunities for advancement. They promised a roof overhead and warmth in the winter. They promised there would no longer be mass deaths from a devastating famine. And as long as they could provide economic growth, then the people agreed that the ends would justify the means.

And so economic growth and stability became the responsibility of the CCP, the sole matter of import. In exchange for this stability, the

Chinese people agreed to surrender quite literally *all* of their social and political liberties.

In China there is no freedom of press, no privacy, no freedom of religion. In China, there is no Bill of Rights to assure the rights of any Chinese citizen. There is no Declaration of Independence to declare that "all men are created equal." There is no Constitution that declares the rights of the People are supreme, no Judeo-Christian values to inform on the importance of human dignity or equality before the law. Little value is placed on honesty or integrity. Enormous value is place on results. Families are nothing but convenient backdrops to help move forward the Social Contract.

Freedom of any sort is viewed with suspicion, if not outright disdain.

There is only the Social Contract.

But are we being too harsh when judging the CCP's Social Contract? After all, the CCP is responsible for bringing millions of people out of abject poverty. They can't be all that bad, right? Perhaps their goals are admirable?

Perhaps...

But in order to truly understand the CCP, one must understand one simple fact: according to the Social Contract, if an act solidifies the CCP's power over its people, it is deemed both necessary and a moral good. If it weakens their grasp on power, it is primeval. Nothing else matters. And if history is any guide, when a government's power is absolute, so is its corruption.

And the power of the CCP is nothing if not absolute.

There are numerous examples that could accurately paint a picture of the soul of the CCP and their Social Contract, but nowhere is it more clearly exemplified than in the internment camps of Xinjiang. Millions of Muslims, Christians, and political dissidents are imprisoned without trial, condemned to hard labor, re-education, and in countless cases, torture and death. Organ harvesting is secretly sanctioned and protected. Members of the CCP, the general recipients of harvested organs, would feel right at home in the Nazi Party. Indeed, these camps are strikingly similar to the Jewish internment camps of World War II.

The question then must be asked: Does China plan on spreading this form of control to the rest of the world? The answer is fairly obvious: Only if it is necessary to maintain their power.

Which, of course, it will be.

HARD AND SOFT

Hard power is a concept most people are familiar with. As a species, we are evolutionarily hardwired to use hard power, and to be afraid of those who wield it. Hard power is the use of violence, or the credible threat of violence, to achieve a desired objective. From the caveman's club to F-22 Raptors flying through the skies, hard power is the possession of more brute force than one's opponent.

But there is another form of power that is spoken of less often, yet is certainly as impactful, or even more impactful in the global theater, and that is *soft power*.

Over the last century, the United States of America has become a master of this art. Soft power is, by definition, never coercive. Rather it consists of cooperation, common goals and concerns, shared trade, business opportunities, cultural overtures, ideals, and diplomatic ties. Americans are masters at creating organizations with incentives that appeal to other countries. The World Trade Organization is an excellent example. Expanding markets from which Americans can sell and purchase various goods results in an economic landscape that is advantageous for all participants.

American soft power boils down to a principle that has run deep in American culture ever since the inception of our country, and it can be summed up by the concept of viewing the world as an environment of plenty, not a zero-sum game. A world where a win-win is generally possible and almost always the preferred solution. Sometimes (the world being a complicated and unpredictable place), a "win" may be no more than avoiding US ire, but even this is likely to be a step toward the goal of global safety and security.

China has watched intently as American influence has expanded through the deployment of soft power, so they understand its importance and potential. And just as they have emulated, reverse-engineered, stolen, or copied many of the things we have created, they have attempted to do the same with soft power.

But where American soft power attempts to be cooperative, the Chinese version of soft power is anything but. Chinese soft power is manipulative, deceitful, and dangerous. Chinese soft power is based on viewing the world as a zero-sum game—as a series of win-lose relationships, in which one side's gain must necessarily come at the price of the other side's loss.

Just as treacherous hands may twist soft silk sheets into a hanging rope, Chinese soft power can also be fashioned to cause harm. Indeed, despite their calm words and soft tones, the reality is that Chinese soft power strangles the life out of all it gets its hands on.

Examples of their dangerous soft power include:

SURVEILLANCE AND ESPIONAGE

Americans have always placed a premium on privacy. When Edward Snowden revealed many of the NSA's supposed data monitoring capabilities, it was the news story of the year. Countless hours of press time were dedicated to the topic, the story quickly becoming a source of outrage from the American public.

The same is not true of China. The CCP's surveillance capabilities make *1984*'s Big Brother look like the JV team of state surveillance. And one of the purposes of developing this technology is so that they can enable other nations to do the same thing.

As of 2019, there are an estimated 626 million CCTVs in China, or one for every three people, each feeding information to the CCP. It's likely now that there are more than a billion cameras, with aerial drones also on the prowl. The purpose of these cameras is to track the masses so as to identify any individuals who might attract the ire of the CCP. And when these high-resolution cameras are combined with AI, as well as state-of-the-art facial and gait recognition, security forces are able to pick a single individual out of a crowd of tens of thousands. This gives them the capability to search for, identify, and apprehend anyone in the city within only a few minutes. No one can hide. It is virtually impossible. And if someone were to attempt to hide or escape the all-seeing eye of the Chinese Communist officials, it wouldn't take weeks for security officials to find them. It wouldn't take days or even hours. Seven minutes. That's all it takes, once given a photograph, for an individual to be identified, located within the sprawling city of twenty million people, and apprehended by Chinese security forces.

But the rabbit hole of Chinese surveillance goes much deeper than this.

Every Chinese citizen is required to own a cell phone with mandatory software pre-installed, whose sole purpose is to ensure the camera, microphone, and GPS are always on, and constantly feeding real-time audio and video to the CCP. It is impossible to say anything in China without the words potentially reaching the ears of the surveillance state. It's also forbidden for a Chinese person to leave their apartment without their cell phone in their possession. Were they to do that, facial recognition cameras and geolocation technology would know and send security forces to intercept them. If the CCP ever suspects that an individual is hiding something from the government, and it doesn't take much to raise suspicions—the CCP will move.

Amazingly, the Chinese people have not only accepted this as part of their lives, many have embraced it as necessary for economic security and the greater good.

Over the past decade, China has convinced dozens of other nations to install similar surveillance technology, all of it designed and manufactured in China. The supposed justification for helping other nations exploit their citizens can be understood simply by considering the name of this undertaking: *Safe Cities*.

Teaming with China to set up police-surveillance states, these nations are given the opportunity to control their citizens nearly as well as China is able to control their own. All of this is done, of course, in the name of safety and security. It's for their own good, you see.

Of course, much of this information is extracted and sent back to China for their own use, enabling Chinese leadership to monitor their partner nations, manipulate their leadership, exploit information for advantages in trade and other negotiations, steal technology, bribe, manipulate, blackmail, identify individuals sympathetic to their cause…the list of uses of this information is very long.

Through the exportation of Chinese surveillance technology to create *Safe Cities*, China has been able to force dozens of other nations, some friends and some rivals, to share millions of bits of critical information. In some cases, the national leaders surely know that China is extracting this information, but they don't care. Some care, but consider the cost worth the benefit they get from having the information.

Either way, this information gives China enormous advantages on the world stage, making this kind of soft power perhaps…well, not so soft.

ECONOMIC FORCE AND DEBT TRAPS

There are numerous ways in which the CCP uses its economic muscle to get what it wants. Perhaps, the most frequently used is to simply cut off access to Chinese markets if a given company doesn't acquiesce to their demands. American Airlines refused to acknowledge Taiwan as part of mainland China, so China shut them down until they acknowledged their crime, publicly begged for forgiveness, and redrew their maps. Marriott was guilty of the same offense, and we saw the same result.

A relatively unknown manager with the NBA Houston Rockets sent out a single tweet, "Stand with Hong Kong" in support of Hong Kong citizens protesting the brutal tactics of the CCP. Chinese leaders blacked out their NBA games in all of China, cut off ties with the Rockets, and demanded that the official "correct the error and take imminent concrete measures to eliminate the adverse impact." In a show of raw courage (kidding!), the NBA quickly caved to the Chinese demands, called the tweet regrettable, and distanced themselves from the official who dared suggest that freedom and human rights were worth supporting.

When it appeared that Norway was going to award Liu Xiaobo the Nobel Peace Prize for his "long and non-violent struggle for fundamental human rights in China," a feat that earned him more than a decade in prison, China threatened Norway with, and ultimately pursued, economic consequences. Liu Xiaobo was awarded the Nobel Peace Prize all the same, though he was not allowed to accept it, nor to send an emissary to accept the prize on his behalf.

South Park aired an episode in which President Xi was compared to Winnie the Pooh. As a result, *South Park* has been outlawed in China, with criminal repercussions for those who disobey.

These, as well as countless other examples, clearly show the Chinese don't merely want to censor free speech, media, art, and political discussions in their own country, they want to do it all over the world. And unless confronted, they will soon have the power to do so, deciding when, where, and who to shut down.

Another tactic the Chinese have repeatedly employed is ensnaring poorer countries in so-called "debt traps," a practice where China lends massive amounts of money to weaker nations, loans which are clearly designed to stretch them beyond their financial limits. It will then use this debt leverage to advance its own agenda, many times against the debtor nation's own goals. These financial contracts are highly confidential, but they often include provisions which allow China to call the loan at any time and for any reason, including if the debtor nation does anything against the "interest" of the PRC. Some of the contracts also require the debtor to keep the borrowed funds in special accounts which the PRC has access to, and with bylaws that allow China to preclude the debtor from having access to the funds.

A good example of this is Djibouti.

Djibouti is a tiny East African country whose debt nearly equals its entire GDP. It recently had the majority of its debt purchased by the Chinese. Shortly thereafter, and not coincidentally, Djibouti agreed to host the first People's Liberation Army military installation outside of mainland China. The base in Djibouti, located in the Horn of Africa, is capable of receiving large warships, likely even aircraft carriers, and is packed with some of the most modern defensive and offensive weapons that China has. Since completion of the installation, China has claimed airspace and port access far beyond what the government originally agreed to in regard to the loan. China has also imposed restrictions on the local government that brings the sovereignty of the host nation into question.

In other cases, if the debtor nation cannot fulfill its obligations, China will appropriate land and infrastructure, resulting in destruction of host nation national assets.

For example, Sri Lanka took out a series of loans from China to build and improve infrastructure for Hambantota, one of the largest ports in the Indian Ocean. When it became clear they would not be able to make good on their payments, Sri Lanka was forced to "lease" the port, the international airport, and the surrounding 15,000 acres to the CCP for a period of ninety-nine years. Though the elected leaders who initially made the deal with China have long since been forced out of office, the current government's pleas to bring the port back under sovereign control have been in vain. The result is that China, an increasingly aggressive military power, now controls a strategic foothold that practically borders its rival, India. Fears that the port has become essentially a Chinese military base are not unfounded, as all indicators point toward a repeat of the situation in Djibouti. Also of note, this would likely never have happened if the CCP hadn't gamed their own man into power in Sri Lanka. In 2015, enormous amounts of money found their way from China directly into the pockets of President Rajapaksa, the Sri Lankan leader who led the country toward China and ultimately signed the agreements for the original loans.

John Adams once said, "There are two ways to conquer and enslave a nation. One is by the sword. The other is by debt." The CCP have taken this teaching to heart, and the list of countries over whom they have leveraged a sovereign-destroying level of debt power is alarming.

Hopefully this is a wake-up call to other potential Chinese partner nations.

The CCP has demonstrated to the world that they are willing to play hardball in other ways as well. For example, shortly after President Trump was defeated in his bid for reelection, Yang Jiechi, China's preeminent diplomat, addressed American businesses. After touting all of the immense benefits to be had from gaining access to the Chinese marketplace, he then proceeded to make it very clear that any entity that so much as breathed the words Tiananmen, Hong Kong, Taiwan, or Xinjiang, would immediately be expelled from the country and sanctioned. The message from China was unmistakable: if you want to do business with China, deviation from Party ideals will not be tolerated; wrongspeak will be punished. Furthermore, it is not enough for you to abandon American ideals when in China; you must abandon them once you have returned home as well. If you don't, we'll close every store and disappear you from the entire Chinese internet (think H&M).

And if you're a politician who speaks ill of China, China has made clear their intentions to get you out of office by targeting your constituents' supply chains and bankrupting anyone who may have otherwise voted for you. (See Australian wine exports for an example of this.)

MANILA, THE PHILIPPINES

September

"There are a few things you need to understand, Mr. Rossi. If you are ignorant of the way the world works, then you cannot make a good decision. So may I tell you something to enlighten you, Mr. Rossi?"

Marco motioned for another cigarette, nodded thanks and touched it to his lips, then flourished his hand as if to say, go on.

"First, anything you think you know about our part of the world is wrong. Indeed, half of what you think about your own country is wrong. Americans put so much stock in their free press. But the term free press is somewhat of a misnomer. Everyone has a price, and as it turns out, the going rate for an American journalist is astoundingly low." Lee paused to light another cigarette and blew smoke in Marco's direction. "Democracy isn't dying, it's dead. It merely hasn't had the opportunity to be placed in the grave. If you want proof, look no further than the

rise of my country. Your nation is no longer serious, Mr. Rossi. Democracy is foolish and lazy and far too shortsighted to have allowed, to have facilitated even, the rise of a power that was destined to become an enemy.

"As we expand our sphere of influence, we find the necessity of expanding our message beyond our borders. You should know that the vulnerabilities of the Western press are far from difficult to exploit. Paid-for advertorials, the state sponsorship of journalists, intimidating partners by denying them access to Chinese markets, purchasing and destroying platforms adversarial to our own views—our tactics are as diverse as they are effective. The Associated Press has tanked hundreds of stories at our request. The Wuhan Virus was relabeled by the entire world at our request. Amazingly, half of the people now believe it originated in America, of all places!

"So, Mr. Rossi, if we want the press to report you as a terrorist, then that's what is going to happen. If we want them to report you were smuggling drugs into our country, then we will. Not only can we destroy you, we can destroy your legacy." He paused and leaned forward. "And don't think we can't do it to your beautiful daughter, as well."

The two men stared at each other.

"Our reach," Lee went on, "is not merely limited to the hypocrites in the American press. There is no person beyond our grasp. This year alone, we have detained hundreds of individuals, from American entrepreneurs to the president of Interpol! The largest of your corporations have bowed to our demands. ESPN, Disney, Versace, United Airlines…all have attracted the ire of the Party, and all of them have folded like a paper tiger. Not only did they concede, they literally begged our forgiveness."

Lee took a final drag from his cigarette and forced himself to maintain eye contact with Marco. "We have forced the closure of dozens of American companies because their CEOs have been critical of our leadership. We have demanded, and received, political dissidents back inside our borders. We have coerced European governments to allow us to buy technology with sensitive military and telecommunications capabilities, stolen foreign ports, and militarized the South China Sea. And all of this has been done with no repercussions." He paused a final time and then repeated. "No repercussions, Mr. Rossi. People and nations bow to our demands."

Lee fell silent as Marco stubbed out the last ashes of his cigarette on the top of the metal table.

Lee chuckled. "There is nothing we will not do to get what we want."

MISINFORMATION WARFARE

It should come as no surprise that Russia, one of our greatest geopolitical rivals, has long sought to sow chaos amongst us. However, over the last decade, as their economic standing in the world continued to wane (they are not even among the top ten economies of the world), and as the pain of sanctions and increasing isolation began to truly sting, the pressure grew for Russia to find a way to weaken their primary adversary.

In 2016, Russia stumbled into perhaps the most successful psychological operation in history. With a handful of operatives, and aided by the American press, their "election meddling" campaign created a political firestorm in the United States. But it turns out that they were passengers and not drivers of the train. Corrupt operatives in the DOJ and FBI took the false narrative and ran.

The CCP watched the disinformation campaign with great interest; then, over the course of the Trump presidency, they adopted and improved on this form of media warfare.

And make no mistake: the propaganda machine of the CCP is nothing short of warfare. In fact, their media dissemination organization is a branch of the government that falls under the direction of the People's Liberation Army of China.

From the inception of the CCP, their primary goal has been the suppression of free press and discourse among their own citizenry, and for decades the CCP concentrated primarily on controlling their own media. The little bit of Western press that made it into their country was heavily redacted, newspapers had stories blacked-out, magazines had pictures and articles literally cut out, television programming had entire segments that were missing, or so heavily edited as to be unintelligible.

But as their power grew, CCP tactics became more sophisticated, and in recent times, they have moved from editing Western press stories to the state-funded creation of content. Today the CCP controls the creation of content for television, internet, print, and radio, whose sole purpose is to craft a message that seeks to advance the agenda of the CCP—or, as President Xi said, to "tell China's story." Their state media reports are carefully designed and meticulously constructed "stories" that only tell what the CCP wants people to believe.

This is the reason we require Chinese state-run media outlets to register as "foreign missions." They aren't independent, autonomous news organizations. They aren't even media outlets influenced by the CCP. They *are* the CCP.

But as China continues to force its way to the front of the global stage, we find they increasingly target their propaganda not toward their own people, but to an international audience. The goals of their media campaign are numerous. First and foremost, they seek to improve the image of the CCP and their standing in the world, to paint the CCP in a positive light, as well as to erase or hide any party flaws. They also seek to shape geopolitical issues, international politics, and opinions toward CCP policies. Perhaps most dangerously, they have increasingly tuned their propaganda machine in order to sow discord among their adversaries, primarily the US and the EU. They seek to influence elections, harm and embarrass those critical of the CCP, and eliminate political rivals and adversaries.

The more experience they accumulate, the more effective they become. Today, their tactics of information dissemination are as varied as they are insidious. A short list of their propaganda weaponry includes:

- Paying supposedly independent Western media to run state-created content. Documents filed with the Department of Justice show that the CCP funnels millions of dollars to newspapers such as *The New York Times, The Washington Post,* and *The Wall Street Journal* through *China Daily.* While these CCP promotions are presented as "supplements," it is nearly impossible to differentiate between these propaganda adverts and actual news pieces.

- Targeting op-eds and ads critical of Western politicians who have taken positions in opposition to the CCP.

- Intimidating or economically coercing platforms that don't censor messages they deem counter to their policies.

- Offering cash and other benefits to American and Western journalists in exchange for "reporting the news from a Chinese perspective" (a tactic that has demonstrated how exceedingly thin the courage and resolve of many in our media actually are).

- Enticing journalists with expensive tours, cash, and free degrees in communications in order to get them to publish articles that are nothing more than state-approved propaganda.

- Bribing, blackmailing, and even threatening journalists. When pressure campaigns haven't worked, they have taken the next step and outright purchased internationally respected media outlets.

As concerning as this list is, news outlets touting Chinese disinformation represent only the tip of the iceberg. The CCP's mission of changing the global narrative runs so much deeper.

Many people around the world have turned to tech giants such as Facebook, Google, and Twitter as their primary source for news. In China, these platforms have been banned. Yet even though the CCP does not allow their citizens to use these tools, they will exploit Western social media to advance their goals. It has been estimated that, in spite of Facebook being banned in China, as much as 10 percent of their ad revenue comes from China.

A glaring example the CCP using social media to influence discourse can be found in the Chinese portrayal of the Hong Kong protesters as terrorists and thugs, all while they hid their own police brutality and suppression of human rights. Over the course of the Hong Kong protests, the CCP paid to promote tweets and other social media posts that targeted political opponents. They have also purchased personal social media accounts to be used as CCP mouthpieces and hacked private accounts to delete or alter posts. More insidious, China has shown an expert ability to identify Western collaborators whose political views are similar to their own, then increasing the volume of these voices by promoting their tweets and subsidizing their stories, thus spreading their message while granting China plausible deniability for spreading their narratives. They communicate frequently with these followers, using encrypted messages, training and coaching them along the way, while paying generously to post views sympathetic to their cause. All the while, hundreds of thousands, if not millions, of bots nudge fake conversations in order to shift the ideological battlegrounds toward the East.

And don't forget, these campaigns could not be aimed at a domestic Chinese audience. All of these platforms are banned in their country. These propaganda campaigns are aimed at you and me.

Examples of these propaganda efforts include:

Exaggerating their economic strength. Impressive as the growth in the Chinese economy has been, thanks in large part to assistance from and trade with the West, the rate of growth in their GDP is nowhere near as impressive as Chinese leaders claim. While it is difficult to ascertain their true GDP, it is likely they have overestimated their growth by as much as 2 percent per year. Combined with the fact they have been doing this for decades, the result is an economy that may be overstated by an eye-popping 20 percent! Some official estimates peg their total GDP as being only half that of the United States. But of course, they can never admit this, having created the impression of their economic might, which explains the necessity for their misinformation campaign.

The CCP convinced Obama and other US political leaders to sign a treaty regarding cybersecurity. But not surprisingly, they lied about their intentions to steal private businesses intellectual property, and in fact, they were observed ramping up their efforts even during the signing of the treaty. The public would have never supported such a treaty were it not for their misinformation campaign.

Their propaganda deceived the world regarding their intentions with the atolls in the South China Sea, allowing them the time they needed to create military installations in international waters and infringe on the sovereign rights of neighboring nations. Despite their assurances to the contrary, China's militarization of the South China Sea is widely regarded as one of the most destabilizing influences in the region.

Perhaps nowhere can Chinese media warfare be better documented than in how they handled the COVID-19 pandemic of 2020. But before we delve into the China's misinformation campaign, let's review some of the things we know about the history and origins of COVID-19.

Lead researchers at the Wuhan Institute of Virology have a well-deserved reputation for being reckless and irresponsible. Before the pandemic, multiple Western officials complained that Chinese researchers there had neither the mindset nor the professional experience and training to safely manage dangerous pathogens. Chinese scientists had also been reprimanded for conducting potentially disastrous research. For example, Zhengli Shi, the director of the Wuhan Institute of Virology, has published articles about dangerous "gain of function" experiments she performed that allowed coronaviruses to more easily bind to human cells.

The WHO-China report on the origins of the virus (completed in 2021) argues that the virus probably spread from bats to another animal species and then to humans. But China barred international scientists involved in writing the report from collecting the necessary data or reviewing critical medical records. WHO investigators also were not allowed access to various labs, nor were they allowed to speak with Chinese scientists without being monitored by CCP officials. Remarkably, the WHO even agreed to give China veto power over any of the report's findings or recommendations.

Furthermore, according to an investigation conducted by the State Department, "Several researchers inside the Wuhan Institute of Virology became sick in autumn 2019, before the first identified case of the outbreak, with symptoms consistent with both COVID-19 and common seasonal illnesses." Even Zhengli Shi admitted to several sleepless nights wondering if the virus had come from her lab, though these communications have long since disappeared from the public eye. Why would she be so worried if the coronavirus were anything other than the same she was studying? During the early stages of the pandemic, and before alerting the world to the threat of SARS-CoV-2, the CCP ordered samples of coronavirus at the Wuhan Institute of Virology destroyed, thus ensuring no outside entity could ever confirm if they had been studying the virus pre-pandemic. The destruction of these virus samples begs the question: why would they have done this if the virus had originated at the wet market? Peter Daszak, the man responsible for publishing the widely read *Lancet* article cited by innumerable news outlets condemning the lab-leak explanation as a conspiracy theory, had an obvious conflict of interest. His group was responsible for transferring hundreds of thousands of taxpayer dollars to the Wuhan Institute of Virology to study coronaviruses. Furthermore, SARS-CoV-2 contains genetic footprints that have never been observed in a naturally occurring coronavirus.

During the initial weeks of the outbreak, Chinese physician whistleblowers and other community leaders were silenced, then forced to acknowledge their "wrongdoings," and/or disappeared. The day after a Chinese physician self-posted the sequence of the virus online, his lab was closed by the Chinese for "rectification." The local governor, after claiming he had long since reported the outbreak, was removed from his position and then silenced.

We also know China became aware that the COVID virus presented a credible threat as early as September of 2019. With each week that passed, more and more information indicated that a worldwide pandemic was becoming increasingly likely.

At that point, two options were available to President Xi.

Option A: Inform the rest of the world about the incident and lock down travel out of Wuhan, thus allowing the world the best chance to prevent a global pandemic and all of its consequences. Though this was clearly the moral thing to do, there were two major problems for the CCP with this course of action. First, they were not willing to accept responsibility for a global catastrophe. Admitting mistakes is anathema to their carefully crafted image of perfection. Second—and far worse—they knew that if they prevented the outbreak from going global, then the only nation that would suffer the devastating medical and economic consequences of their mistake would be China.

No way they were going to let that happen!

Option B: Admit no fault, silence or disappear all whistleblowers, pressure the WHO to fall in line, and then reassure the rest of the world that not only was SARS-CoV-2 not a credible threat, but that it was also not spread via human-to-human transmission.

So it was that the CCP made a number of decisions that guaranteed the virus had opportunity to be seeded throughout the rest of the world, thus ensuring that the consequences of their recklessness would be suffered by all. Simply put, they decided that if they had to face the economic and medical consequences of their own recklessness, then so would the rest of the world. The best evidence of this is the fact that China officials shut down all domestic travel to and from Wuhan, while still allowing international travel from the province, thus assuring the virus would be spread around the globe.

Think about that for a moment, then consider the obvious question: did China try to protect or *infect* the rest of the world? Allowing a pandemic to spread unchecked is an action so terrible that many Americans refuse even to acknowledge it as a possibility. Surely such an accusation is nothing but a wild conspiracy.

But that is almost certainly what happened.

As the world began to realize that a global pandemic was in the making, the CCP worked to suppress the truth. According to German and American intelligence, President Xi managed to convince Dr. Tedros, the president of the World Health Organization, to delay labeling it a global health threat, despite all evidence to the contrary. Xi also convinced the leadership of the

WHO to praise Beijing's response to the virus, to laud China's own travel restrictions while condemning President Trump's decision to ban travel from China, to insist there was "no evidence of human-to-human transmission," and, in a stunning display of ironic dishonesty, to praise the Chinese for their "transparency." (It should be noted that Dr. Tedros hails from Ethiopia, a nation that landed itself in the one of China's "debt traps." He also has deep financial ties to China and secured his position as head of the WHO with the explicit backing of Beijing.)

While the Chinese leaders worked with the WHO to suppress critical information, their global media campaign kicked into overdrive, launching a veritable war on truth, their goals being to polish their own image, shift blame, and challenge any political leaders who were critical of the CCP.

With the help of Western apologists, the CCP managed to convince the world that the term "China Virus" was racist. They condemned any news outlets that ran articles exposing their bio labs as the source of the virus. The World Health Organization, as well as the social media giants willing to acquiesce to Chinese pressure, became complicit in China's coverup. Any media that attempted to even discuss narratives that ran counter to those of the CCP were ridiculed, silenced, blocked, and banned. During this time, a network of high-ranking Chinese officials and thousands of bots waged social media warfare to distance the CCP from responsibility and shift the blame to others. They purchased ads in social media that praised China's response the outbreak, falsely linked COVID to vaping, compared the Western response to the pandemic as "apocalyptic," promoted the absurd claim that the United States military was the true source of the virus, praised Western media figures that were critical of the US administration's response to the outbreak, and spread false rumors of an impending US nationwide military quarantine.

There is no question that if the CCP had let the world know about the threat posed by coronavirus in a timely manner, it could have certainly mitigated, if not outright prevented the ensuing loss of jobs, wealth, and life. The obvious denial of biological facts and the condemnation of opposing viewpoints demonstrates the incredible power the CCP, Western media, and tech giants possess. For more than a year, only a minority of Americans believed the coronavirus leaked from a lab, despite mountains of anecdotal and scientific evidence to the contrary, most of this evidence freely available since the earliest days of the pandemic. And in large part due to their propaganda campaign, China has received little, if any, meaningful condemnation for their complicity in allowing the virus to spread.

Former CDC director Robert Redfield has noted that the wet market theory doesn't make "biological sense," and has gone on record to say that an escape from the nearby virology institute was almost certainly the source of the pathogen.

Former lead State Department investigator David Asher stated, "[The Wuhan Institute of Virology] was operating a secret, classified program.... And if you believe as I do, that this might have been a weapons vector gone awry, not deliberately released, but in development and then somehow leaked, this has turned out to be the greatest weapon in history. You've taken out 15 to 20 percent of the global GDP. You've killed millions of people. The Chinese population has been barely affected."

Sir Richard Dearlove, former head of M16, the UK's Secret Intelligence Service, has said that the WHO's probe of the virus's origins was a "farcical investigation," and that it was "far more likely" to have been a lab leak. Even CNN's celebrity physician Sanjay Gupta said that he had reason to believe COVID-19 originated from the Wuhan Institute of Virology and not from natural origins.

The CCP's efforts at suppressing the truth, as well as the abject failure of our own media to investigate the origins of the virus, are nothing short of malicious. The fact that the CCP was so successful at manipulating public opinion is alarming, if not unexpected. But how did our own media fail so miserably? Are they really so incompetent they were incapable of connecting the dots of anecdotal and scientific evidence? Or perhaps they were so anxious to condemn every action of President Trump that they were blinded to reality?

The CCP has a lot of questions that need answering.

So does the Western press.

MANILA, THE PHILIPPINES

September

"Are you familiar with Xinjiang?" Lee asked.

"I know it's where your government kills Muslims," Marco answered.

"Hmmm…" Lee frowned, then went on. "Many years ago, I was one of the captains of a camp there. Just over ten million Uighur Muslims live in Xinjiang. Since the Party decided that Muslims were a problem, about ten percent of them have been relocated into a network of internment camps in the region. Conditions

there are…" He paused, brow furrowed, tapping his chin as he thought. "Well, I am not sure exactly of the perfect word in English to describe the hell that occurs there, but suffice to say, it is pure misery for anyone who has the misfortune to find himself in one of our camps. Of course, the party calls it re-education for extremists, but anyone with experience in these camps knows it is little more than punishment for not being sufficiently Chinese. Sexual violence, torture, murder, forced labor, and organ harvesting are the day-to-day norm. The worst horror movie you've ever seen can't even begin to compare to the depravity that occurs there."

Marco only stared at him. The man was enjoying himself, and he shuddered as Lee pulled deep on his cigarette.

"The internment camps are not just for Muslims, either. Christians, capitalists, corrupt party officials, enemies of President Xi…anyone the Party deems a threat to its power winds up there. The exact number of prisoners is unknown, but I've spent a fair amount of time there, and I believe my estimate to be quite accurate. Your nation guessed there to be about a million prisoners, but they fall short by half!"

"I know about your concentration camps," Marco said. "It disgusts me to think—"

"It disgusts you, Mr. Rossi? Maybe it does. But it doesn't disgust your government. It seems they don't care.

"Which is an interesting thing, Mr. Rossi, for it's clear that for all your arrogance, you Americans are nothing more than hypocrites. What does the West do about our internment camps? No sanctions. No reprimands. Nothing. You know we torture; you know we rape and murder. But you do nothing. Organ harvesting among the Falun Gong? You say nothing. What does your country do when we humiliate your friends and turn them into vassals? Nothing. We take ships in the open seas. You do nothing. We attack you ten million times a day with cyber. Nothing. Claim the South China Sea? Nothing. Steal your technology? Manipulate our currency? We even took Hong Kong, and you uttered not a peep!

"You say you care about freedom and human rights, but you really don't. You claim that you care about social justice. You say that you care about civil rights and the lives of innocents. But you really don't. Some say it is because Americans are slaves to the dollar, but I don't believe that. I think it's something else. I think you have grown lazy. You can't be bothered. And if you need any more proof of what I'm saying, look at what is happening to your country now. A botched election. Riots. A civil war in the making. You are not a serious nation any longer, that is clear.

"And Mr. Rossi, if we can get the Congress of the United States of America to turn their heads while we murder millions of Muslims and Christians, then what

makes you think they are ever going to change?"

Marco didn't answer.

"I spent several years as an officer in one of the camps," Lee went on. "With the Uighurs, I mean. At first, the sheer level of violence that occurs there was shocking. Many soldiers were not able to stomach it and requested to be transferred. Such requests are usually honored, but almost always result in demotions. Fortunately, I grew a thick skin. I never exactly enjoyed my work there, but I recognized its necessity.

"At one point, I was asked to escort a child to her execution. When I opened the door, I was taken back. The child was young. Eight years old. A beautiful little girl." He paused. "She was my niece."

Lee's eyes drooped behind heavy hoods, black and soulless. Marco dropped his head into his hands.

"You see, I knew immediately it was a test," he continued. "My brother had been a party loyalist, but after a few too many ill-conceived social media posts, the Party decided he'd crossed a line. He was killed, his wife as well. And I knew I would find myself in the firing line if I didn't pass this test."

"Did you really kill your niece?" Marco asked in disgust.

"Would I be here if I hadn't?" Lee answered coldly.

Marco could only shake his head. He already knew how this conversation was going to play out. He'd known ever since he'd asked Lee for the cigarette. "Why must you tell me this?" he asked in resignation.

"Because I need you to understand, Mr. Rossi. Our commitment is absolute. There is no cost we are not willing to pay, no sacrifice we will not willingly make, to see the ascension of the Chinese people and the fall of American hegemony.

"And now, unfortunately for you, Mr. Rossi, your daughter, Victoria, such a beautiful girl, has appeared on the radar of the Party. She claims to be working for a bio lab. We know that's not true. And yes, it's the perfect cover. International travel. Access to the most inaccessible places. But we know she has followed in your footsteps, Mr. Rossi, and that's a risky proposition, working for the government agency she does. And now we need something from her. Something very simple."

Lee pulled out a highly detailed satellite picture: Darkness. A group of soldiers. Desert. Two large vehicles along a road.

"These were taken some time ago," he said. "Some days after this picture was taken, a US team received some information about your president. We think it's tied to the bombing at the US Cathedral. It's important for us to know. Important to our relationship with your president." Lee tapped his finger on the picture of the tallest soldier. "Your daughter knows him. We know they worked together on

a special CIA team in Syria. All we want is—"

"She'll never help you. I will never help you," he sneered.

"We think she will, Mr. Rossi. As long as we have you, we think—"

"She…will…never…help you!" Marco shot back, emphasizing each word.

Lee stood abruptly, pushing the chair back across the cement floor. His face hardened as he searched Marco's eyes. Looking for fear, Marco thought. He would not give Lee that satisfaction. He kept his face blank, and watched as the expression on Lee's soured.

Marco shifted in his seat, turning away from Lee. He stared across the room. He had known it would come to this, and he was calm. At peace. His heart had slowed down, and he almost felt relief.

Lee's voice jarred him back to the present. "Mr. Rossi, you have two options. The first option is to agree to our proposal. I will not ask you to hurt your daughter. Never would I do that. All I ask is for a little bit of information. We can do it in such a way that she will never even know."

"What happens if I don't?"

Lee sat down again, leaning across the table. "Your daughter has a weak spot for you, Mr. Rossi. We will take advantage of that weakness until she gives us what we need. The result will be that you will make a traitor of your daughter. You will ruin her professionally. Scare her with guilt forever. And maybe get the both of you killed.

"I am not your friend, Mr. Rossi. You know that. But you can minimize the pain you and your daughter are to receive if you will cooperate."

Marco had already done the math in his head. Four seconds for the guards behind the mirror to get to the door, another three to open it, four to enter the room and shoot him. Marco might not be as fast as he once was, but that was enough time.

He leaned forward as if he were going to share a secret.

"Mr. Lee, I think you are not as smart as you think you are," he whispered so quietly that Lee had to lean forward even further to hear what he said. "You see, I didn't allegedly quit smoking for my daughter. I would never lie to her. So you made a mistake when you set my hand free." With the strength of a man who knew he was about to die, Marco reached up, grabbed a fist full of Lee's dark hair and slammed his head onto the steel bar that ran across the top of the table. Again, and again, he bashed. Bones and cartilage shattered, fountains of blood painting the room in scarlet red.

The guards shot him nine seconds after the attack began. But Marco Rossi died with a look of satisfaction on his face.

Victoria would have been proud.

WHAT WILL WE DO?

In many ways, our approach to the power that is rising in the East mirrors the world's approach to the Nazis before the outbreak of the Second World War. Much to the chagrin of Winston Churchill, most of his contemporaries throughout Europe and the United States believed that confronting Germany was simply too inconvenient. Too hard. Too high of a price to be paid. Because of this, Hitler and the Nazis were allowed to grow unchecked for far too long.

And now, with our nation so divided and weakened by emotion and discord, and as we go screaming down a path that is designed to fracture us even further as a nation, it's fair to ask: are we prepared—or even able—to defend our freedoms any longer?

At a time when we seem far more interested in the latest emoji, calling each other racist, waiting for the government to announce the next round of funding, and trashing anyone who disagrees with us on every matter, including those issues in which we have no real knowledge, are we ready for the full-spectrum warfare that is at our door? As other countries wonder if we could look any less serious as a nation, we have to wonder if we are ready for the asymmetrical attacks that will surely come if our adversaries conclude that we are weak.

Or will we simply fade away, another great nation that met the end of its natural life and divided into tribes, too exhausted to go on?

In considering the answers to these questions, it seems that one thing is clear. Before we can be ready to fight our adversary, we have to settle the war within ourselves.

Two wars. Ten years. That seems to be the timeline we are on.

Book Three

WAR

I do not know what weapons World War III will be fought with, but one thing is certain: World War IV will be fought with sticks and stones.

— Albert Einstein

To be fair, the above statement is an anecdotal paraphrasing of something Einstein said to a handful of friends, not a direct quote. Regardless of the fact that his exact words have been lost to time, the implications of the statement are still true. During the life of Albert Einstein, nations developed weapons with the capability to destroy most of humanity and all of civilization.

That was eighty years ago.

We've come a very long way in our capabilities for destruction since then. And China is at the tip of the spear in many of these capabilities. They clearly have ambitions and military capabilities in the South China Sea. Their intentions on Taiwan cannot be achieved without military force.

But does that mean China will be sending warships to the East Coast? Will Chinese combat aircraft be observed flying over Washington, DC, or CCP soldiers be seen landing on the pebbled beaches of San Francisco?

Almost certainly not.

They don't need and they don't want to do any of those things. They know they don't have to occupy us to destroy us. They don't have to defeat us militarily to bring us down. They can replace us as the supreme power in the world without ever firing a bullet at a US soldier, aircraft, or ship.

If we, as a nation, continue down the path we are on, if we weaken ourselves to the point that we are unable or unwilling to defend ourselves, these are some of the weapons that will be unleashed against us.

QUANTUM TIME, SPACE, AND MAGIC

L eading quantum physicist Richard Feynman once said, "I think I can safely say that nobody understands quantum mechanics." That may not be exactly true, but it is probably true that at any given time, there are fewer than five people on the planet who truly understand quantum mechanics.

Quantum physics is vastly distinct from classical physics. Classical physics is based on principles that are intuitive to humans, and deals with things such as force, acceleration, and energy. If you pick up a baseball and throw it to a friend, you know it will fly through the air based on the amount of force you applied when you threw it. You know that a headwind can slow the ball down, and eventually gravity will pull the ball back toward Earth. Even if you had never had a formal education, you intuitively understand that force is equal to mass times acceleration. In other words, the bigger and faster the ball is moving when it hits you, the more it's going to hurt.

Now take all of these classical physics principles and throw them out the window. Entirely forget them. Not a single one of them applies in the quantum realm.

The quantum realm is ruled by a collection of bizarre principles that run so counterintuitive to the human experience that it's nearly impossible to resolve the contradictions.

A few examples of these strange rules:

Quantization is the principle that, in the quantum realm, energy, momentum, and a slew of other properties are restricted to discrete values— meaning that when subatomic particles move between energy levels in an atom, they make abrupt "quantum" jumps between the different energy levels and do not cover the space in between them. *Wave-particle duality* teaches us that objects can have the properties of both particles and waves. According to the *uncertainty principle*, we cannot accurately predict both the position and momentum of a particle; we can only predict them with some characteristic "uncertainties." For example, in classical physics, if you know the direction you threw the ball and how much force it was thrown with, you can calculate when it will arrive at its destination and how fast it will be going when it gets there. Yet, this is entirely untrue in the quantum realm.

But perhaps the most curious aspect of quantum mechanics—and one of the fundamental principles upon which quantum computing is based—is that of *quantum superposition*, a principle that states that in the quantum realm, subatomic particles are capable of existing in two places (or states) at the same time. The importance of this principle when discussing computing power cannot be overstated.

In classical computing, when solving an equation or storing information, it is done so as either a zero or a one. That is, there are always exactly two, and only two, options by which classical computing can communicate. This is referred to as a *bit*. Quantum computing does not work in bits, but rather in something called *qubits*. In quantum computing, because these subatomic particles are capable of existing in two places (or states) at any given time, they are also capable of existing anywhere in between these two states at the same time. This is what is referred to as a qubit. Furthermore, qubits are capable of existing as a combination of two states—or places—at the same time. As an example, at any given time, a qubit is *not* either one or zero. Rather, at any moment in time it can be a one *and* a zero, or 90 percent a one and 10 percent a zero, or 50 percent a one and 50 percent a zero, or any percentage of one or the other. This means that rather than performing a single action at a time, when a qubit is stored, it can be stored not just as one of two options, but theoretically, as an infinite number of different combinations—anywhere in between zero and one.

(The enemy of superposition is something called *decoherence*, defined as: when a quantum superposition occurs, it is destroyed by an experimenter observing the atom. This is one of the primary difficulties that researchers face in their attempts to create a true quantum supercomputer.)

If the true potential of quantum computing is ever realized, the result will not just be a "faster computer." It will be a *fundamentally different machine*, as different from the computers that sit on our desk as the principles that define them. And it's impossible to overstate the importance of getting there first.

Quantum computing has been described as the Manhattan Project of our day, and for good reason.

Though its full potential is yet to be defined, its primary application is in the realm of *encryption*. This alone makes the race to be the first to master quantum computing an existential threat. There is no second-place winner. The nation who first masters quantum will, through its use, be able to preclude another nation from completing their research and development.

Which leaves us with this urgent fact. Whoever solves the riddle of quantum computing may rule the world.

BERLIN, GERMANY

October

Jackson was a man who had become used to the absolute finest things that life had to offer: the fastest private jets, the most luxurious of getaways, the most remote islands with the most spectacular views…the most incredible women. He was a man who had quickly become acclimated to opulence, a man who had come to demand things he couldn't even have imagined just a few years before. All of this left him in a state where scarce few things could make him blink, much less pause.

And so, the young woman took it as a personal accomplishment that she caused him to do both. His eyebrows rose as he sucked in his breath. Around them in the bar moved dozens of the most powerful and beautiful men and women in the world, dressed to kill and drinking spirits worth more than the average American car. But as he took in the sight of her, she could tell that all of it became nothing but background noise.

Not that she was surprised.

Victoria Rossi (unaware yet of her father's death in the Philippines) had been called many times one of the most beautiful women in the world. And tonight, she'd actually made an effort. The stakes demanded nothing less.

"I think we both know why I'm here," she said, sending her voice through the air like a symphony as she took the vacant seat beside him. "And I think we both know you're going to agree to my terms. So, let's just jump straight to it. When can you come back to work for us?"

Jackson might have been taken off guard, but he hadn't acquired his station in life by chance. Less than half a second passed before she saw him reclaim his composure, assuming a poise so arrogant it bordered on disdain of all things not him.

"I was told the Company would be making another offer," he began. *"I never would have guessed they were going to send. . ."*

Jackson paused. His face had become an emotionless mask, sterile as an operating table.

"A woman?" she offered. It was a ridiculous thing for him to say.

"A trap," he clarified.

Victoria smiled. She knew even her fake smile was a thing of dreams for a man, and she imagined that it made his heart skip a beat.

"I guess you're just lucky," she said as she leaned toward him.

As dangerous as her smile was, Victoria was well aware that by any rational standard she didn't stand a chance in the contest between herself and the quantum genius. He had all the money, all the power. The best friends. The powerful people. But more than anything else, he had an entire nation intent on keeping him in their fold.

Mr. Jackson had been recruited by the Department of Defense straight out of high school and had worked for them for five years, during which time he'd finished a bachelor's and a master's program in theoretical computations, graduated from law school (for something to do on the weekends), and almost completed a PhD, quitting only after he'd realized that his superiors had nothing more to teach him. Despite his enormous value to the US government, he chose to leave their employment as soon as his contract expired. He then went to work for one of the biggest technological companies in the world, started a tech company of his own (which burned through two hundred million dollars of other people's money before it failed, proving that not all quantum geniuses were good at marketing), was pulled back into US government for another four-year stint, then back into the private sector once again. Each time, he was given more power, more responsibility, more money, more fame. Each assignment taught him something, honed his skills, and allowed him to move higher in the ranks—an easy thing for one of the most intelligent men in the world to do.

After becoming a technological "free agent" for the second time, he'd been courted by every entity on the planet who'd had a hand in the quantum computing game. Google had offered him seven figures in salary and eight figures worth of stock as a signing bonus, and Microsoft had offered him stock options that would have landed him on the Forbes list.

But the Chinese were waiting. They'd had him in their sights for years. And they made him on offer that no man could refuse.

Come work for Tencent, the technological industrial arm of the Communist Party, they said, and we will make you one of the wealthiest people in the world.

At first, he didn't believe it. But they had proven their intent. Then they gave him twenty-four hours to decide.

Initially, he'd resisted. Working for the Chinese government was anathema to everything he held dear—or at least what he thought he held dear, until he learned how dear real money could be. China had even proposed that he could work for them out of California, allowing him to keep his life in the States—though when the US government got wind of that, they made it very clear that they would revoke his US passport, place him under constant surveillance, and impose a long list of other detriments if he took the job with the Chinese.

During hour twenty-two, he made his decision.

The money was just too much to resist. And besides, the US wasn't the only acceptable place to live. For the money he was offered, he could buy his own island. His own country. He could pretty much buy any place, anyone, anything that he desired.

Upon agreement, his new Chinese bosses determined the wealth of the world's top twenty richest people and gifted him stock, property, and cash to make him number ten on the list, plus one dollar to start him on his way to number nine.

But only if he was able to produce.

Which he did.

He met productivity bonuses every six months, making leaps and strides in the field of quantum that were previously unprecedented. Not only did he make Forbes, but he also was currently listed as having more wealth than the yearly GDP of the poorest dozen countries combined. And with that sort of wealth had come power. He had the ears of more government officials than the next ten men behind him. And one wouldn't be faulted for mistaking his "personal security" for a private army.

With such a background, the odds certainly did not appear to be in Victoria's favor. But her confidence was anything but false. And she hadn't come unarmed.

"I'm a woman who happens to know exactly what you want," she said and arched a pretty eyebrow. As she spoke, she exposed her long neck beneath golden curls. Her analysts had perused his search history and told her he preferred brunettes, but she had disregarded the advice. She would make him want blonde.

"That's a confident claim."

"I've never been accused of humility." She paused to consider as she touched her thin fingers to her chin. "Nor do I recall ever having been accused of being wrong, if we're being honest."

"I'll hear you out for curiosity's sake," Jackson said as he glanced down at his watch. "But you'd better hurry. My bodyguards won't hurt you unless I tell them to, but when my employer gets wind of this conversation, and they will, I won't have the power to protect you. The CCP are beyond even my influence. If history is any indicator, I'd guess you have less than fifteen minutes to make your case."

Victoria knew the man's words were no idle threat. She didn't so much as spare a glance in their direction, but her training had allowed her to take notice of the two men at the far end of the bar. They were dressed in fine suits and appeared deep in conversation, but she had spotted them as Jackson's men the moment she had entered the room. Two more were near the glass waterfall. Two of the women whispering over a small table were certainly his as well. And there were probably several more she didn't have time to tag in the three seconds she'd had to look around the room. All of them were dangerous.

But Jackson's men weren't the true threat. That honor belonged to Jackson's employers, the Chinese Communist Party. They were here in Berlin with him, of course, but at this moment they were nowhere to be seen.

At least not yet.

If the Chinese caught her talking with Jackson, she was dead. Her only hope was that the microphone in her ear would warn her before it was too late.

"I seem to remember hearing something about knowing a man by the company he kept," Victoria said as she twirled her finger to indicate the girls around the bar. Any one of them would have cost more for a night than the yearly salary of the average blue-collar worker, but they were bought, nonetheless. "I can't imagine this is how you pictured your life."

"You do realize I just finished lunch with the king of Saudi Arabia, and tomorrow I am having dinner with the pope," Jackson replied. But there was little conviction in his words. "And next week I plan to—"

Victoria cut him off with a genuine laugh, sending the sound of it splashing against his ears. Jackson couldn't help but smile. Anything less would have been inhuman, and she thought there was still a corner of his heart that could feel. "If you find either of those men intellectually engaging, then I've severely underestimated you," she said lightly.

His smile began to broaden, but he chewed his lip to bite it down.

She stared into his eyes and smiled. With every word he spoke, she got a better read on him, which, in her line of work, was a more powerful weapon than anything that could explode. As remarkable as her appearance was, her high cheekbones and curved hips were only distractions from her true power. Her real talent was the way her mind could assess all of the pieces of the human puzzle. She had been selected for the job because she could read a man's emotions as easily as a book. She could know his thoughts, his leanings, his intentions, usually before he did.

"The pope—" Jackson started again before Victoria cut him off once more.

"—doesn't understand the world the way that you do."

"Hmmm…" He mused for a moment. "Maybe you're right. But even if the company I keep does little to stimulate the mind…well…that's what all of the other stuff is for."

He smirked, half-friendly, half-dismissively, but with a sadness in his eyes. Anyone else would have missed it. But Victoria didn't.

The microphone in her ear clicked, and a quiet voice sounded, "You've got to work him faster."

She lightly touched her left ear, the signal for her director to calm down. Leave me alone…don't distract me now!

Ignoring her instructions, he spoke into her ear again. "They're five minutes out."

Victoria heart slammed in her chest, fear knotting in her stomach.

She needed more time!

Jackson started to make some vague argument about heaven-only-knows what, but she barely heard him as her mind raced in fear.

"Money is power," he told her. "In fact, at this moment, with what I have, with the things I know, the things I understand that only a few humans are even able to comprehend, I am one of the most powerful men in the world. Certainly, the most powerful man you will ever meet. I have the power to unmake you. I could buy your home, your family, your entire town, and turn it all into something for my pleasure." His voice was hard now, a bit angry. Normally he was more restrained, but she could see she had unnerved him. She saw the tightness of his lips and knew it was a dangerous omen.

"Is all that not power?" he demanded.

"Yes. I suppose it is. But it's not the right kind of power," she answered quietly.

"What other power is there?"

"Three minutes!" the voice in her earpiece hissed. "Two teams. Three men each. Contractors. The best."

She shook her blonde hair from her face and touched her ear again as she listened. "You don't have enough time. They are coming for you. Get out of there!"

She leaned forward until she was only inches from his face, grabbed his jaw in her warm hands and locked eyes. "What good is controlling an army if someone else is making you dance? What good is all this money if you owe everything to them!"

She paused, looking deep into his eyes. she gave him a look of pity that was obvious and sincere. She wasn't acting any more. "I have the power to choose my own destiny," she whispered. "You surely want that, too." And before she could think better of it, she added, "Unless you are a moron."

His eyes turned dark and wolfish.

"So, let me get this straight," he hissed. "You think I'm going to come work for you! You think you can get the blueprints and codes for Quantum?"

She didn't answer.

"Even if I wanted to help you, do you think we could simply board a plane and go back to America? Do you think it is that simple?" His face suddenly drained of color. He had realized the real stakes of their conversation, and he took a step back. "You are insane," he said softly. "You can't win against them. Don't you know that? No one can."

PHYSICS CLASS

Robert Oppenheimer was a brilliant physicist born at the turn of the last century. His achievements include work in molecular wave functions, nuclear fusion, quantum field theory, cosmic rays, quantum tunneling, and more. He is also credited as being the father of the Manhattan Project. At the height of the Second World War, he and his colleagues worked furiously toward the creation of the atomic bomb, one of the greatest weapons humankind has ever known. If they ever took time to consider the long-term implications of their work, the destructive power and death they were going to unleash, it didn't appear to slow them down, for they understood the importance of their work to winning the war.

After the first nuclear detonation made clear to him the implications of what he had accomplished, Oppenheimer uttered the chilling phrase, "Now I am become death, the destroyer of worlds."

It's quite clear he didn't utter this phrase hyperbolically. After the fateful day, regret appears to have directed his every professional action. In an effort to limit nuclear proliferation, he spent the rest of his life lobbying for the international control of nuclear weapons, becoming such a vocal critic of the government that his security clearances were revoked. Despite his efforts to curb the proliferation of nuclear weapons, by most reasonable measures his mission was a failure. From the very moment his creation lit up the Japanese sky with thermonuclear fire, the cat was out of the bag. There currently exists enough nuclear weaponry to destroy all human life several times over.

Now we find ourselves in a similar struggle, a race to be the first to harness a technology that is critical to the defense of freedom. And though only history can prove whether Oppenheimer's regret will be shared by those who achieve quantum supremacy, one thing is certain: if we are not first, our regret will be forever.

And our enemies understand this. They know this is an existential threat for both nations.

To achieve this goal, our Chinese adversaries are illegally appropriating our intellectual property, recruiting our best and brightest, educating their students at our finest universities, demanding associations with our premier NGOs, and stealing our research at an astounding rate. If anything, we've underestimated the lengths to which they will go to gain the high ground in the race to complete the first quantum computer. And how could they not? Quantum computers will be to classical computing what an F-22 Raptor is to a caveman's club.

To understand why, we have to go back to physics.

Encryption consists of using Shor's algorithm to convert a desired piece of information into a secret code. Shor's algorithm, invented in 1994 by American mathematician Peter Shor, appears as a simple equation: $N = P \times Q$. If I tell you the number N, for example the number 21, then ask you to solve for P and Q, with the mandate that P and Q are both prime numbers (a prime number being a number that is only divisible by itself and 1), the answer is fairly simple: 7 and 3.

The answer to the equation seems uncomplicated at first glance. And the method to find the answer is also quite simple: the only way to solve the problem is to divide sequentially by prime numbers.

But when the numbers get large, it becomes *extraordinarily* difficult to solve. As a matter of fact, it becomes so difficult that it's the principle upon which encryption is based. This is because as N increases in size, the number of possibilities grows at an exponential rate. And exponential growth is *very fast*. It is so fast, it begs an example of how quickly numbers grow any time exponentiality is involved.

Let's say I discover a zombie. His bite always turns its victims into zombies. But he's also kind of lazy. He only bites a human every six hours. His offspring zombies are also lazy, only biting every six hours as well. As such, the number of zombies on the planet doubles every six hours. How many zombies would infest the earth after a single month?

More than 1,000,000,000,000,000,000,000,000,000,000,000.

Perhaps an unlikely example. But it does illustrate the point that when dealing with the principle of exponential growth, the numbers get *very* large, *very* quickly.

When dealing with mathematical problems that have exponentiality baked into them, it makes for problems that are nearly impossible for a classical computer to solve, because the number of calculations it needs to perform is simply overwhelming. Not even the fastest supercomputers on the planet are capable of hacking an encrypted message in anything close to an efficient manner. Give our most powerful computers a couple weeks, a couple months, maybe a couple years, and they might break the code... eventually (if they get really, *really* lucky). But the purposes for which we need encryption broken very often require that we need answers right now!

With our current technology, all we can do is turn our most powerful computers on the problem, fire up the generators to produce a massive amount of electricity, then sit back and wait. And hope.

And it's not that the super computers we have now are slow. Indeed, they are fast. Like, really fast.

The fastest nonclassified supercomputer on Earth is Fugaku, a behemoth of a machine that is larger than two tennis courts and capable of performing 415 petaFLOPs per second. A computer capable of doing even a single petaFLOP is able to perform 1,000,000,000,000,000 calculations per second.

But even with this speed, while it's theoretically possible to hack a highly encrypted target, for most decryption purposes we don't have the time.

Enter quantum computing.

The theory—and at this point it remains only a theory, though a widely accepted one—is that if the power of quantum mechanics can be harnessed, it would be able to do these sorts of calculations very quickly. The logic behind this theory is that, for classical computing, each possibility must be performed in sequential order. Even the fastest supercomputers on Earth fall woefully short in achieving these tasks. They are limited by classical physics, principles which dictate that they still must perform each calculation, every time, one after the other.

But remember, in the quantum realm, particles are capable of being in two different places (or states) at the same time (as well as all of the places and states in between...all at the same time). The theory goes that if a qubit can be in two states/places at the same moment in time, then they could logically perform multiple calculations *at the same time!* If theory holds correct, this means that a quantum computer would have the capability of performing more calculations per second than the number of atoms that exist in the universe.

Wrap your head around that thought for a second.

Which means that whoever has a quantum computer would be able to effortlessly hack encryption.

But why is hacking encryption so important? On a scale of one to the Manhattan Project, does that really rank as a critical undertaking?

Absolutely yes.

BERLIN, GERMANY

October

Jackson pushed himself away from the table and stood. He nodded to his lead man, and it seemed that half the bar stood and began making their way toward him, hands at their hidden weapons.

Victoria nearly panicked. The moment was slipping. Had she misjudged the man?

"You're right, Jackson," she said in fear. "They will not let you come with me. They will kill you. And no one in the world can stop them." She took a step toward him. "Except for me."

Jackson turned back to her, his eyes glaring.

"Come with me!" she begged him. "Come with me! I know you can feel it burning in your bones. You can feel it pounding in your chest. You hate this empty cage they've made for you."

He looked at her and shook his head. "I'm flattered you think I have that kind of heart, but I haven't gotten to where I am by being sentimental. You can't convince—"

"I don't have to convince you!" she shot back. "You already know! Even if you can't admit it, you know that I am right. With all the things you own, there is one thing you don't have. And it's the one thing you need more than anything else in this world!"

"You know nothing of what I want," he hissed.

But she did. She understood him very well. And she also knew if she couldn't convince him now, she would never get another chance.

He nodded to his men, who had surrounded him in a circle of protection. Together, they started walking toward the door.

"They are on the stairs," the voice in her earpiece sounded. "Get out of there, Victoria. Get out of there NOW!"

She ignored the screaming in her ears.

"SECONDS! YOU HAVE ONLY SECONDS!"

She moved after Jackson. "I know that when you sip the best wine, it tastes to you like ash," she called out to his back.

Jackson stopped and didn't move.

"I know when you breathe in a tropical breeze, it smells like smoke," she said in a softer voice.

He stood frozen, his eyes dropping to the floor. The room seemed to fall silent, every eye on him.

She took another step toward him and extended her hand until it touched his shoulder. "I know when the sun touches your face, it does nothing more than make you itch. I know you'd give all the wealth in this world to hold a woman who doesn't feel like plastic." She stepped slowly to his side and he finally turned to look at her.

"I know," she said, staring into his anguished face. "I understand. You may have all of the pleasures in this world, but you enjoy them less and less. Every day that passes, you find the world a more dead and empty place. Do you want to spend the rest of your days in the desert, dying of thirst and drinking sand?"

He shook his head. "You don't make a deal with the Party and then back out of it. They will find me. They will kill me. And they will kill me hard and slow."

"GO! GO! GO!" the voice screamed in her ear. "They are assembling at the doorway. You've got to use the back door!"

She glanced in fear behind her. If she left now, there was a chance she could get away. But she couldn't leave without Jackson. She ignored her supervisor's commands.

"If you come with me, you can have the one thing in all the world you crave the most," she told him. "The only thing that matters. I can give it back to you."

Their eyes met. He seemed to choke. The fear on his face was replaced by a deep sadness that pulled the light from his eyes.

"You have always been a warrior," she concluded. "But now you have no cause."

He stared at her in silence. She leaned forward and whispered in his ear. "I can give you freedom."

And there it was.

The truth.

Jackson took a breath, his shoulders trembling. He put his hand to his face to cover the quiver in his chin. A tear formed in his eye and he quickly wiped it away.

He knew what he'd done. It was devouring him, eating him from the inside. The CCP was soon going to rule the world because he had crafted for them the most powerful sword the world had ever known.

His mouth moved to speak, but no sound came out.

"Come with me," the woman said as she held out her hand. "Please!" Her eyes were deep and shining. She was weeping too.

He reached out and took her hand. "It's too late," he said.

The men poured into the room, tactical gear and black uniforms flashing in the dim light. Their weapons ready, they moved like spiders through the room.

The shots rang out. Blazes of white light amid the darkness. Dozens of them. Far too many. The sound was nearly deafening. Smoke and acid filled the air....

In the end, it turned out that Victoria's supervisor was right. She was in great danger. They weren't only after him.

Their thinking was pretty simple: if they couldn't keep him—and they realized that he wasn't going to stay, fool as he was for freedom—then no one would. And they'd kill anyone who came to take him, be they American or not.

So it was that Jackson lay, along with most of his bodyguards, dead on the floor.

Victoria saw him fall, then turned and ran.

* * * * *

In the modern world, cryptography is everywhere: bank accounts, financial records, medical servers, intellectual property of nearly every business, military secrets in the most secure vaults, nuclear launch codes on submarines. From biomedical research being conducted by DARPA at sites whose names we don't even know, to a simple iMessage sent on your phone, our entire world is blanketed in a layer of encryption. Without the key, anyone who intercepts an encrypted message would see nothing but gibberish. The receiver of the message presumably has the "cipher" (one of the prime numbers needed to crack the code), which is the key to turning the gibberish code back into meaningful information.

The power of quantum computing may revolutionize countless fields, from pharmaceutical studies and financial modeling to weather predictions. But more than all of these, whoever develops this technology first will have the power to crack encrypted codes without needing the cipher. Meaning they will have unfettered access to…well…*everything*.

Want to hack into the private servers of an American company and steal all of its intellectual property? It would take the amount of time it took you to type the commands on the keyboard. Want to hack Wells Fargo or Bank of America and mess with every dollar in every account? Go right ahead. Want to force your way into the New York Stock Exchange because you want to steal a billion dollars' worth of stock? Want to hack into the American power grid to bring it down? Plant a computer virus that would destroy the nation's financial sector? How about a nuclear reactor? Want to infiltrate Northrop Grumman's or Boeing's servers and steal some of America's most tightly guarded military secrets? How about the CIA, so that you could reveal the name, location, and mission of every undercover agent on the planet? The Fed? DARPA? NASA? The NSA?

Nothing will be safe.

And again—there is no second place. The nation that masters quantum first will be able to hack and destroy a rival's efforts, keeping them from developing the technology themselves.

WASHINGTON, DC

End of November

Darren stood in the middle of the room, his face pale, his breath short, his hands trembling at his side. He was surrounded by half a dozen of the family empire's senior executives, another half dozen accountants, a couple secretaries, and two guys who did computer security or something like that, he didn't know for sure.

"We don't know how it happened," his senior advisor tried to explain. "The Fed is being very quiet. It seems that some of the banks are unaffected. I don't know how many…half? A third? Very little information is getting out. But many have been taken down."

Darren stared at him and gulped.

"Perhaps you could talk to your associates at the FBI," the advisor suggested. "I know that you and the director have become friends."

Darren shook his head in anger. "I tried. He told me nothing. Not a word. Or at least nothing of any value."

"Perhaps if you explained it wasn't for your reporting. Strictly off the record. For your own benefit is all. If you were to—"

"He's not going to help me!" Darren screamed. "He won't tell me anything. And I don't think…" He hesitated. "I don't even think he knows."

"Impossible," the advisor muttered.

"No, I really don't think he understands what happened. He sounded rattled. No, he was more than rattled, he was straight-up terrified. He stammered and spat out a few things that made no sense, but I really don't think they know."

The room was quiet for a horrifying moment.

"Two billion dollars," his old man muttered as he leaned his head against the leather couch.

Good thing he's already drunk, Darren thought sourly. His father had been worthless at pretty much everything since it all had started to unravel. He wasn't going to survive this, Darren knew that. He wouldn't live another week.

The old man sat up and leaned toward him. "How much cash have you got on you?" he demanded.

"What difference does it make!" Darren shot back.

"Because that's how much we are worth now."

"Sir," the adviser muttered to the old man, trying to reassure him. "We are going to get it back. It might take time, but it's not impossible. In fact, it'd be impossible not to get it back. There are backups to the backups to the backups—"

"And all of them are gone," Darren muttered.

The advisor turned to face him. "They can't be gone, sir. That's kind of like saying the sun has disappeared."

Darren turned to look at him and smiled weakly. He didn't know how he knew it, but he knew his advisor had it wrong.

In his mind, he thought back on his frantic conversation with the FBI director. The director had only given him five minutes, which offended him deeply, as much as he had helped them, but it turned out to be worthless anyway. The director had sputtered about backbones and blockchains and curation and servers and encryption and a million other things that neither of them understood. And he had muttered something else…something Darren knew nothing about. What was it?

It came to him. He turned to his advisors. Surely one of them understood.

"What is quantum?" he asked.

DNA CRISPR
TOOLS OF LIFE

Just because we are not ready for scientific progress
does not mean it won't happen.

— Jennifer A. Doudna *(Recipient of 2020 Nobel Prize in*
Chemistry for her work on CRISPR)

GENETIC MODIFYING TOOLS

The potential of CRISPR and other genetic modifying tools to change the world is so incredibly revolutionary that it is difficult to describe.

To do so, as with quantum, we have to provide a little of the science first, beginning with the DNA that makes us who we are.

DNA is a double-helix assembly of four different nucleic acids whose purpose is to store and transmit biological information, making it the "blueprint" of life. Just as the twenty-six letters in the English alphabet can be rearranged in infinitely different ways to create different words, different sentences, different thoughts and ideas, stories, and concepts, the nucleic acids that make up DNA can be rearranged in infinitely different sequences. Each different arrangement of nucleic acids (a.k.a. the genetic "code") results in a different message to the cell. Therefore, DNA is responsible for every trait of every living organism that has ever graced our planet; everything from the rigidity of a bacterial cell wall, to the orange and black stripes of a tiger's fur, to a bird's lightweight bones, to the intelligence of a dolphin. Every living organism's DNA contains the entirety of information that is needed to grow, develop, function, and reproduce.

And humans are no different. Genetic sequences code for the color of our eyes, the strength of our hearts, the pigmentation of our skin, our height, our intelligence, our creativity. DNA is largely responsible for whether or not we go bald, have a crooked nose or irritable bowel syndrome, or develop Alzheimer's. Even our personality is influenced by the DNA in our cells.

Scientists have long understood this, and ever since DNA was discovered by Watson and Crick in the 1970s, they have spent countless hours peeking under the hood of our genetic engines in an effort to manipulate the genetic code. They did so with relatively limited success.

Until CRISPR.

CRISPR (or CRISPR-Cas9 if you want to be academic) is a collection of proteins that can be programmed to do one thing: identify a particular sequence of DNA molecules (as determined by the scientist), and to then remove the particular piece of DNA from the cell. After the undesirable part of the genetic blueprint has been removed, CRISPR then fills in the gap in the DNA sequence with whatever piece of genetic code it was loaded with by the scientist.

And we aren't merely on the cusp of the genetic alterations' horizon; we are already there.

For example, CRISPR has been used to alter crops in a number of different ways. Scientists have managed everything from creating larger vegetables, to enhancing their ability to be pest-and-weather resistant, to creating fruit that doesn't spoil for months. In addition, there is research being done to change the allergen content, flavor, and taste.

Spicy strawberries, anyone?

And the ability to modify the basic building blocks of life is not limited to plants. CRISPR has been used to create microorganisms capable of creating biofuels, as well as mosquitoes incapable of carrying human diseases like malaria, or, in a stroke of genius by one scientist, a mosquito whose progeny self-destructs. Scientists in China recently created monkeys with genetic code responsible for human intelligence, resulting in animals that performed significantly better on intelligence tests (as well as causing us to wonder if *anyone* in China has ever seen *Planet of the Apes)*.

In our lifetime, we will see everything from faster racehorses to more intelligent breeds of canines to more friendly felines. One day we may even possess the ability to bring extinct species back to our planet. It's nearly impossible to enumerate all of the incredible things that may be accomplished during our lifetimes through genetic modification.

The first major advances for humans will occur in the fields of health and medicine. Currently, research is being conducted on a number of different genetic diseases, such as sickle cell disease, cystic fibrosis, and muscular dystrophy, all with incredible promise. The power of CRISPR is also being used to excise cancerous chains of genetic code, and preliminary results from research in this field appear to be quite encouraging. Today, because of CRISPR, we stand on the cusp of not merely an evolution, but a revolution, in the field of medicine.

However, as much as genetic-modifying tools will be used to benefit mankind, the God-like power of genetic manipulations is accompanied by a number of very troubling ethical concerns.

Should you be allowed to choose the traits your children have, or should this power remain with the Deity? Would it be immoral to accept a genetic-modifying treatment for your unborn child if the treatment infers a 99 percent chance to create a genius, but a 1 percent chance he will die before age five? What if you knew the technology was safe and your child was guaranteed to have the trait you selected, but you also knew it came about as a result of questionable research by governments not restrained by Western ethics? Would you select the genes for your offspring knowing that only a small percentage of the human population will have access to this very expensive technology, only furthering the divide between the haves and the have-nots? Will we become a society where sex is no longer the primary means of human conception? With approximately 3 percent of children born with a significant genetic defect, what if it were deemed "too risky" to have a child by natural conception, and insurance companies were allowed to refuse coverage to any children not created in a lab? And who should be the regulators of this technology?

We will be forced to reckon with these questions within our lifetime.

And even if the United States is able to regulate the most troubling aspects of genetic-altering technology, there are numerous countries that have no regulatory ethics or moral standards that prohibit them from forging full steam ahead with the goal of creating a superhuman race.

Which then leads to a chilling question: what if the United States falls behind in the genetic arms race? What if we "lose" the coming biological war?

Then the greatest story of the twenty-first century will be the rise of China and its power struggle with the United States. It is primarily through their relationship with Western universities and research centers that they have become masters in gene manipulation, and in many ways are beginning to eclipse their Western counterparts. Furthermore, they are unencumbered by Western ideals, traditions, and morals. In an op-ed discussing CRISPR and similar technologies, former director of national intelligence John Ratcliffe stated, "There are no ethical boundaries to Beijing's pursuit of power."

The CCP have clearly demonstrated they are immune to restraint when it comes to advancing their agenda, and that they view the creation of a master race as a very high priority.

Dr. He Jiankui, a Chinese biophysics researcher, shocked the world when, in 2018, he publicly announced that he had created the first genetically modified babies using CRISPR-Cas9 on a pair of fertilized eggs, twins named Lulu and Nana. Initially he received praise, but sentiment quickly soured, and as Western public opinion turned, so, too, did the favor of the Communist party. His research was allegedly disbanded and disavowed by the Chinese government. However, not only were multiple Chinese government institutions aware of his research, and had been aware since its inception, the overwhelming evidence points to the fact they funded it.

The intelligence regarding this topic is very sensitive, but there can be no doubt that the CCP has recognized the near-limitless potential inherent in manipulating the human genome. They want the most durable and athletic super-soldiers, the most brilliant scientists, the healthiest race. As confirmed by the former director of national intelligence, we know they are years into their experimentation of "super soldiers," as well as the creation of a master race. In short, they want complete and total "biological dominance."

The rest of the world is finally becoming aware of China's determination to press forward in this field. Several advanced Western nations have thus concluded that they, too, must conduct similar research in order to stay competitive in the coming decades. For example, France has publicly given the green light for the development of augmented soldiers, the French minister for the armed forces publicly stating, "We have to be clear, not everyone has the same scruples as us and we have to prepare ourselves for such a future."

But as we struggle with the complicated ethical and moral implications of CRISPR research, while understanding the potential good that CRISPR might lead to, we also have to recognize that some of the potential applications of CRISPR are pure evil.

WASHINGTON, DC

December

Darren slowly came awake as the banging echoed through his historic brownstone; someone knocking on the front door. He looked at the clock. Three-thirty in the morning. His heart raced. He got up, checked the security camera, saw it was Irene, and moved toward the enormous metal front door while pulling a T-shirt over his head.

Irene, a post-grad programming engineer who looked like she was eighteen and couldn't have weighed more than a hundred twenty soaking wet—which she was—looked up at him through the security camera, a little girl in her arms. She shivered as he opened the door, rain dripping off her shoulders, her waterlogged hair sticking to her forehead. She had on a designer jacket, $10,250 at Jeanne Lanvin on Park Avenue, good for getting noticed but worthless at keeping her warm.

Irene, the mother of his daughter, used to be the beneficiary of $200,000 a month of hard-earned child support. She had received it every month until the financial collapse. Since then, she hadn't received a dime, because he had not a dime to give.

She pushed into the entry before he could say anything. Maddie, the only person in the world Darren cared about more than himself, clung to her with the determination of a terror-stricken child.

"I was afraid you'd be in New York," Irene said in relief.

"Why are you here?" he demanded.

"You don't know yet?" she answered incredulously. "You really don't know what's going on?"

Maddie was shivering as well, a scared and confused look on her face. He reached out to take her and she fell into his arms. He looked at their wet clothes. "You walked here in the rain?" he asked.

"I didn't have any cash for gas."

"You couldn't take a cab?"

"Listen to me, Darren. I have no cash. Most of the banks are down. That means I have to walk."

He stared another minute. "Let me get you something to dry yourselves."

"We don't have time, Darren," Irene said fearfully.

Darren shook his head. "Hang on…hang on…our daughter is freezing!" He moved into the foyer bathroom and grabbed a couple of thick, white towels, threw one to Irene then started to towel-dry Maddie's hair.

"She's fine, Darren," Irene said. "I can't believe you haven't been following this. Don't you have staff to notify you—"

"I was asleep."

She eyed him suspiciously, then glanced back toward the narrow corridor leading to his bedroom.

"Go into the living room. Turn on the fire. Give me a minute." He turned toward his bedroom.

"You have to see this right now!" Irene almost shouted. She was a timid person, and it was entirely out of character for her when she stamped a foot and stared him down.

Ignoring her, he hurried to his bedroom, Maddie still in his arms. Grabbing his cell phone, he discovered twenty-seven messages. Nine missed calls.

Darren froze.

Why did he take the Ambien? And the whiskey too!

He noted the time of the last call. More than three hours before....

He called his executive assistant. An unfamiliar tone was all he got. He called his personal assistant. The call didn't go through. He swore again. Turning, he walked back toward the front of the house. Irene had moved into the living room. "What's going on?" he demanded.

She took the remote from the coffee table and turned on the television. Darren immediately noticed the emergency broadcast chyron scrolling along the bottom of the screen. The midnight anchor, a man he'd worked with for years, but whose name he didn't know, spoke in deliberate tones. He was interviewing a woman with red curly hair, the text on the screen identifying her as a government official from the CDC.

Darren felt a coldness grab his belly, and without realizing, he stepped closer to the TV.

"...is the thing we fear," the official was saying, "Since the virus was first detected in Boston seven days ago, it has obviously spread. And spread with a vengeance. The R-naught on this...I'm sorry, the expected cases from exposure to a single infected person, is frightening. Tonight, the government announced that all modes of public transport have been shut down. This will only be for a short time, just while we get a handle on the virus, but we need to do it for a while. We're calling on people not to leave their homes unless absolutely necessary. At this point, any and all means of travel will only help to spread the pathogen.

"Currently all of the nation's airports and other means of interstate travel are under military quarantine. This won't affect many people, since there have only been limited flights since the financial attack. The only airports we have collected data from are JFK and Reagan in Washington, DC. Approximately three hundred people reported flu- or cold-like symptoms at JFK. And in the time since the quarantine was initiated, forty-seven of them have died from seizure-like episodes and uncontrollable fevers."

The news anchor was silent for an awkward moment. The fear in his eyes was real. "How did this happen?" he asked. "How could something like this take us by such surprise?"

Darren felt his spine grow cold. The CDC spokesperson went on. There were multiple theories about the origins of the virus, she explained. Some said the wet markets, yet again, but it was way too early to know. She paused, her face suddenly taut. "Preliminary information reports about a quarter of people die, half of the survivors have fever-induced brain damage, and it's nearly as contagious as the common cold."

"God save us," the news anchor whispered. "So, what are we to do?"

The woman's bland expression returned as she forced herself to regain her composure. "In the short term, we quarantine. Trace contacts. We stabilize. We research. We just went through this with COVID-19. If we can contain it…"

Darren turned away from the TV and tried his phone again. Still no service. He had to get to the studio. It was the biggest story of the decade. How was he going to get a driver? Who would pick him up? Where was all of his help, the people he paid a lot of money to…well, used to pay a lot of money to.

"Cell towers are overloaded," Irene said as he continued poking at his phone. "Millions of people are jamming all the lines. That's why I came here. I couldn't call you."

He paused, then turned back to his phone and kept jabbing at the numbers.

"It's too late," she whispered. "They imposed a quarantine around the airport where the virus was detected. Another around the George Washington hospital. We're inside the parameters. Trapped inside the zone—"

"They what?" he shouted.

Irene nodded toward his phone. "I know what you're thinking. You've got to get to the studio. You've got to get to work. A big story…history in the making… you've got to get on screen. But let me tell you, father of my child: you're not going anywhere. The world out there has gone bat crazy. And we're way past the point where news reports even matter. People only have to look out their front windows to see what's going on."

Darren dropped his arms to his side, feeling his face grow slack.

She was right. The world as he knew it was gone. After a generation of weakness, after years of buildup and then months of falling, they were about to hit the ground. And in that moment, he knew such fear as he had never felt before. Fear of the unknown. Fear of death. Fear of pain. Fear for Maddie. Fear of being powerless to do anything to prevent what was going to happen.

His gut grew tight with a knot fear and helplessness.

He knew what was coming.

The FBI director hadn't returned any of his calls. And the last time he had spoken with his other contacts, they had been distant, anxious to get off the phone. They'd certainly refused to offer any information.

The initial cases had been reported about a week before. Boston was the first. Then New York and Chicago. Detroit. L.A. At first there were just a few curious cases of a new and aggressive flu, hardly more than a short mention in the news. But then the reality hit, the exponentiality becoming real. And the people were primed to fear it, COVID having sensitized them to the reality that a deadly virus could erupt.

But they had crossed a new boundary now, one they had never crossed before.

Quarantines. Forced separations. Protecting those who had not been exposed, but trapping others inside a quarantine zone.

No way…he knew it…no way they would not become exposed….

He moved his eyes toward the windows, looking out on the street. He lived less than two miles from Reagan National Airport. If the quarantine at the airport failed…if infected people got out…

"We have to go," he said. "We have to leave the city."

Irene frowned and looked away. "I don't think that's a good idea. I think we should stay here. All of Maddie's things are here. All her clothes. Her toys. Her friends."

Darren stared at her in disbelief. "Her friends! Her toys and clothes!"

"I have food, enough for a few days. A week at least. We can probably get some more from the market if we get there first thing in the morning. The city water is still running. And besides—"

Darren shook his head in frustration. Irene had always been a good mother for Maddie, and he knew that she had been careful to gather whatever food and staples that she could get, being especially vigilant since the grocery stores had become undependable and the restaurants had shut down. But the little bit of food she had stuffed away in her pantry was not going to help them now.

"We have to go," he said again, interrupting. "We have to get out of the city." He made his voice hard.

Irene frowned. "The authorities—"

"The authorities are going to lie to us! The media are going to lie to us. Trust me, I know. If what you said is true, if they have forced a quarantine…if the virus escapes the quarantine zone, and it will, and if we stay here, we'll die."

He started to move through the room, looking for a notepad to write a list of things to take with them, his mind racing.

Irene's frown deepened and she stepped back. "You heard the CDC person. She said they could contain it."

Darren swore angrily and motioned to his daughter, who had curled in the white towel on the couch and closed her eyes. He took a step toward Irene and lowered his voice to a whisper. "I may not know anything about molecular biology, but I know people. Humans are predictable. Everyone—everyone—is going to try and get out. They won't just stay here and die! This thing is going to spread. How long until they quarantine the whole city? We have to get out of here before they do."

Irene didn't say anything, her eyes staring at the far wall. "That is exactly how the virus spreads! Your plan isn't very…altruistic. But if everybody just stayed in place and did what they were told—"

"My plan is the only way we are going to live!"

"Where will you go?"

Darren didn't answer her. He didn't know.

He sat a moment to catch his thoughts. To plan. But his mind kept racing back.

There had been rumors. Whispers from the Pentagon and FBI. Nothing concrete. And they all seemed so outrageous. Simply unbelievable. He had not even considered they were anything but just that, rumor. Something about a biological agent that China had created. Then they had made demands of American leadership—outrageous demands, impossible for any US president to agree to.

And there was more, things that simply could not be real. And even if real, they certainly couldn't be…wouldn't be used. Was it even possible? A virus that only attacked certain people! It made his skin crawl.

Darren hadn't believed it at the time, but the moment he saw the newscast he knew it was real.

He moved to the back of his house and began grabbing the things he would need. He emerged from his bedroom with his warmest clothes and started layering them on. He took his backpack from the closet and stuffed it full of food, then filled a water bottle. He grabbed all of his cash and put it all in his front pocket, remembering what his dad had said. "How much cash do you have on you? Because that's all you're worth."

He hesitated for a moment before grabbing the largest knife in the kitchen and slid it in the outer pocket of his backpack.

"Okay," Irene said. "I'm coming with you."

Darren met her eyes and offered the best smile he could. She was the mother of his child, and it felt good to know he wasn't going to be alone.

Irene had already changed out of her wet clothes and into an ill-fitting pair of jeans and a heavy jacket. They bundled Maddie up, stepped outside into the frigid air, and nothing could have prepared them for the mayhem that ensued.

CRISPR: WMD

In 2016, the United States intelligence community classified genetic-altering tools such as CRISPR as potential weapons of mass destruction.

At first glance, this might seem odd. You have a tool for the use of modifying living genetic material on the national list of WMDs, a list that includes atomic and hydrogen bombs, anthrax, ricin, and sarin gas? It seemed that one of these things wasn't like the others.

The reaction from the scientific community was mixed. For some in the world of molecular biology and research, such tools as the ability to manipulate DNA are compared to some of the greatest discoveries of all time and viewed as being on par with the invention of the wheel. Others thought the classification was overblown at best and almost certainly premature. But the overwhelming majority of academia simply ignored it. Nobody cared; or if they did, they still did nothing to address the threat. To date, very little has been done by the academic community to contain or limit access to this powerful tool.

But what the academic community failed to understand was that the United States government put CRISPR on the list of potential weapons of mass destruction not because they thought it might one day—in the distant future, and only hypothetically of course—be a threat to national survival. They didn't fear that something dangerous *might* be created from CRISPR one day.

They knew it had already been done.

One example that is in the public realm: In 2016, Canadian researchers were able to recreate a virus known as horsepox using nothing but a mail-order form and a few months' work. Unfortunately, these rather myopic individuals then published their research, making their work available for anyone to study and repeat. The methodology is shockingly simple and incredibly cheap, so much so that it wouldn't require much more than a high school education and some internet research to replicate.

For the first time in human history, a weapon of mass destruction was available to just about anyone with a few thousand dollars and an Amazon account.

There are a number of qualities that make genetic-altering tools uniquely dangerous. First, when compared to other WMDs, the sheer life-ending capacity of genetic-altering tools places them on a very short list of destructive capabilities. Short of global thermonuclear war, no other man-made threat in the world can compare with the loss of life that CRISPR has the potential to achieve.

For example, CRISPR could be used to recreate the human smallpox virus, and to do so with relative ease. Eliminating smallpox from the planet was arguably the greatest medical achievement in history. This monumental success could be undone with a shoestring budget, a little time, and a mail-order form. But who would do such a horrible thing, you might ask? Consider this: even though true psychopaths only make up a very small portion of the population—about 1 percent or less—with seven billion people on the planet, that adds up to a lot of unstable people. The fact that any one of them could purchase and play with arguably one of the most powerful weapons in the world scares the life out of intelligence and law enforcement officers. How long will it be until the next school shooter or foreign terrorist decides to buy a CRISPR set instead of a bomb or AR-15?

If a couple of researchers at a Canadian university could recreate extraordinarily dangerous pathogens, it's obvious that Russia or China could do the same. Have they already done it? What about North Korea? Or ISIS? It would be much easier for a terrorist organization or rogue nation to create a global pathogen than it would be to build a nuclear weapon. With a few alterations to the smallpox virus, one could yield a new disease that would exceed the potential for global human suffering over the most powerful nuclear device.

Which brings us to our second, and perhaps even more frightening, point about the destructive power of CRISPR.

Gene-editing technology has the versatility to create exquisitely targeted weapons, the potential applications limited only by the creativity of the person who designs them. In theory, it could be used to create plagues that target only US grain or corn production. It could be used to wreak havoc on a specific regional ecosystem, but leave others alone. It could create killer mosquitoes that are resistant to abatement techniques used in the US, or nanoweapons that shred specific human DNA...the possibilities are nearly endless.

And if an adversary could target specific grains or agricultural products, how much more specific could they be?

What if one of our adversaries created a novel pathogen whose purpose was to target a specific ethnic or racial group? What if China could create an infection for which anyone of Asian ancestry was immune, or a virus that attacked only Caucasians or people of European descent?

There is no doubt that it is possible; indeed, we've seen it before, even if not by design. For example, while the Spanish conquest of Mesoamerica was aided by their advanced weaponry, it was primarily a series of epidemics that wiped out the indigenous peoples, diseases that took a significantly more costly toll on the Aztecs and other locals than it did on anyone of Western descent.

What if a similar pathogen could be replicated in the lab? How would we respond to an enemy if they created a pathogen that would only infect someone of Northern European descent? What if they could create a disease capable of targeting a specific individual? Could you assassinate the president of the United States by giving him a CRISPR-created cancer, and thus maintain plausible deniability? Could you give him Alzheimer's? Or schizophrenia?

As early as 2012, Russian president Vladimir Putin mentioned the danger of falling behind in the next generation arms race. Among the next-gen weapons systems he mentioned, he included the term "genetic weapons." He didn't mention biological or chemical weapons. He said *genetic*.

And if one day we find that these weapons have been aimed in our direction, one can envision what it would do to a society already on the very edge of a cliff.

WASHINGTON, DC

December

They moved through the narrow streets of the residential neighborhood, making their way west. The rain-soaked streets were dark and empty, with only few lights showing the way.

But hitting Georgetown, everything changed. What started out as a small crowd on one block exploded on the next. Hundreds of terrified people were moving in every direction, shouting, running, fighting. Some moved alone, some in groups. A mass of people. The noise. The emotion. The air seemed to crackle with the building threat of violence. Every storefront window had been boarded up long before. In the distance, against the backdrop of the storm, he could see the orange glow of a distant fire burning in the east, toward the Capitol.

Irene took his hand and Darren held it tight. "Stay close," he said.

The CDC hadn't just quarantined the hospital and the airport, they had quarantined everything within a two-mile radius of both, essentially fragmenting the city. The zones had been determined, and they were on the wrong side.

He led them down 34th. The next block felt like moving through a war zone. He turned west on M Street. Another half mile, and it grew worse. They hit the first barricade of steel fence, razor wire, military vehicles, and guns, forcing them north. Another barricade. They circled back, heading toward the Francis Scott Key Bridge. A crowd of angry people rushed by them and Irene was pushed to the ground. Darren helped her to her feet, and they jogged toward the bridge that would take them out of the city.

And then they hit the final barricade.

Darren stared at the frightening wall before them. Stunning, he thought. They erected this in a few hours! Shaking his head, he climbed on top of a stranded car to get a better view. It was unlike anything he had ever imagined. The National Guard had created a barrier along the entire width of the bridge, six lanes of steel, spikes, and guns, all of it ending with an impenetrable fence topped with concertina wire.

How had they done this so quickly! How much advance warning did they have?

Thousands of people pressed around them, pushing forward in a mindless mass, desperate to get past the blockade, across the bridge and then to freedom.

Behind the barrier, a hundred armed National Guard soldiers stood in riot gear. Over loudspeakers a voice demanded calm, explaining they needed time for the CDC to sort things out, time to treat those who'd been infected, time to protect those who'd been exposed. No one would get hurt if they complied with the instructions; but if they didn't, they were authorized to use force.

As Darren watched, a wave of terrified people stormed the barricade. Tear gas rained upon them. Half of the on-rushers pushed through the pain, only to be greeted by the full force of water cannons that tore them from their feet and sent them skidding across the pavement in a torrent of dirty water and blood.

A second wave of desperate people rushed the barricade, trampling those from the first. Rubber bullets began to fly. Dozens were felled in their tracks. One man charged and opened fire with a pistol. A hailstorm of rubber bullets sent him flying back and he didn't get up. One woman charged while holding a child before her as a human shield. She made it through the tear gas, but the water cannon took her feet out from underneath her and the child went tumbling to the asphalt.

The violence was shocking.

Darren turned away and climbed down from the car.

"What did you see?" Irene asked, her eyes filled with terror. She was shaking so hard he wondered if she was going to collapse, Maddie's arms wrapped around her as if she were clutching to her life.

"We can't get through," he said as he turned and started walking.

"Where are you going!" Irene demanded.

"Back home," he said in defeat.

CYBER

THE TINIEST WAR

Crime is a problem that has plagued every species since the primordial soup first spat out the precursors to modern life. Microorganisms steal the molecules necessary for life, vegetation will rob sunlight from their neighbors, hermit crabs will socialize in order to steal another's shell. Animals swipe food from each other every chance they get. Apes will take territory from another. Cavemen stole food. African tribes stole water, pottery, and weapons. From the ancient pharaohs to the modern armies, humans have used violence to take from other people. Indeed, we have a long history of stealing from our neighbors, taking everything from territory to grain, from sheep to cars, cash, and computer code.

But when it comes to stealing, modern day thieves are in a league of their own.

Today, when one thinks of grand larceny, our minds naturally wander to a thug in a ski mask robbing a bank, or possibly the plot of a Hollywood movie. But the type of crime that has the largest impact on our society today is cyber crime.

It is difficult to find the appropriate adjective to describe the sheer quantity of cyber crime that occurs today. Staggering is a start, but even this word is inadequate in describing the level of cyber theft that plagues our internet-dependent society. Cyber criminals are as intelligent as the crime enforcers who track them. They are also well funded—often state funded—and they adapt quickly to whatever countermeasures law enforcement may take. In many ways, it is difficult not to appreciate the elegance with which they approach their profession, taking as much pride in their craft as any artist or doctor.

Worldwide, millions of personal records are lost per day. This data often ends up for sale, where it can be bought for only a few pennies on the black market. A few cents may not seem like much, but when tens of millions of records are bought and sold, these pennies add up to a substantial amount of money.

FBI director Christopher Wray has gone on record saying that the majority of American adults have had, or will have, their personal information stolen, including their healthcare records, Social Security numbers, birthdates, addresses, and everything in between.

Another increasingly frequent crime that plagues the internet is ransomware. Ransomware attacks are malware that infiltrates a computer or other electronic device, taking control of the user's files and encrypting them, essentially holding the information hostage until the attacker is paid the demanded ransom (sometimes in cryptocurrency). Once the fee has been paid, the attacker may (or may not) decrypt the files and return them to the user. Billions of ransomware attacks occur per year, and the cost is staggering. The city of Atlanta was victim to just such an attack, and they shelled out seventeen million dollars to recover files. In 2019, Baltimore paid over eighteen million dollars. In one of the most expensive losses, privately owned Danish company Demant paid an eye-watering eighty-five million dollars to recover files encrypted by malware. But cumulatively, small and midsize businesses are the most common targets, and with nearly 40 percent of victims paying the ransom (regardless of the fact that most experts advise them not to), ransomware attacks cost businesses billions of dollars every year.

Altogether, according to Cybersecurity Ventures's Official Annual Cybercrime Report, it's estimated that in 2021, the worldwide cost of cyber crime will be around six trillion dollars.

And things get far more devastating when nation states, most notably China, are involved in criminal enterprises.

The FBI director has revealed that at any given time, there are approximately five thousand active FBI counterintelligence cases underway, and "almost half are related to China." It's difficult to appreciate the economic damage we've suffered at the hands of the Chinese Communist Party, which accounts for as much as 80 percent of all theft of intellectual property. Cyber economic espionage—infiltrating a private company's networks to discover trade secrets and other valuable pieces of intellectual property—costs Americans hundreds of billions of dollars.

In fact, China considers cyber espionage an essential component of their economic development. And with spy networks and technological data-gathering capabilities that are in some ways equal to or better than our own, they have enjoyed great success. They have forced their way into most of the telecom companies on the planet, and exploited vulnerabilities in every operating system from iOS to Windows to Android. In 2019, the United States Department of Justice made public a fifty-five-page document detailing numerous ways in which the Chinese Communist Party had committed intellectual property theft for the sole purpose of allowing Chinese enterprises a leg up in the competitive world of tech. The 3PLA and Chinese Ministry of State Security (Chinese equivalents of the NSA and CIA) have stolen source codes, specifications of innovative hardware, pharmaceutical research, surgical equipment, and vaccinations (think COVID-19), as well as US research on internal strategies, cost, logistics, and pricing information for hundreds of thousands of products. From tech to aviation and everything in between, the CCP will steal anything that can give them a competitive advantage.

And it's important to realize that many of their communications networks are specifically designed to infiltrate military, government, businesses, and American universities.

Commenting on the topic, former deputy attorney general Rod Rosenstein stated, "This is outright cheating and theft, and it gives China an unfair advantage at the expense of law-abiding businesses and countries that follow the international rules in return for the privilege of participating in the global economic system." In the words of FBI director Christopher Wray, "Healthy competition is good for the global economy, but criminal conduct is not. No country should be able to flout the rule of law. [This behavior is] illegal, unethical, and unfair. It's going to take all of us working together to protect our economic security and our way of life, because the American people deserve no less." More recently he stated that the theft is "on a scale so massive that it represents one of the largest transfers of wealth in human history," and that the theft of American intellectual property, research, and innovation is the "greatest long-term threat" of any foreign spy institution.

With their denials and protestations of innocence, it's clear the CCP has no intention of changing their behavior.

And why would they? Under current conditions, they are able to accomplish their goals with little pushback or meaningful consequences for their actions. As an example, in 2015 President Obama and Chinese president Xi signed an agreement to define international norms regarding cyber espionage. The sole purpose of this agreement was to curb the government-funded cyber theft of IP. Yet we know that the wholesale theft of intellectual property continued, even during the signing of the agreement.

The long-term plan of the CCP is not simply to hack their way into another nation's systems, but to provide the hardware so that backdoor access and hacking is no longer even necessary. With Chinese equipment in place, stealing information is no more than a single click away. Huawei, a Chinese technology firm that has grown faster than any company in the history of the world (think about that for a moment), has managed to do so because China knows the control and distribution of hardware and technology infrastructure is one of the keys to expanding cyber theft. So they have committed enormous subsidies, state-funded infrastructure, markets, technology, and global incentives to make companies such as Huawei enormously successful. The valuable information they collect is one reason the CCP is willing to provide these technologies at subsidized prices, which explains, for example, why a Huawei phone, which is nearly identical in performance to an iPhone, can be purchased for about a third of the price.

There is little doubt that Huawei has built back doors into their products. The private information they collect passes through their devices and is funneled to the Chinese Communist Party, allowing them to steal intellectual property, spy on individuals, and learn sensitive government and business secrets. The irony that the vast majority of their "cutting-edge" technology has been stolen from Western "partners," and is the primary factor in their ability to build competitive smartphones and servers, should make all Americans furious.

While the theft of IP, illicit surveillance, and market manipulation by the CCP has garnered bipartisan condemnation, little has been done about it.

And finally, in a remarkable push for control of information, China has declared their intention to exert control over the very foundations of the global internet. As *The Epoch Times* reported (*"Chinese Leader Xi Jinping Lays Out Plan to Control the Global Internet: Leaked Documents,"* May 2, 2021):

> Chinese leader Xi Jinping personally directed the communist regime to focus its efforts to control the global internet, displacing the influential role of the United States, according to internal government documents recently obtained by *The Epoch Times*.
>
> In a January 2017 speech, Xi said the "power to control the internet" had become the "new focal point of [China's] national strategic contest," and singled out the

United States as a "rival force" standing in the way of the regime's ambitions.

The ultimate goal was for the Chinese Communist Party (CCP) to control all content on the global internet, so the regime could wield what Xi described as "discourse power" over communications and discussions on the world stage.

The statements confirm efforts made by Beijing, in the past few years, to promote its own authoritarian version of the internet as a model for the world.

Having successfully built the world's most sprawling and sophisticated online censorship and surveillance apparatus, known as the Great Firewall, the CCP under Xi is turning outwards, championing a Chinese internet whose values run counter to the open model advocated by the West. Rather than prioritizing the free flow of information, the CCP's system centers on giving the state the ability to censor, spy on, and control internet data.

The report added, "'American companies should be used by the regime to reach its goal,' Xi said."

THE AMERICAN GRID

There are two reasons why an attack against the American electric grid would be so destructive.

The first is that the grid is as vulnerable as a spider web in the wind.

Our nation's electrical distribution system is a series of variously secure and disparately functioning private companies, quasi-government producers, government regulators, and tens of thousands of computers—all connected via the internet—whose sole purpose is to deliver electricity to consumers. Breathtakingly complex, the grid is composed of millions of individual parts and shifting components that provide, consume, and transfer various measures of electricity. Numerous checks and controls are constantly shifting and self-correcting for any imbalances in supply and demand. In the name of competition, any company that sells or distributes electricity can purchase it from any number of producers, resulting in a hodgepodge of interconnected parties, each racing to provide a stable supply and the lowest price to the American consumer.

An example:

Let's say it's a devastatingly hot summer in the Southwest. Heat leaves Tucson in a pool of sweat. Every air conditioner in the city is on full blast, forcing the demand for electricity to skyrocket. The city needs more than can be provided on a local level, so they shop around for additional power. But they want it at a good price. Phoenix, being in a similar crisis, offers outrageous prices, and neighbor Albuquerque won't even come to the table. The further north they shop, the more power becomes available and the lower the price. Ultimately, they get in contact with their counterpart in Oregon where they reach an agreement. A quantity is agreed upon, as well as the time of transfer: every afternoon for three hours for the next two weeks.

But how does the electricity get to Tucson? It's not as if a power transmission line runs from the power plant in Oregon to Tucson's distribution center. The Regional Transmission Organizations, the equivalent of air traffic controllers for electricity, find the best route, moving the electricity through the maze of interstate power lines that stretch for thousands of miles across each state. At the scheduled time, the power providers in Oregon dump the specified amount of electricity into the system, which is routed through a series of dozens, if not hundreds, of jumps through numerous cities, cables, and high-tension wires. At precisely one o'clock, the power arrives at Tucson, ready to blast away the sweat from the salty brows of some hot Arizonans.

The modern grid allows energy providers to efficiently generate, manage, and transfer electricity, a science so perfected and efficient that barely a penny is wasted.

But this marvel of efficiency has come at a cost: immense vulnerability.

Each transfer box, access point, transformer, and safety system is a potential entry point for a talented hacker.

Making matters worse, there is virtually no vertical integration of the grid. Hundreds of small, privately or municipally owned producers, some of them little more than mom-and-pop shops, are among the primary providers of electricity to Smalltown, USA National regulations are insufficient, at best, in monitoring these independent producers. In fact, many critical federal regulations don't even have jurisdiction over local providers.

The federal government does provide recommendations regarding cybersecurity; but in reality, many of the smaller electrical companies simply can't afford the type of cyber protection required to harden their infrastructure against a sophisticated attack from an aggressive nation such as Russia or China. Efficiency and profit are the primary business drivers, leaving regulations regarding cybersecurity poorly enforced, each state and individual company accessing the grid with a different standard.

Like a series of chains crisscrossing the nation, the grid is only as strong as the weakest link among them. If a single one of these entry points is penetrated, then unfettered access to the entire national grid could be achieved. While the amount of work required to bring down the grid would not be small (think reconnaissance, research, a reasonable understanding of weak points and integrated vulnerabilities), according to a bipartisan report, it has *already been achieved* by multiple overseas adversaries. Because of this, our electrical grid is staring down the barrel of a loaded gun. Our adversaries might not have pulled the trigger yet, but unless we are able to measurably improve our defenses, timing is the only question that remains.

The most likely target of a successful operation would be the enormous power transformers that dot the grid. These transformers are massive pieces of custom-built equipment, some of them weighing nearly a million pounds. They are responsible for increasing the voltage of electricity before it is transferred over long distances, a critical step in achieving maximum efficiency. They are not cheap. They are not interchangeable. And they are not mass-produced. In fact, only a handful of companies in the world can manufacture these massive transformers. Perhaps most concerning, they regularly take a year, and sometimes up to two years, to replace. And that's under normal circumstances and normal demand. Imagine if some event suddenly destroyed a substantial number of these transformers, substantially increasing demand. The time to replace them could quickly turn into a very long time.

With the interconnectivity of the national grid, the loss of even a handful of these transformers would be catastrophic, potentially affecting the entire nation.

Frightening as this sounds, many still wonder: can it really be done?

Russia demonstrated to the world in 2015 that it possesses the capability to attack an adversary's electrical system. In late December of that year, a power plant worker in Ukraine was startled when he lost control of his computer cursor. Moving without his input across his screen, the cursor responded to commands from some force unseen. His computer began performing a number of dangerous actions. He could only watch in horror as it wreaked havoc on systems that were vital to the Ukrainian power grid. The cursor logged him out, changed his password, shut down the backup generator, and then began systematically dismantling the region's power distribution system, taking down the power for more than 200,000 people.

But it could have been much worse. Russia could have taken down their entire grid. But they didn't, seemingly satisfied to have sent the message.

What would be the result if Russia initiated a similar attack against the United States? What would happen if President Xi decided that China's time as the world's dominant superpower had finally arrived? Similar to what happened in Ukraine, electricity could be incorrectly routed through weaker points of our grid, resulting in an overwhelmed system, melted wires, drooping power lines, devastating fires, and, ultimately, the destruction of the irreplaceable transformers.

Think Stuxnet. Think kaboom.

And then darkness.

WASHINGTON, DC

December

For five days, they hid in Darren's apartment, each day bringing a new heartbreak and fear.

On the first day, Darren was forced to come to terms with the fact that, in all likelihood, the world was never going to go back to how it was.

On the second day, Irene woke up with a fever. She had two seizures by the afternoon and was comatose before he tried to turn in for the night. But of course, sleep never came.

On the third day, none of that even mattered, because a stray bullet from one of the mobs took her life.

On the fourth day, Maddie's belly began to hurt.

On the fifth day, the power went out.

BETHESDA HOSPITAL, WASHINGTON, DC

December

In spite of the ocean of caffeine pumping in his blood, Dr. Johnathan Wilson's mental reserves had been long since depleted. He hadn't slept in three days, eaten a meal in two, or used the restroom in more than fourteen hours, which, as it turned out, didn't matter, for he was as dehydrated as a rock. The day before, as he was leaving the hospital to walk to his apartment, he had been informed that one of his colleagues had quit, and of course, his boss had asked him to take another twelve-hour shift. And so here he was, with only one more hour to go. He headed for his office for another cup of coffee.

As bad as things were when the virus began, the bad dream turned into a nightmare when the power went out. Like a patient gasping for breath in the final stages of pneumonia, the national power grid had painfully struggled to provide momentary gasps of electricity, the rolling blackouts increasing in intensity and frequency until the strain proved too great and the grid simply collapsed. What little power the hospital had from the emergency generators was now being used for respirators and other forms of life support, but Johnathan knew they only had enough fuel for a week. They had been told the electricity would turn back on in a few days, but he no longer believed it. Worse, they were no longer receiving any shipments of medications or supplies. Johnathan's good friend, an ER physician, had told him he'd had two patients die the day before from asthma attacks. An asthma attack! Something so simple. But without meds, there was nothing that could be done. If things didn't improve soon, and he saw no indication that they would, he would see more people die of curable diseases like asthma and ear infections than from the new virus.

He collapsed into his office chair with a sigh. He didn't know how much longer he could go on. For now, he just needed two minutes to sit down and close his eyes....

A knock on the door startled him awake. He hadn't realized he had drifted off, and he could tell from the fog he had slammed into REM, the deep sleep he desperately needed. He struggled to stand, opened the door, and found one of the ER nurses.

"Dr. Walker was wondering if you could come down to the ER and see a patient. He's not real comfortable managing kids, and she sounds pretty sick."

"Sure," he said as he reached out to take from the nurse the sheet of paper with the consult on it.

Maddie Hardy, ER Bed 24, six-year-old female with abdominal pain and intractable vomiting. He read the details of the case as they walked.

He didn't even try to log onto a computer to look at the child's medical chart before entering her room. The servers had been shut down for days. And anyway, it didn't matter. The case was going to be just like every other he had seen in the last couple days. No functioning equipment, no meds, no scans, no surgery.... The hospital had become little more than a third-world palliative care unit.

Glancing around, he saw that the emergency room was full. An elderly woman in the nearest bed, makeshift bandages across her shin. A grimy middle-aged man grimacing in pain as he breathed. A young man with a horrific laceration across his forearm. It was ironic, the hospital had never been so unable to provide even basic medical care, and yet they had never seen so many patients coming through their doors in urgent need of help.

"Hi, I'm Dr. Wilson. I need to give you a quick exam," Johnathan said as he pulled back the privacy curtain around the bed. He didn't make eye contact with the patient. He was simply too burned out.

He was surprised to see that no one else was in the room. "Where's mom and dad?" he asked in his doctor-talking-to-a-child voice.

The little girl didn't answer.

"You just missed the father," the elderly nurse told him.

Johnathan forced the frustration away. "It's okay. I can get what I need from the exam." He reached for his stethoscope and placed it on her chest, "Take a deep breath."

She didn't answer. In fact, she held her breath instead.

Johnathan clenched his teeth on the urge to say something sharp and patiently said, "Could you take a deep breath, little girl?"

The child pulled even farther away and folded her thin arms across her chest. Realizing he would have to engage her if he wanted her to participate, Johnathan pulled the stethoscope away. "Hey there," he said while forcing a smile. She turned to face him and for the first time, he looked into the little girl's eyes.

Oh man, she was going to be a firecracker.

CYBER-DESTRUCTION

When envisioning a cyber soldier, some people think of a sloppy, middle-aged man sitting at his computer in a basement, eating Cheetos while creating a few lines of code that, once downloaded, slow down your already aging computer and obligate you to buy a replacement a few months sooner than you otherwise might have. This time, as you unbox your shiny new computer, you promise yourself to install malware protection and not to visit so many shady websites.

But this caricature of a computer criminal could not be farther from the truth. Cyber weaponry is, in many ways, not dissimilar from the arsenal of weapons used in kinetic warfare. In the hands of capable cyber operators, the goal of a well-crafted virus isn't just to slow down a computer or even to momentarily disable it. They can literally make things explode.

The Stuxnet virus was proof of concept.

The details surrounding Stuxnet are highly classified. Very few people in the world really understand the operation. We certainly don't. We have no inside knowledge on the virus at all.

But we can take the information that is available, and with a little imagination, create a reasonable scenario as to what happened.

Let's suppose that, toward the end of his presidency, George W. Bush realized that he had invaded the wrong country. Yes, Iraq was a mess, led by a tyrant who was a constant menace to the US, but they were not the primary threat to our national interests. Iran was the problem. A huge problem. The mullahs were fanatical zealots helming one of the most powerful countries in the Middle East. Bent on destroying Israel and the United States, they were on the fast track to developing nuclear weapons that, by their own admission, they fully intended to use. And their nuclear facility in Natanz was nearing their goal of enriching enough uranium to make the first nuclear weapon.

But the president's hands were tied. America was tired of war. Tired of warmongering. Exasperated with the commander in chief. The president couldn't possibly order the invasion of another Muslim country. Not after Iraq.

So, some of the brightest minds in the intelligence community came up with a plan.

The question was posed to POTUS: why risk the lives of American soldiers, the support of the American people, and spend billions of dollars when there was another option? Why not simply code Iran's nuclear facility into oblivion from a few thousand miles away?

Let's suppose the potential was immediately recognized, and the cyber warriors got the green light to begin a project that would disrupt the future of non-kinetic warfare. As expected, there was no great fanfare when the Stuxnet weapon was finished—and certainly no mushroom cloud, as in Nagasaki. But when the Stuxnet virus was delivered to the nuclear facility in Natanz, the principle of destructive cyber warfare was taken to a level never seen before.

Unlike most malware at the time, Stuxnet was programmed for a very precise purpose. But before it was able to accomplish its mission, it had to spread. And so it did, becoming a promiscuous virus that spread very quickly across the globe. One report by Symantec showed it affected nearly 10 percent of computers in the world. But the virus had no effect on any computer it infected that did not meet very specific requirements. Even more impressive, it was programmed to erase itself in 2012.

The targets of the virus were the computers that controlled the uranium-enriching centrifuges at the Iranian nuclear facility in Natanz—more specifically, the small black boxes known as PLCs, or programmable logic controllers. A PLC is not a full-sized computer. It doesn't have a screen, and there's no keyboard or mouse. It is little more than a small device with circuits boards, wires, and controllers that connect various components of the facility, allowing the physicists to use their computers to control the centrifuges. Once the Stuxnet virus gained access to the PLCs, it would intercept and manipulate the signals being sent between the computers and the centrifuges.

The first command the Stuxnet virus issued caused the centrifuges to spin much faster than their normal operating speed, and then caused them to slow down. Centrifuges are incredibly precise machines not capable of withstanding such dramatic changes in speed so quickly, and the stresses caused the tubes to expand. Sensing this, fail-safe mechanisms in the centrifuges alerted the physicists to the problem, and they immediately began the emergency power-down procedures. But the Stuxnet virus intercepted these emergency messages and sent a reply to the physicists that the centrifuges had indeed begun to power down, while simultaneously sending a command to the centrifuges to speed up a second time, which ultimately led to failure and the destruction of the centrifuges.

No nation in history had ever been the victim of such a focused and powerful cyber weapon. The Iranian scientists had no idea what was going on. It never entered their minds, nor the minds of the Iranian military or political leaders, that a few digital assassins on the other side of the globe had the ability to nearly decapitate their nuclear program.

They ordered new centrifuges. They fired the physicists. They replaced every tube and cord and machine and computer in the facility. According to one report, over a two-month period, 10 percent of the centrifuges were destroyed. All of them were replaced, spun up, then replaced again. Uranium enrichment ground to a halt.

Though much of the reporting on the Stuxnet virus is incomplete, and many reported "facts" are just plain wrong, one thing is obvious: it was a very successful cyber attack.

And this was a *first-generation cyber weapon*, in many ways little more than a proof-of-concept demonstration.

But the success of the attack left us with a problem.

Stuxnet was a stone thrown by people who live in glass houses. Very large, very fragile, very valuable glass houses. The more interconnected and modernized a nation is, the more vulnerable it is to a cyber attack. And no nation is more connected nor technologically dependent than is the United States.

China, Iran, North Korea, Cuba, and Russia have developed incredibly sophisticated cyber weapons. And when you consider that Stuxnet was created many years ago, by computer pioneers who were operating on a minimal budget, it isn't hard to imagine how sophisticated and destructive cyber weapons are today.

There are few international norms, guidelines or treaties that regulate the proliferation or deployment of cyber weapons. And even if there were, cyber attacks come with the principle of plausible deniability built into them. Even with the most powerful detection tools, it can be very difficult, and sometimes impossible, to trace the source of an attack. Compared to kinetic warfare, cyber weapons are relatively cheap and easy to create. And a well-crafted and cleverly implemented cyber attack could prove to be as destructive as any conventional attack.

Defense from a cyber attack can be far more difficult than creating an offensive capability. There's a common complaint among cyber experts who focus on defense: a malicious cyber attacker only has to get lucky once. Those defending our nation must be right 100 percent of the time. It's kind of like this: you can purchase a .38 bullet for a dollar, whereas a bulletproof vest costs hundreds of dollars and protects only a small portion of your body. And the more these weapons proliferate, the more we realize just how vulnerable we are.

To put it in military terms, we present our enemies with a target-rich environment.

A successful attack on our financial system could achieve anything from massively inconveniencing millions of people, to complete economic carnage. At attack on our telecoms could take down our communications. An attack on our air traffic control system could lead to thousands of deaths. The number of daily attacks on our military and national intelligence agencies is so large that it's nearly impossible to keep up. Gas and oil pipelines, as we saw in the Colonial Pipeline attack. Cell towers. Even our water and sewage systems are vulnerable. In early 2021, a town in Florida was the victim of a hack that altered chemical levels in its water supply to potentially lethal levels. If not for an attentive employee, the result could have been catastrophic.

But the most likely target we present our adversaries is our electrical grid.

WASHINGTON, DC

December

Maddie had olive skin, a firm mouth set in a determined clench, and black diamond eyes that sparkled with absolute defiance.

"South Carolina," Maddie said suddenly.

"Huh?" he asked.

"You may be as rude as a New Yorker, but you have a southern sound." She spoke confidently even if through clenched teeth.

He found her confidence amusing, but he was simply too tired to smile. "I'll tell you where I'm from if you can take a deep breath," he bargained.

She frowned and studied him with bright eyes for a solid five count before answering. "Deal," she said, and then did as he had instructed. Jonathan listened for half a dozen breaths then asked her to roll to her side.

"Aren't you going to…" She paused, wincing as an apparent wave of pain passed. "Aren't you gunna ask where I'm from?" She sounded disappointed he had not shown interest. Her voice was tired. Soft. Raspy as a gravel. Not a healthy voice. Still…amazingly…there was a playfulness to the disappointed look on her face. He didn't answer as he listened to her lungs.

"It's polite to ask about other people," she scolded him. "You tell me. I tell you. Then we're friends."

He shook his head in shame. Her enthusiasm was intoxicating. Playful and hopeful. What kind of person, what kind of doctor, wouldn't respond to that!

Johnathan felt the hours of exhaustion and thankless toil wash away, and he gave in to her game without even realizing what was happening. "Do you want to be my friend, Maddie?" he said, offering a smile.

"Of course, I would," she answered.

He motioned for her to roll onto her back. "That will help you to breathe a little easier." She did as he instructed and Johnathan pressed gently on her belly. "Pray tell, Maddie, would you do me the favor of telling me where you are from, then?" he asked.

"Well, I would think it's pretty obvious to anyone smarter than your average fifth grader," she said matter of factly. "I'm from Texas, duh."

Johnathan had to smile again.

"And you know what they say about Texas?" she said as he continued the examination.

"Can't say I do."

"Very well. I suppose it's my duty to inform you. Never ask a girl if she's from

Texas, because if she is, she'll tell you, and if she isn't from Texas, well, you don't want to embarrass her."

Johnathan couldn't help but laugh. It was a rich and delicious thing, cool water down a parched throat.

She smiled at his laughing. "But not really," she quickly said. "I'm not from Texas. That's just a joke. I'm glad you got it. I think it's funny. I'm from DC. And sometimes New York. But I like DC better. It's not so—" Maddie suddenly made an awkward sound and grimaced. She grabbed at her belly as a flash of pain spread across her abdomen.

He waited a moment until it passed.

Maddie forced a smile and asked, "When do you get to go home, Johnny? All of you doctors are working too hard." Her face was suddenly serious. Soft with empathy, a caring in her eyes that was far too great for one so young.

"So now we're on a first name basis, are we?" he asked.

"Sure. I made you laugh. That makes us friends, remember?"

"I can go home anytime I want. I'm actually on vacation right now. I just came in to the hospital because I heard the famous Maddie was admitted, and I wanted to meet her in person."

Maddie looked over to see her father come into the room.

Johnathan thought he recognized the man, but it took several moments to place him. Heavy stubble splashed across a face that was dirty and covered in a painful sunburn. Hair unkempt and disheveled, Darren Hardy, the rock star news anchor, was a barely recognizable shell of his former self.

"How are you going to help my daughter?" he demanded as he entered, his voice equal parts entitled and desperate.

Johnathan closed his eyes and gathered his thoughts, then motioned for Darren to follow him into the hall where they could speak without Maddie overhearing. Johnathan looked around for any place where they could find even a modicum of privacy, but there was barely an inch of hospital tile that wasn't filled with the sick, scared, and dying.

"What is happening to Maddie? Does she have the virus? How are you going to help her?"

Johnathan took a deep breath and steeled himself for the conversation. He'd had similar conversations before, but experience didn't make it any easier, and he felt a tightness in the back of his throat. "The differential diagnosis for abdominal pain in a child is broad. Her history, the fact she is febrile, and positive Psoas sign indicate likely appendiceal pathology. Normally, we'd get a CT scan, but given everything going on around us I think—"

A surge of anger flashed across Darren's face. "English, please!"

Johnathan paused. "It's not the virus. There's something wrong with her belly. I don't know what it is."

The frown on Darren's mouth deepened dangerously. "I don't believe you."

John shrugged. "Feel free to get a second opinion." He turned to leave.

Darren reached out and grabbed his arm. "Wait. Stop." His face washed in pain and depression, a shadow of guilt darkening his eyes. The doctor stared. He'd seen it too many times before.

"I…look, I'm sorry…I'm sorry…I'm scared," Darren stumbled. "We all are. But can you blame me? I didn't mean it." His voice was heavy with sincerity and desperation. "Please forgive me. The world is burning all around us. I just lost my wife. Maddie is all I have left. Please help me…us…please help her…I'll do anything for her!"

Johnathan swallowed and nodded slowly. He wished he was too tired to care, but the truth was, he did. He didn't want Maddie to have to go through what she was experiencing. He didn't want the child to be in pain; he certainly didn't want for her to die. He'd gone into medicine because he wanted to help.

Darren reached into his pocket and removed a handful of cash. He looked anxiously up and down the hall. It was dangerous to have money. Dangerous to flash it around. "I have resources," he whispered.

The doctor stepped back. Darren's breath smelled like he hadn't eaten in days, but when he flashed a smile, his teeth were still as white as snow.

"If my baby girl needs a CAT scan, then we're going to find a way to get her one."

The physician lifted his hand. "Sir, I'm sorry—"

Darren interrupted the doctor with a firm voice. "I know electricity is worth its weight in gold, but like I said, I have resources." He removed the gold Rolex from his wrist, then two rings from his fingers, both studded in diamonds.

Johnathan took another step back. "Your daughter is sick, Mr. Hardy. And I do not know what is going on. She needs imaging, but we simply do not have the power for it. Even if we did, we don't have contrast. I could fake my way through an abdominal CT interpretation, but she may need a skilled radiologist to diagnose the problem, and our only radiologist quit three days ago. Your daughter might need antibiotics, but the inpatient pharmacy was raided last night, and we don't even have Tylenol—a few Advil, maybe. She may need surgery, but we haven't performed a single surgery since the power went out, and frankly I doubt we could even find any sterile equipment."

Johnathan paused to take a breath. He could have gone on, but he chose not to. The obstacles that would need to be overcome to get Maddie what she needed were simply insurmountable. It was clear by the expression on Darren's face that his point had sunk in.

He could tell that this father's mind was simply broken, now. He stared at empty space, his eyes blank, a wad of spittle forming on the corner of his mouth. He thrust the rings and watch forward, stabbing at the air, then shook his head and dropped them to the floor. Then he turned, leaned his back against the wall and slid to the cold tile, his legs stuffed awkwardly beneath him.

Johnathan blinked the tears from his eyes as he left the emergency room. But instead of returning to his office, he walked out the front door of the hospital and began walking toward his apartment. He told himself he just needed a little rest, a little time to sleep. He just needed to regroup, to collect himself, to rest his mind and aching muscles.

A little time. That's all he needed.

But as he walked away from the hospital, he wondered if he would ever go back.

A CROWD-PLEASER OF DESTRUCTION

What would it look like to be thrust into a nationwide grid failure?

As the sunset, we would experience a darkness that hasn't been seen in more than a hundred years. For a short time, those fortunate enough to be connected to an independent source of power, for example, a generator, would have limited power. Hospitals, for example, have emergency generators that may keep them running for a few days, or in some cases even a few weeks. But eventually, these diesel-powered generators would go dark as well.

Perhaps worse than the lack of light would be the information vacuum. In the immediate aftermath of an attack, people will invariably turn to the internet for answers—an internet that will simply be gone. No TV. No radio. No means of communications. Cell phones can't connect to a tower that has no power.

Any city without a gravity-fed water source will dry up almost instantly. Even those fed with gravity will likely not have more than a few days' worth of water. The production and distribution of food, water, fuel, antibiotics, pharmaceuticals, sanitary products, and pretty much everything else, will be devastated. Banks would close. Grocery stores wiped clean. With no ability to pump fuel, gasoline stations would have to close. And you wouldn't be the only one to run out of gas. So would the police. Fire trucks. Ambulances. The food in our refrigerators would spoil within a few days. Many commercial buildings would be uninhabitable without power to light, heat, or cool them. Homes would be ice-cold in the winter. The list goes on....

No society has ever been so dependent on the power grid, and so incapable of living life without modern conveniences, as we are today. What will happen when it's gone? What happens when people realize that it might be months, or maybe years, before the power comes back on? What happens when they realize that very little, if any, help is on the way?

What happens when the lights go out, the taps go dry, and the grocery stores are picked clean—something that, for large cities like New York City and Los Angeles, will likely occur within the first hour?

Some people will wait for the government to restore order. They will remain in their homes waiting for the world to return to the way it used to be. But help may not come. Or it may be weeks or months away. FEMA has proven that they struggle to respond to local emergencies involving a few hundred thousand people. How can they respond to an emergency that involves an entire state? The entire East Coast? The entire nation?

Discouragingly, it turns out FEMA doesn't even have a plan to respond to a nationwide power failure.

WASHINGTON, DC

December

Darren remained on the floor for a few minutes. Then he gathered himself and stood. Maddie had fallen asleep, her body curled underneath the hospital sheets, her forehead dripping with sweat. He approached the nearest nurse and begged her again but got the same response. Her eyes were moist in pain and sympathy, but there was nothing she could do. Nothing the hospital could do. They could wrap a bandage, set a broken bone, but anything internal...she was sorry...so sorry.

He approached another nurse and got the same story. "Take her home," she told him. "Keep her warm. Keep her hydrated. Give her Advil for the pain. Here are a few I managed to scrounge up. If she gets worse, bring her back, and we'll see what we can do."

Which is nothing, Darren thought bitterly.

A final nurse, a final plea, the same answer. He rested on the floor once more, leaning against the wall opposite Maddie's bed, nurses and orderlies stepping over his outstretched legs. A couple times he was asked to stand up, but having nothing better to offer him, no one really seemed to care. After an hour or so, he gathered his strength, picked Maddie up, and left the hospital, heading home.

For the next five days, Darren stood and stared out the front window of his historic brick house, watching his city being torn apart by the fighting and violence. Maddie struggled for the first few days, but then suddenly turned, the fever breaking, the pain passing. He wondered what had ailed her, but figured he would never know.

He had waited long enough, perhaps too long. He didn't know how far he'd make it, especially if he had to carry his little girl in his weakened state. But he knew if they stayed, they were going to die here, hungry and alone.

After gathering what supplies he had, Darren scribbled a note to Peter—a note he knew his brother might not ever receive, but knowing that with Peter, there was at least a chance—saying that he and Maddie were alive, telling him their whereabouts and plan.

He drank what was left of the water he had stored, picked up his sleeping daughter, stepped out the front door, and started walking.

Like millions of others in his country, he was now an American refugee.

They spent much of the rest of the day hiding behind a dumpster as a gang looted what remained on the shelves of a small market, hoping he could slip in unseen and get some food for themselves. But the opportunity never developed, and soon the food was gone. The sun went down, leaving them just as hungry, and now cold.

As the frigid air numbed his brain, a dozen questions kept fighting for his attention. And Darren had an answer for exactly none of them.

What he would give for a single can of soup! But what if he tried to search a house, and there was someone inside? On the other hand, how long could he and Maddie go without food? Would he be able to defend himself and protect Maddie if he ran into someone who was dangerous?

But the first question he had to answer was, where was he going?

And then it came to him. The doctor at the hospital. He was caring. Level-headed. Capable and kind. Head over to the hospital. Try to get some help.

As the last ray of sun slipped away and left their surroundings in profound darkness, a powerful new emotion surged through his body. As he looked around at this new world and all of the terrible people who possessed it, he realized that he hated them all.

After all he had done for them…this was the result!

More than ever in his life, stronger than any emotion he had ever felt, he hated the American people….

A crashing noise echoed through the streets and startled him from his thoughts. Eyes wide with terror, he carried Maddie to the side of the street and cowered against the wall of a building that bore the blackened marks of fire.

And in that moment, Darren knew he was never going to make it out of the city, and much less to a place where he could build a life again.

The sinking realization put tears in his eyes. But they weren't tears of sadness for what they'd lost. They were tears of abject fear.

Another thumping sound echoed in the distance. Two men shouting at each other. The explosions of gunfire. His daughter began to cough, and then to whimper, and then to cry.

Death came for Darren later that night. One block from the hospital.

He'd almost made it.

Early the next morning, Dr. Jonathan Wilson found Maddie huddled at the hospital door. Picking her up, he gently carried her inside.

FULL SPECTRUM
WARFARE

No country on Earth spends as much as the United States does on its military budget. But it's also true that, once adjusted for the value of the dollar, stolen technology, poverty wages paid to enlisted personnel, and quasi-military spending not included in their military budget, China is closing the gap at an alarming rate. Still, the US remains the largest spender on its military. And when one considers our global commitments to stability, freedom, NATO, freedom of navigation on the seas, the containment of Russian expansion, narco-terrorism, the rise of China, North Korean nuclear arms, the mullahs in Iran, the global war on terror, and a dozen other responsibilities, it's no surprise that we spend a huge sum on defense.

As President Reagan reminded in his farewell address, "Because we're a great nation, our challenges seem complex."

A single aircraft carrier, the definition of global power projection, costs billions. And that is to say nothing of the sophisticated weaponry aboard the ship, bringing the total value of a carrier to ten or twelve billion dollars. Russia has one aircraft carrier. China has two. The United States has twelve. The money spent on research and development for the B-21 is greater than the entire yearly military budgets of many other nations. Our nation spent more than twenty billion dollars in 2020 on missile defense alone. And with America's decades of head starts in critical technologies, and countless hours of actual war-fighting experience, our adversaries have long known that in a head-to-head confrontation of a conventional war, we would surely—and gratefully—be able to defend ourselves.

But nothing in warfare is conventional any longer. So, while they cannot match our defense budget dollar for dollar, in the world of asymmetrical and full-spectrum warfare, our adversaries don't need to spend as much as we do.

All they need to do is spend it smarter. All they need to do is change the game.

And the game has changed.

A US aircraft carrier is nearly defenseless against a single hypersonic missile. Twelve billion dollars. Five or six thousand lives. The destruction of the concept of power projection. The destruction of the reputation of the US military.

A single missile....

Yes, the game has changed.

While we currently hold advantages in most land, sea, and air operations, all of those domains are being challenged. In some critical areas, we have moved from superiority to near-peer, and in some cases, to operating from a position of technological weakness. And perhaps more importantly, the next war will involve multiple domains, many of which have never been tested in a military campaign: sub-oceanic and extraterrestrial, psychological, genetic, biological, and cyber.

Has Russia developed a portable Pulsed RF weapon with the capability to target a specific person and damage their brain? We don't know. But press reports indicate that it's a possibility. And that's just one example of the things we're up against. In a world where our adversaries have access to hypersonic and cyber weapons, tools of economic sabotage, Little Green Men (think Russian soldiers in Crimea), and Little Blue Sailors (think Chinese naval forces dressed up as civilian ships in the South China Sea), all of whom operate outside of the normal spectrum of war...these, plus a dozen other asymmetrical weapons, force us to reconsider what we used to think of as impossible.

We could actually lose a kinetic war.

And while we currently hold supremacy in many of these domains, a weakness in any of them could cause a collapse in the rest.

Why spend billions on advanced fighters when a drone fleet could accomplish the same task for a fraction of the cost? Why spend billions on reconnaissance satellites when a cyber attack can make all US satellites go blind? Why spend money on incredibly expensive stealth technology when quantum radar could negate any American supremacy? And as already expressed, why spend twelve billion dollars on a single aircraft carrier stacked to the brim with anti-missile technology, rail and laser guns, and the world's most impressive fighter jets, when it turns out all you need is a really fast missile to send the massive ship to the ocean floor?

Over the past decade, a number of profound technological weaknesses have emerged in our war-fighting capabilities until, like the Death Star, we are facing the reality that a smaller, more nimble, more committed, more creative nation could bring down the greatest military power on the planet.

SPACE WAR

Long has space captured our imaginations, as evidenced in everything from Hollywood movies to the choice of children's action figures from all over the world. Our ancestors gazed in awe into the expanse at night, giving the stars names and histories, even making gods and legends of the twinkling lights. And as they stared at the night, they always wondered what lay beyond the seemingly inescapable pull of Earth's gravity, the last frontier constantly beckoning us to rise. And we answered the call, sending the brilliant, the explorers, and the brave into the cold expanse with the mission of conquering the empty blackness.

As a result of the research generated by the desire to explore space, our quality of life has been enriched in ways our ancestors never would have dreamed possible. With a modern smartphone, small enough to hold in our hand yet with more computing power than was on the space module that took men to the moon, we have access to instant communication across the earth. We have more movies, music, and other forms of entertainment at the tips of our fingers than could ever be consumed in a lifetime. GPS coordinates span the globe and establish our location down to a fraction of a meter, any time, any place, and under any atmospheric or meteorological conditions. From ATMs that give us cash, to the ability to order specialty items from anywhere on Earth, to the capacity to forecast weather and monitor crop yields in the Sudan and pollution levels in Beijing, all is made possible because of the assets we have in space. They allow us to do things that would have boggled the mind only one generation ago.

But we are also left with the hard reality that we are extremely vulnerable because of our dependence on satellites.

Space, or what the intelligence community calls overhead architecture, will be one of the most critical arenas in a future war. But it's also one of the fields most deeply shrouded in secrecy. TS/SCI, or Top Secret/Sensitive

Compartmented Information, is the normal classification of space assets, and many of their capabilities are well protected, as they should be.

But we do know this: the United States military has made use of space's potential every bit as much as the civilian sector has. Indeed, our long-held supremacy in this domain has been vital to our military's war-fighting capabilities. Space assets allow war fighters to update targeting information, then to use GPS-guided weapons to strike a target to within a few feet, all while being in communication with covert targeters who may be in the vicinity of the target. Satellites provide real-time and strikingly detailed feeds of the planet, allowing us to receive, among other things, early warnings of missile launches or other potential attacks. Space assets allow us to monitor weapons production, mobile nuclear launch vehicles, naval assets, and troops' movements down to the squad level. They allow us to track the location of known terrorists, estimate how much cobalt the Russians are importing, know how much oil is being snuck into North Korea, and how many portable crematoriums Wuhan brought in to handle deaths for COVID. And this information is all from open-source reporting. Imagine some of the information that is available from the highly classified applications of our space assets.

If the F-22 Raptor represents the sword of our modern military, then satellites are our eyes and our ears. Which begs the question: how well could even the best swordsman fight if he became blind and deaf?

Yet our ability to defend our critical assets in space—assets without which our national security is greatly diminished—is very limited. Targeting a multi-billion-dollar satellite may be the equivalent of shooting fish in a barrel when it comes to full spectrum war.

So, what is very difficult to physically defend, we have sought to protect through other means.

For decades, we have relied on a number of treaties to defend our assets in space. The Outer Space Treaty, which 109 countries are party to, has provided the basis for international space law since it went into force in 1967. Among other things, it specifically prohibits nuclear weapons in space, bans military activities in space (of which an attack upon a satellite would surely be one), and limits the use of the moon and other celestial bodies to "peaceful purposes only." However, as America's reliance on satellites in both the civilian and the military sector has increased, it has become increasingly clear to our enemies that, treaties aside, the extraterrestrial domain represents a phenomenal weakness that would be very easy to exploit.

The means of attack on our satellites are diverse. Probably the easiest (and the method that has been employed the most often) is jamming.

Saddam Hussein employed such tactics to jam GPS-guided weapons, as has Russia during the recent Ukraine skirmishes. Cyber is also an enormous concern. Any entity that could gain access to a satellite could employ a cyber attack that could put the satellite out of commission. Adversary satellites could approach our space assets and hover adjacent to them without being detected. From this position, they could commit any number of nefarious acts, from planting malicious spy code to outright destruction. Lasers have also been demonstrated to be efficacious. When fired from Earth, they can damage the most fragile parts of a satellite. When fired from another space asset, lasers have even more destructive capability and, because they lack the dangerous recoil of a conventional weapon, they are not a threat to other satellites. (In the frictionless arena of space, even a few rounds fired from a conventional weapon could be enough to cause a satellite to spin dangerously out of control.) In addition, with non-kinetic weapons such as lasers, debris fields are generally not a factor. There is also a component of plausible deniability built into these attacks, as they are notoriously difficult to prove as being anything other than a malfunction. Finally, lasers come from the invisible spectrum of light, rather than the bright reds and greens we normally think of, making them more difficult to detect.

But as tantalizing as a laser attack might be, what many experts fear most is a kinetic attack, such as from an anti-satellite missile.

The potential use of anti-satellite missiles extends back decades, and both Russia and China, as well as the US, have demonstrated such a capability. But anti-satellite missiles have never been used in an intentional offensive maneuver. Part of the reason for this is because, while operating in the frictionless environment of space and at overwhelming speeds, it's not the loss of a single satellite that is most concerning, but the debris field that would be created from the explosion. Even a small shard of shrapnel could spell disaster for anything nearby, given the fact it would likely be moving at something like 20,000 miles per hour. There currently exists no ability to clear space junk from orbit, and if the attack were not well timed (or very well timed, depending on the situation), the debris field could cause a chain reaction that could destroy multiple satellites.

Which is a little bit like MAD, or mutually assured destruction. Yes, an anti-satellite missile attack by one of our adversaries might also take out some of their own satellites. But if our adversaries are less dependent on space assets for their war-fighting capability than we are, they would suffer much less, making it the equivalent of sacrificing a bishop for the queen.

If the world ever entered a full-spectrum war that involved the physical destruction of assets in space, what could we expect to see from the earth's surface? The answer is, not much. As the debris entered the earth's atmosphere, we would most likely see a few dozen "shooting stars," but otherwise we wouldn't even notice, until we tried to use a GPS, ATM, smartphone, TV, anything connected to the internet, or a hundred other things we rely upon each day to live in the modern world.

And while we were trying to get our cell phone or the ATM to work, our military would be trying to get many of their weapons systems to work as well.

ARTIFICIAL INTELLIGENCE

For the past century, most war-fighting technological breakthroughs have been developed in top-secret military labs. However, there has been a meaningful shift in recent years to where many of the most creative and dramatic innovations that will define how the next war is fought have been created in the private sector. Artificial intelligence and machine learning are two of the most dramatic examples.

Artificial intelligence is defined as computer programming that creates intelligent machines that imitate human behavior and learning. Basically, it's using computers to do things that, in the past, humans were required to do.

Machine learning is much the same thing, but with the additional goal that the computers will actually "learn" and improve as they do their tasks.

Few innovations have the potential to change the battlefield as much as AI/ML do. Shamefully, some American companies that have benefited from all of the blessings of living in a free and capitalistic society, and that are now leading the way in quantum computing and artificial intelligence research, are selling some of their best technologies to our adversaries overseas. Another concern is the partnerships that are forming. For example, Google recently cancelled their AI research contract with the Pentagon and then immediately opened an AI research facility in Beijing, where they are currently working for a company with deep ties to the Chinese military—a move that could nearly be described as the modern-day equivalent of the founders of the Manhattan Project moving to Nazi Germany in the 1940s.

Of course, Google and Beijing affirm that their intentions are benign, if not actually charitable, but only a fool would deny the military applications of the technologies that Google is working on with their Chinese partners. As the battlefield of tomorrow takes shape, there can be no doubt that AI will not merely play a role; it will be one of the pivotal technologies that determines the victor. It is not hyperbole to argue that every piece of AI code should be viewed through the lens of its potential as a piece of military technology.

One of the primary military uses of AI and ML is the ability to scan incredible volumes of mostly meaningless data in search of a single piece of critical intelligence. And when you consider that we have generated more data in the past eighteen months than in the entire history of mankind (think about that for second), it's easy to see there is no possible way we can sort through it all. For example, if every image recorded by our surveillance satellites over the course of just a week had to be analyzed by humans, it would require hundreds of NSA analysts working for months to go through the data. As one National Reconnaissance Office leader recently described it, we are swimming in an ocean of information while dying of thirst for actual intelligence. And not only is finding the proverbial needle in the haystack impossibly inefficient, far too often human error (i.e., boredom) causes us to miss the critical links or indicators that are so important.

Let's say we knew that a small group of terrorists was hiding somewhere in the remote mountains of Afghanistan, mountains that can best be described as vast, harsh, and seemingly unending. The entirety of the mountain range is being surveilled by our satellites, some of which are capable of resolution down to a very small range. Yes, it would be possible for an analyst to search through the satellite images to find evidence of human activity; but the time required to do that is such that, barring a lottery-winning amount of luck, she would die of old age before sorting through it all. But AI is capable of searching through petabytes of satellite imagery very quickly, the vast majority of which would consist of nothing more than rocks and brush. Through all this sameness, AI is able to find a few telltale signs left by an otherwise careful terrorist. The program would then flag the photos for manual inspection by an analyst.

Perhaps even more impressive, as AI/ML applications become more intelligent, we find that not only are they faster than humans at picking up suspicious activity, they are actually better at it. It is not uncommon for an AI program to flag a satellite image for human inspection, telling the analyst there is something there to look at, but for the analyst not to be able to find it. Ironically, the computer has no method for informing the analyst exactly what it found so concerning in the photo, sometimes leaving the analyst to scratch his head. As the computers learn, we find that sometimes we don't even understand *how* it identifies human activity. But we have also learned through hard experience to trust the program. When the analyst cannot find any sign of human activity, and yet the program is insistent the terrorist is nearby, more often than not the AI is right!

And searching through countless satellite images is only one of many applications for which AI can be employed. AI/ML can be used to search through overseas phone calls or emails for suspicious statements, flight paths and vehicle traffic patterns for anomalous behavior, and waves on the ocean for indications that submarines are deep beneath the surface. On the battlefield, it can be an absolute game-changer. It can be used to sort battlefield communications, track enemy forces, project the movement of artillery and men, estimate fuel consumption, calculate weapons inventories, and consider a vast array of factors, such weather forecasts, enemy drone locations, reinforcement dispositions, angles of sunlight, Predator munitions and times on targets, command and control priorities, communication frequencies, and many other things. It can then prioritize the most critical elements and present the information to the individual war fighter in such a way that it makes sense, telling him the things he needs to know and see and do right now in order to minimize the threats to his life while accomplishing his mission.

It's impossible to convey how AI/ML changes the battlefield. It will give more information to an individual soldier than what used to be provided to an entire battalion command and control center. It does it instantly. It makes it all make sense. It changes the battle. It saves lives.

But, like all military applications, it also can be abused.

One of the more horrifying applications of AI programs lies in their ability to perfect the surveillance state. As an example, the same program used to search satellite imagery could be used to search through communications to find anyone who is deemed a "domestic terrorist," or to search through CCTV footage in search of anyone exercising their Second Amendment rights. Because once the initial code has been written, bending the program to a different application is only a minor detail, not unlike pointing a loaded weapon at a different target.

Machine learning and artificial intelligence have applications with far greater implications than merely finding the proverbial data-needle in the haystack. Using a combination of different AI programs, machines can interpret data from their surroundings and then act in a pre-programmed manner, becoming automated weapons systems. Think smart drones, in swarms—some of them controllers, some of them ISR (intelligence, surveillance, and reconnaissance), some of them communicators, some of them shooters—all of them acting in unison and without input from human commanders.

There is growing consensus that at some point in the near future, air, land, and sea battles will be heavily "populated" with fleets of autonomous drones, each machine having the capability not only to kill, but to *decide* who to kill without direct human guidance or intervention.

So yes, humans may start the next war, but once the battle begins, there are certain parts of it that will make us nothing more than bystanders. And targets.

Russian president Vladimir Putin believes (as do many who have a deep understanding of the capabilities of this technology) that future wars will be fought by two sides relying primarily on autonomous weapons systems. He stated that "when one party's drones are destroyed, it will have no other choice but to surrender."

The moral implications of autonomous drone warfare are sticky, the ethics gray. But the fear of wading into these morally murky waters can't be allowed to put us in a position of defeat. Our enemies have no qualms with such use of drones, and the race was started long ago. The question that must be answered is not: should Americans possess this power? The question is: should we be the only ones without it? Because time will likely prove that Putin said it best: "Whoever becomes the leader [in artificial intelligence] will become the ruler of the world."

BERLIN, GERMANY

May

To the never-ending disappointment of his father (a man who grew up on a ranch in Wyoming but went on to become one of the richest men in the country), Peter had joined the army. But his skill soon became simply impossible to ignore. Green Berets before twenty, then Delta. Recently he'd been recruited to an organization given the very unsexy name of INTER-AG, or Inter-Agency, meaning his team worked with the CIA, DIA, NSA, SpecForce, Navy Seals—anyone who needed something special and needed it now.

It wasn't Peter's strength or speed that made him an amazing soldier; it was his mind that made him truly dangerous. And today, he had only one job. One simple task. To get the officer safely to the US embassy.

No way he was going to fail in such a simple mission.

But tonight, as he stared at Victoria and listened to her tell him what they were up against, he was smart enough to know both of them were almost certainly going to die.

"We only have to make it four blocks," Victoria told him. "Four blocks to the embassy, and we'll be safe. It's not that far."

Peter looked at the CIA officer and smiled. He'd worked with her a couple times before. He knew she was fiercely intelligent, crafty, and always fearless. Truth was, he doubted that his rifle was as dangerous as her wicked smile. But she was a spy, not military, and this wasn't an arena with which she had enough experience.

"Four blocks, soldier. Can you get me another four blocks to safety?" she asked a second time.

"How many swarms outside?" Peter asked.

"Two."

Two Chinese swarms! He shook his head. There weren't words in the English language to describe how completely screwed they were. "Have you ever seen a swarm in action?" he asked.

She pressed her lips together but didn't answer.

"Swarms are...intense. One single Chinese drone would be more than enough to take either of us out. Each swarm consists of fifty football-sized machines of death. Faster than us. More agile. More coordinated. And once they lock onto a target, they move like a bullet from a gun. That's to say nothing of the two dozen oversized B-drones floating half a mile above us, each of them capable of launching enough explosives to take out a convoy. And that's not the worst part." He paused. "They are smarter than us, too. Like...lots smarter."

She frowned and started to interrupt, but he didn't allow her the chance to speak. He wanted her to know what they were up against.

"Each of the drones is controlled by an AI algorithm called Laozi, named for the Chinese god of intelligence. Laozi is three times more intelligent than you or I and becomes smarter over time. Each drone can move independently, each in a different direction, each with a different task; and yet they always behave as one, perfectly coordinated and intent on a single goal: the destruction of the target."

Victoria frowned again.

"And you said they were Chinese, right?" he asked.

She nodded, the worry lines between her eyes deepening.

"Okay, well, that makes matters worse. Since Germany, the cowards, started kowtowing to the PRC, they allowed Huawei to create the infrastructure for their telecoms. Which means the CCP now has access to every single camera in the city. Which means they see us. They'll always see us. Berlin has...I don't know how many CCTV cameras per block, each of them funneling pictures of our faces to Laozi. In a city this size, assuming the drones are spread out evenly—which they won't be, they'll be concentrated in the few blocks around the embassy—I would *guess that gives us about...I don't know...six seconds to get to there. Can you run four blocks in six seconds?"*

"Of course, I can," she said. She finally smiled, defiance in her eyes. "Can't you?"

"Of course."

"Okay, let's say you can't. You don't look that fast. Can't you just shoot them?"

He laughed. "One drone I could shoot. Maybe. If we were in broad daylight, and if I knew it was coming, and if I had a shotgun. But an entire swarm? At night? While they're shooting back? I'd have a better chance of shooting a sniper's bullet out of the air than stopping a swarm with my pistol."

He watched her process what he'd told her, the defiance fading to despair.

"But...you're supposed to be my exfiltration. You're the best. I've seen it before. You can get me out of here!"

He watched her carefully, her teeth grinding as she seethed. "What information do you have? What do you know that has made the Chinese so desperate they would resort to violence on European soil?"

She stared at him, then swallowed and answered with a soft voice. "They're going to attack the Ford. And the rest of the carriers. Within the hour."

His eyebrows shot up.

Which meant was there was no way—no way—he could get them out of the dingy apartment building and to the embassy alive, not with their comms being jammed and no way to communicate.

But still, he had to try.

DRONES, HIVES, AND SWARMS

When one hears the words *military drone,* one generally thinks of an awkward-looking, fixed-wing craft such as the Predator, with its fifty-five-foot wingspan and loaded to the teeth with 450 pounds of explosive weaponry and millions of dollars of sophisticated technology. But the drones in a swarm more closely resemble the three-hundred-dollar drone purchased for Christmas than the military drones used over Afghanistan or Iraq. And the truth is, in the face of drone swarms, such large, expensive, and sophisticated weapons as the Predator are flying at Mach speed toward obsolescence.

The key to the effectiveness of a drone swarm is what is called collective consciousness, or shared organization, or the hive mind: the ability of AI-controlled machines to make individual decisions based on collective consciousness and the shared sensory input of the entire swarm, and then to carry out the mission based on an intelligent assessment of the situation.

In many ways, drone swarms are quite comparable to the primal swarms found in nature. When hundreds of animals, or millions of insects, work collectively toward a single objective, it can be both beautiful and terrifying. These "swarms" in nature require unique and sophisticated communication channels between individual parties so that the swarm can maintain cohesion and achieve its objective. And in many ways, electronic drones have already surpassed anything found in nature.

Another reason that drone swarms are such an appealing option is the sheer number of drones that swarms can contain, each providing information to the hive mind as well as being capable of carrying out individual objectives.

Even caveman warriors knew that numbers mattered when it came to warfare. This principle hasn't changed in the last ten thousand years. China has publicly discussed having successfully tested drone swarms of up to a thousand individual units, and there is little reason why swarms wouldn't be able to increase in size. It doesn't take much imagination to envision a scenario where an enemy force deploys thousands or tens of thousands of small, low-cost, expendable units, attacking an objective and overcoming its defenses through the use of overwhelming numbers. With the reality of low cost and production-scalability, drone swarms hold the promise of being an absolutely terrifying weapons system. One can envision a scenario in which the United States spends tens of billions of dollars on sophisticated missile defense systems, only to be overwhelmed by a cloud of buzzing drones, each one no larger than a child's toy.

Much of the research into this promising technology is classified, but some information is open sourced. A good example:

In 2016, DARPA and the US Air Force released video demonstrations of a project appropriately named *Gremlins*. The videos showed hundreds of small micro-drones being dropped out of the cargo bay of an F/A-18. (In theory, the Gremlins could be launched from a number of different platforms, including fighter jets, larger drones, and any transport aircraft.) After being ejected from the fighter plane at more than half the speed of sound, the drones flew as a single, cohesive unit and formed up at a preselected area. If a drone was damaged or dropped out for any reason, the swarm "self-healed" and rearranged the individual units to maintain the swarm. After grouping in formation, they moved in an intelligent reconnaissance pattern, scanned the area, found the objective, circled it from above, and eventually annihilated the target in a simultaneous attack, all without human intervention or guidance.

And these technologies are not merely experimental. Drone attacks in Ukraine date back to 2015. Syrian-backed rebels used a swarm of low-tech drones to attack a Russian ship. ISIS has employed these both effectively and frequently. In 2017, Russians used drones carrying thermite grenades to infiltrate a Ukrainian ammunition depot where they destroyed a *billion* dollars of Ukrainian ammunition, dealing a severe blow to their enemy (as well as creating a video of some very impressive explosions!).

The technologies of AI-controlled weaponry will continue to grow, and will almost certainly replace a number of complicated and dangerous tasks currently done only by humans. For example, the United States Air Force is years deep into the creation of autonomous, AI-piloted fighter jets capable of air-to-air and air-to-ground combat. The Air Force has publicly discussed their goal of very soon pitting experienced fighter pilots up against drones. And though only time will tell who the ultimate victor will be, on paper the well-trained pilot is almost certainly doomed. The combat capability of a human pilot is largely based on experience, a talented fighter pilot having logged thousands of hours of flight time. But due to the nature of machine learning, the drones would have access to *millions* of hours of training and experience. When this is combined with a machine's ability of instantaneous reaction, the fact that they are capable of receiving information from far more sensory inputs than humans can, the fact that drones are fully integrated with other autonomous machines and can communicate instantly with the smaller drone fleets that are part of the swarm attack, as well as the final fact that drones aren't distracted by illogical emotions such as fear and the desire to live, it's easy to assume that the pilot is going to have a very difficult time.

Indeed, AI-controlled fighter jets could prove to be the most significant advancement in aerial combat since the inception of the jet engine.

AI-controlled autonomous weapons represent a true revolution in other areas of the field of battle. Drone swarms will provide reconnaissance for our troops and surveillance of battlefield environments. They'll search oceans, roads, and landmine-laden fields. They'll be equipped with sensors that can detect the presence of chemical, biological, or nuclear weapons. They'll fly with networks to enhance communication between friendly units while their jamming technology disrupts enemy comms. They'll provide an additional layer of missile defense by jamming incoming sensors, or simply be deployed in the path of the oncoming missiles. Cameras, facial recognition, and other means of identification will be employed to find human targets. They'll integrate with manned fighters and bombers flying above the battlefield, helping them to rain death down from above.

Given this, it's easy to understand why President Putin stated that he believed future wars will be fought by two sides using nothing more than drones.

BERLIN, GERMANY

May

"Hold still," he told her as he grabbed her by the chin. In the other hand he held a syringe. With great speed but little gentleness, he pressed the needle against her upper cheek and began injecting the dermal fillers, then repeated the process at other points in her face. He could feel her clench and her pretty face paled, but she didn't complain. He was no plastic surgeon, and she looked a little goofy by the time he was done, but he hoped it would be enough to fool Laozi's facial recognition for at least a few minutes.

"Don't you need some?" Victoria asked.

"No," he told her. "I'm a ghost."

She frowned, but didn't argue.

He took her shoes and placed four sharp tacks strategically along the inner linings. Laozi's gait analysis was even more difficult to trick than its facial recognition, and he didn't know how much time the pins would grant them. He reached into his backpack and threw her a form-fitting black Kevlar suit. Covering her from ankle to neck, it wouldn't stop a swarm, but it would mitigate the damage from a single drone.

She pulled it on, threw her coat on to cover it, and they left the apartment.

The Berlin night was dark, the streets wet, the air tainted with the smell of dog feces, which always happened when it rained.

He told her not to speak. With China's access to the telecom network, all it would take was the stray phone of a single passerby to pick up her voice, and Laozi's voice recognition would mark her as the target. He told her not to run or limp. Laozi would flag her behavior as abnormal and focus the unseen drones on them.

Their only defense was to be invisible. And so, they walked casually, a couple out for a late-night stroll. Victoria started to clench her teeth from the pins that were embedded in her shoes, but she didn't limp. Instead, she casually reached out to grab his arm for support.

One block. Two blocks. Three. Almost to the embassy. Still no sign of the swarm. They were making good time. They might make it!

Some might have called it instinct, others might have said it was exceptional eyesight, but more likely than not it was pure luck that saved them. As they turned the final corner, he saw the glint of the streetlight as it reflected off a small ball flying through the air toward them.

"Run!" he roared.

Peter sprinted to the nearest storefront window, shattered it, and jumped through, Victoria close behind. Alarms shrieked furiously as he scrambled to regain his feet and escape the incoming attack. They ran through the clothing displays and into a hallway at the back, slamming the door behind them.

Crash!

The drone exploded against the center of the door, sacrificing itself to make a hole. Other drones shot through the jagged hole, chasing like a pack of flying wolves.

They reached the end of the hallway. Peter kicked the door open and they rushed into a large reception area. Looking over his shoulder, he grabbed a small grenade-like object from his belt, armed it, and threw it down the hall.

There was no explosion. There wasn't even any noise. But the drones fell to the ground, lifeless as they rolled down the hall. The shrieking alarms went silent, the background noise of ventilation shut off, and everything around them went utterly black.

"What was that?" Victoria asked through heavy panting.

"E-grenade," he said.

"They gave you an E-grenade!" she asked incredulously from the dark. "And you used it?"

"We're alive, aren't we?"

"You, my friend, just used an E-pulse in downtown Berlin. The chancellor is not going to be happy!"

"It won't take out anything beyond two hundred feet," he argued. "No biggie. They'll get things fixed. But it only bought us thirty seconds."

He removed a hardened flashlight from his pack and started running again. Victoria followed. They found a stairwell and ran up. He stopped at the second floor, then turned and ran down a hallway, east, toward the embassy. At the end of the hall, he kicked in a door and ran through the office toward the window.

He could see the embassy.

Half a block away.

Might as well have been across the Atlantic.

Given a month, and if he'd had access to the best weaponry the Agency had to offer, he might have been able to come up with a clever plan to get them down the street. But he knew the drone swarms too well. He knew what they were capable of. Frankly, he was amazed they'd gotten as far as they had.

The drone came crashing through the window and kamikazed directly into Victoria's foot.

Clever, Peter thought angrily. Laozi and the swarm must have realized that they were wearing the upgraded Kevlar, and the best way to achieve their objective was to slow them down, crippling her until the rest of the swarm could arrive and take her out.

Victoria groaned as she collapsed to a knee and grabbed at her injured foot. Not a second passed before Peter picked her up, ran to the window, and jumped through the glass, shards raining down around them as they landed on the roof of a car.

Victoria was up before he could even roll over. She knew what she had to do. She hobbled to her bloody feet and ran toward the embassy gates. "American! I'm an American!" she cried as she ran.

Peter stumbled off the roof of the car and watched. He felt an icy hand grab his gut as a band of glistening black projectiles converged on Victoria's position. He grabbed his pistol and began firing hopelessly at the hovering balls.

The marines on guard jerked the gate open and ran toward her. But she wasn't going to make it. Peter closed his eyes.

Nobody beats the swarm....

But Victoria wasn't just a nobody. Three seconds later, she fell into the arms of the waiting marine.

But then she looked at her watch and realized that it was too late.

HYPERSONIC MISSILES

Short of a full-blown nuclear detonation, hypersonic missiles are the world's most powerful kinetic weapon.

Unfortunately, while the United States has been dabbling in the science of hypersonic flight, our enemies have been intensively researching these technologies for years. When the US hypersonic program was defunded under the Obama administration, both China and Russia saw an opening that could lead to them winning the race in a critical military area. They dumped huge amounts of capital into hyper R&D, and they have outspent, out-researched, out-innovated, and out-built us in hypersonics for nearly a decade. Tactically, this decision made perfect sense. Why build a full array of anti-aircraft systems—burdensome, complicated, and expensive—in order to shoot down a single aircraft, when you can destroy them all, plus their carrier, with one hyper strike?

But at the time, the US decision to defund the program wasn't without merit. The world of hypersonic flight is such an unforgiving realm, and the technology required to create a viable weapon so overwhelmingly difficult, it didn't have the powerful supporters within the DOD that were required to move such an expensive and uncertain program forward. And there were a dozen reasons why hypersonic was such a technological challenge. Engines. Maneuverability. Stability. Control. Materials. Metallurgy. Fuels. The list is long, the aerodynamics extremely complicated. Thin, shock-layer, viscous interaction and high temperature dynamics. Chemically reacting and radiative effects. The assumption that air is a slightly viscous, heat-conducting, continuous medium that obeys the laws of a perfect gas was put to question. And these are just some of the aspects that distinguish hypersonic flow from supersonic dynamics.

Perhaps the greatest challenge was the question of how to build a missile that didn't simply disintegrate in flight. At hypersonic speeds, dissociation of air occurs very quickly, a process in which the air molecules split apart into their individual atoms. When this process affects a considerable proportion of the gas molecules, the gas is said to be dissociated. Sudden spikes in turbulence occur as the boundary layer of dissociated air compresses and then suddenly breaks into eddies, a layer of superheated molecules sent tumbling down the body of the missile. The friction, thermal stress, and heat load on the projectile is enormous, putting the missile under constant threat of fracture, deformation, and disintegration. The slightest miscalculation is disastrous.

As difficult as these challenges are, it's still easy to see why hypersonic technologies are the proverbial pot of gold at the end of the kinetic warfare rainbow. A first-generation hypersonic missile is capable of Mach 5, or five times the speed of sound. That is nearly four thousand miles per hour, or New York to L.A. in about forty minutes. And Mach 5 is only the beginning. In 2018, Russia successfully tested the Kinzhal missile, and we know that it has reached speeds of Mach 10. It has been reported to be capable of Mach 27. Nearly six miles per second! New York to L.A. in seven minutes! China's hypersonic program is probably a little bit behind Russia's. Or maybe a little bit ahead. We really don't know. The secrecy around their programs makes it nearly impossible to evaluate their progress in finite detail. What we do know is this: they are years ahead of us, and moving forward. Which means we have to catch up, and catch up fast.

A hypersonic weapon has a number of advantages that, in today's battlefield, are difficult to overstate.

First, they could be equipped with nuclear weapons.

Second, even if the missile is not tipped with a nuclear warhead, its incredible speed grants it unmatched destructive power. No military target could survive a hit with a hypersonic weapon.

Third, with the exception of intercontinental ballistic missiles, no other weapon has the ability to fly trans-theater, giving them enormous range.

Fourth, hypersonic missiles move so fast that they essentially negate any meaningful warning system. If a hypersonic missile can reach a target anywhere in the world within a matter of minutes, the target is much less able to defend itself. They wouldn't have time to mount an escape plan or counter the attack. An aircraft carrier would be a great big, beautiful hunk of sitting duck. An airfield would have no time to get planes into the air, and the Pentagon or White House would not be able to evacuate before they would be demolished by the incoming barrage. Due to the unmatched speed and resultant "simultaneous effect," a reasonable argument could be made that hypersonic weapons negate the entire doctrine of mutually assured destruction, the governing principle that has prevented nuclear war for decades. If every American nuclear launch and control facility is destroyed before we even realize we are under attack, then MAD has essentially become obsolete.

Finally, and most importantly, hypersonic missiles are nearly impossible to shoot down, even with the most advanced missile defense systems available today. That's because current systems are based on the principle that missiles follow a predictable flight path, a smooth and unchanging parabola. Because it is predictable, defense systems are able to calculate that path and intercept the missile based not on where it is now, but where it's going to be. But hypersonic missiles are not only faster than anything else in the world, they can maneuver, making their flight paths unpredictable. The United States military is many years away from fielding a missile defense system capable of intercepting a hypersonic missile.

This becomes extremely important, for example, when one considers the United States Navy's primary mission of power projection. For decades, the aircraft carrier, essentially an entire military base that can move around the world, has allowed our nation to protect our interests overseas. Carriers are manned by more than six thousand sailors, pilots, and Marines. They carry bombers, fighters, long-range missiles, ISR aircraft, watercraft, and everything in between. Because they are considered national assets, we have spent billions in an effort to defend these naval behemoths. They are surrounded by a carrier task force whose primary purpose is to protect the carrier and its air wing, and it includes an array of the world's most sophisticated defensive systems. There is nothing we won't do, no money we won't spend, to protect a US carrier.

But all the defense technology in the world won't make any difference when a projectile comes screaming through the atmosphere, friction heating it to more than two thousand degrees, turning and maneuvering as if flies, loaded with explosives and hurtling toward its target at 20,000 miles per hour, a powerful hypersonic boom following in its wake.

And on the day we lose an aircraft carrier, the world will change forever.

WASHINGTON, DC, "BLUE HOUSE" BUNKER

December

As he made his way into the president's emergency command center in the "Blue House"—the White House having become too perilous to stay in a long time before—General Hammond, chairman of the Joint Chiefs of Staff, pondered the question, "Which is worse: evil or stupid?"

His son had asked the question just a few days before. He didn't know the answer. But this much he knew: the evil he had been warning about for fifteen years had just attacked his countrymen. And they were stupid to have let it happen.

He shook his head to clear it before he walked down the narrow flight of steps that led to the command center. He knew he was entering a place where he didn't have any friends. And what was worse, he wasn't sure he had any solutions either.

He didn't feel it was hyperbole to describe his country as in the final stages of its ignominious death. Many thought it already dead. The sole remaining hope had been the United States military. In no small part due to his own leadership, the military had maintained at least a semblance of unity through all the madness and destruction, including piecing together small pockets of functioning power grid, enough to communicate with most of its troops across the globe.

An old-fashioned warrior, Hammond was considered a relic in the administration. And with what had just happened, he wasn't sure he even deserved his job anymore.

Walking in, he saw there were more people packed in the small room than he thought would fit. He could feel dozens of vengeful eyes settle on him, full of suspicion. He ignored them and moved to stand directly in front of the president.

They had all been through so much in the last few months. The stress. The fear. Facing the destruction of their nation. Some had become diminished. But not the president. She was still an imposing figure, tall and stony hard.

"Thank you for joining us, Jacob," she said, every syllable calm and sure. "Care to explain to us what has happened?"

The president handed him a stack of photographs, and he flipped through them quickly. He'd heard the news, but he hadn't seen the images. And even though he knew what he was about to see, nothing could have prepared him for the shock.

The smoldering wreckage of the United States fleet in the South China Sea was seen drifting in the dark waters of the unforgiving ocean. Fires and rubble bobbed in the current, smoke still rising in the sky. A few sailors were seen clinging to debris. But there were far too few, which meant that thousands were now drifting silently to the bottom of the ocean. More photos, this time of Korea, Japan, and Australia, revealing hundreds of American military planes that were now craters and melted steel.

Once upon a time, the United States military had been the most powerful force in the world. But in the matter of two minutes, all of it was gone.

And in that moment, General Hammond's heart broke. He loved every one of the stricken military personnel. And he had let them down. He felt the tears brimming in his eyes and he quickly blinked them away.

"Well, Hammond?" the president demanded, glaring at the man whom she blamed for the attack.

He had briefed the president no less than three times in the past week on exactly this possibility. Or at least he had tried to brief her. She had cut the briefings short and seemed to take little interest. No questions. No follow up. America was falling apart at home. Who cared about a few aircraft carriers thousands of miles away?

"The attack appears to have had two components," Hammond began. "The first was a kinetic assault on our naval forces in the South China Sea. At 0114, local time, the People's Liberation Army deployed their hypersonic missiles to bring down the USS Lincoln, the Ford, and the Reagan. The attack was so well timed we hardly even realized it had begun before it was over. With their hypersonic missiles, the entire attack lasted less than a minute and a half." He paused and swallowed dryly. "It was...it was an extraordinary achievement," he whispered painfully before continuing.

"They have also destroyed approximately eighty percent of our forces in South Korea and Japan. The runways have also been decimated. It's likely that the remaining twenty percent of our aircraft in the hemisphere have sustained damage *of some sort, although we may have a few assets in Guam that were unharmed. The loss of life for the Air Force was significantly less than our Navy, but with no functioning aircraft in the region, they are essentially useless as a fighting force."*

"How did this happen?" she screamed. "How! How!"

The general didn't flinch. A solid fifteen count passed before she spoke again.

"Is there anything else I need to know?" she seethed.

He paused a moment, the sadness welling around him like a cold blanket. Tears still threatened to spill, and he blinked them away again.

There was so much more he could have told her. Because of quantum, the Chinese had managed to infiltrate even their 512-encryption, meaning that no intelligence or communications was safe from their prying eyes. Whatever response they decided on today, they had to do so knowing the Chinese would be aware of it, making surprise retaliation impossible. A number of critical reconnaissance satellites had been destroyed by unmanned extraterrestrial vehicles, and it was clear that other satellites were being jammed. The list was seemingly endless....

One of the men in the room began speaking, but Hammond didn't turn to look at him as he spoke. Something about sanctions, and needing medical equipment produced in China, and needing them to loan the US money, and needing the rare earths and other materials to keep their manufacturing base intact.

Hammond barely heard a word.

"So, what would you have us do?" the president snapped. "And before we even discuss military options, you need to convince me of one thing." She paused, their eyes locking for a cold second. "Some in this room feel we have no choice," she went on. "We have to allow the Chinese some of the things they are concerned about. They get Taiwan and the South China Sea. After all, their claims do have history. Other reasonable elements of truth. Who are we to—"

"They attacked us, Madam President!" Hammond cut in.

"I know that, of course. But our purpose now is to save American lives. Preserve American stability. We are dying here at home. Why send more Americans to die overseas? The future of our children..."

As she continued, General Hammond felt a surprising calm come over him. But it came with a terrible realization that he knew was true.

Nothing they were going to do would matter, anyway.

This war was over before it began. This war had ended about ten years before. America slept while China worked. Americans fought each other while China worked. Americans flipped the bird at their future while China worked.

And it was only just beginning. With America knocked down, the dominoes had started to fall. Iran and Israel were already hours deep into the most violent Middle East conflict in a generation. Firefights in the DMZ on the Korean

Peninsula had been going on for weeks but were now escalating by the hour. Taiwan was now under CCP version of martial law. In spite of never having fired a weapon, Japan had unconditionally surrendered to China. The grid in Poland and Ukraine had evaporated several days before, and now Russia was advancing. More than half of the nations in the EU had declared they would be exiting the union and turning their attention inward, which was code for, "We know there is a limited amount of food, and we're preparing to do what we need to in order to survive." Half of the peoples of Mexico and Central America had flocked across the American border, only to find things in the US were as bad as anything they left behind.

Hammond stared at the dark blue wall over the president's shoulder.

He said nothing as he removed the stars from his shoulders and excused himself from the room. There was nothing he could say. And the president would never listen to him, anyway.

He was going to go find his family down in Georgia. He made sure to bring his weapons.

He ended up walking the entire way.

Book Four

HOPE

The powers not delegated to the United States by the Constitution, nor prohibited by it to the States, are reserved to the States respectively, or to the people.

— Tenth Amendment

The ancient Persians had a law imposed on them by their warrior-king, a man they considered a god, which stated that it was unlawful to talk of anything that was unlawful to do.

Pretty cool, huh? *It's illegal even to talk about things that I forbid you to do.*

Of course, when you've convinced the people that you're a god, you can get away with that.

And the law actually went further than just mere talk. Under the Persian rulers, not only was it illegal to talk about things that were against the law, but it was also illegal to *think* about them as well.

Speech is illegal. Thought is illegal too.

King Xerxes was one of the most powerful men ever to live on the earth, monarch of one of history's greatest kingdoms. Yet powerful as he was, even he was unable to enforce his own dictates, for it turns out that you can't control what your subjects think and say. Such a thing was simply impossible.

Until today.

Because we are on the cusp of exactly that. Totalitarian governments, working in conjunction with totalitarian tech, old media, compliant business leaders, industry, education, and entertainment, are on the verge of demanding just that. *Watch what you say. Watch what you think. Because we are watching you.*

It's interesting to note that the word totalitarianism didn't exist in the English language until the past century. Those who sought to describe a powerful or abusive government used words such as tyranny, despots, and autocracy. But never totalitarianism.

Why?

Because no government had such absolute power over their people so as to totally control them. That has been true throughout human history. Despite the evil or oppressive demands of the most powerful of kings, gods, or tyrants, it wasn't possible. From the first civilization to crawl out of Mesopotamia to the fall of the inhumane and oppressive Soviet empire, no government had the ability to be a true totalitarian government.

Once again…until today.

When we look at what is coming, it reinforces the desperate need to find the off ramp for the path we are on. To find the answer to these challenges.

To find the thing that gives us hope.

TOTALITARIANISM NOW

Everything a Chinese citizen writes, watches, reads, or searches for has the potential to be detected and recorded. This information is then used to control their citizens in such a way as to make even the man-god Xerxes jealous.

Based on what Chinese officials observe, each citizen is given a social score. Social scores are then used to determine which citizens are allowed to travel, how they can travel, whether and where they are allowed to go to school or move to another city or into a better apartment, what kind of job they can get, what kind of luxury items they can buy, and who they are allowed to associate with. The Party will decide everything, good or bad, that happens in their lives.

Those with a low social score are given a unique and easily identifiable ringer on their phones. This special ringtone cannot be changed or muted, allowing everyone around them to know they are insufficiently loyal to the Party. Those who socialize with, or even briefly associate with those with a low social score, then have their own scores lowered, forcing a completely dehumanizing isolation of low-score individuals, making them pariahs within their own families and through the entire society.

And now Chinese officials are tying their citizen's social scores to their digital wallets—which soon will be required—allowing them to enforce their edicts not only through social shaming and isolation, but by imposing financial costs as well. Jaywalk in Beijing? Facial recognition cameras and AI identify you. Your social score and digital wallet take a hit. Say something critical of President Xi? Your social score collapses. Your digital wallet goes empty.

To those who continue to demonstrate "anti-social," in other words anti-party, behavior, Chinese re-education camps will put a final end to their misbehavior.

The control is complete. Merciless. Crushing to mind and soul.

The dystopian world that Chinese citizens are forced to live in is a perfect example of what Alexis de Tocqueville warned us of:

"Go in peace, I will not take your life, but the life I leave you with is worse than death."

Remarkably, most Chinese citizens don't object. They were promised security. They have been given security. They were promised a job. They have been given a job. They face no real crime or threat from terrorism. Their lives are safe and secure.

And yet their lives are also so meaningless and hollow, so indoctrinated and controlled in thought and deed, that they don't even realize that they *should* object.

Which is the ultimate example of what the Greek god Xerxes was hoping to accomplish.

But is this really so different from the conditions we are beginning to place ourselves under here in the United States?

Who Will Fix This?

Consider the soul-sucking world we just described, then ask yourself: do you think the elites in Washington, DC, have any desire to fix this trend in the US? Do you think they care about these abuses of power? Of course, they don't. Why would they ever agree to any changes that would weaken the laws that help to keep them in power? Quite the opposite; the measures they put forward are designed to increase their power, not to empower you or me. If you think the elites in Washington, DC, will fix any of the enormous challenges before us, you don't understand Washington at all.

But there is a way to save our country. There is a way to change the terrifying future that is coming.

Simply put, we have to do two things.

First, we have to recognize the problem. We have to have a real understanding of what we are up against, the real challenges before us. That is part of the purpose of this book.

The second thing we must do is realize the answer to many of our problems lies *within the states.*

Federalism

If we want to save our country, we have to give states back the power that our Founding Fathers intended them to have. Indeed, the individual states have the power to fix most of the problems that are ripping our nation apart. The states have the power to fight back.

This power is called federalism. In its most basic form, federalism means that everyone gets their say, the federal government and the states. A more technical definition (given by *Britannica*) is a...

> ...*mode of political organization that unites separate states...within an overarching political system in a way that allows each to maintain its own integrity. Federal systems do this by requiring that basic policies be made and implemented through negotiation in some form, so that all the members can share in making and executing decisions... they stress the virtues of dispersed power centres as a means for safeguarding individual and local liberties.*

We are a group of freely united states. We are not serfs living under an all-powerful federal government, subject to its whims and dictates. Our Founders asked, and the people agreed to voluntarily, but reluctantly, surrender some of their power and authority to the federal government, while reserving the remaining power to the people and the states.

The American Revolution was unique in history. Most, if not all, previous revolutions were the "have nots" trying to take things from the "haves." They were fights over land, money, resources, power. But the American Revolution was not an economic or social rebellion. It was a fight for rights and liberties—the natural rights of men. It was about philosophy, ideas, and practical politics.

So, when the Founders had the opportunity to secure these hard-won rights, they desperately wanted to create a system that would ensure that no single person or cabal could destroy what they had fought for. They were political *Newtonians*. Philosophically based on the natural law that for every action there is an equal and opposite reaction, they sought to set up a system of government where actions would be countered by equal reactions. They sought to separate power both horizontally between the three separate branches of government, but also vertically between the federal government and the states. This is what we mean by "checks and balances."

And though it's true that we can't guarantee the states will always counterbalance the national government's lust for power (it turns out states can fall into fellowship with federal overreach), they are our only option to apply an opposite reaction to federal overreach or its affront to individual rights.

This concept was generally accepted among our national leaders until the early 1900s, when it began to fall into disrepute. Teddy Roosevelt called federalism a "fetish." States were, to him, nothing more than mere administrative units. Decisions should be made in Washington, DC, he thought. President Woodrow Wilson thought the idea of balance of powers was nothing but "Constitutional witchcraft," going even a step further than Roosevelt by insisting that decisions should not only be made in DC, but by the president himself, or at least by the "experts" he had placed in the executive agencies. These presidents, and many others that were to follow, certainly didn't trust the riffraff that the people sent to Congress.

Which is why the Tenth Amendment is such a critical thing:

> *The powers not delegated to the United States by the Constitution, nor prohibited by it to the States, are reserved to the States respectively, or to the people.*

It's hard to appreciate what a revolutionary idea this was when first presented during the formation of our nation. The Declaration of Independence. The Constitution. The Bill of Rights. Together, they put forward a concept of government that had rarely, if ever, even been considered, let alone actually put into place.

God gave rights to individuals. Not to the king. Not to the Parliament. Not to the military. God gave rights to *the People*. Then, in order to form a more perfect union, the People conceded to the government certain rights. Limited rights. Definable rights. But the federal government had to share even those limited powers with the states. The states were coequal partners to the central government, not junior or inferior in any way. Federalism isn't state defiance of the federal government. Federalism is the states fulfilling their constitutional purpose, allowing citizens to achieve more of their desires than rule under a national government ever could.

Today…right now…individual states could fix most of the deadly challenges we are facing.

And the beautiful thing is, Democrats and Republicans agree with this. Many progressives may deny it, but their actions show they know it is true. Indeed, over the past several years (and accelerating rapidly during the Trump administration), progressive leaders in blue states have exercised their own form of liberal federalism, arguing aggressively for the preeminence of the power of the states, proving that federalism is not conservative or liberal, Republican or Democrat.

BLUE STATE FEDERALISM

Perhaps the best example of blue state federalism lies in some states implementing healthcare policies that lean hard to the left. Romneycare in Massachusetts, for example. Dozens of states have also expanded Medicaid far beyond what the federal government provides. In 2011, Vermont began to offer a state-financed, single-payer health care system which guaranteed all Vermonters universal health care (although it was abandoned in 2014, because, as it turns out, it was kind of expensive).

Currently there are eleven left-leaning states (as well as Washington, DC) that have legalized recreational marijuana—this despite the fact that it is against federal law to be in possession of the drug.

What is this other than liberal federalism at play?

It's also an example of what Supreme Court Justice Antonin Scalia once said about how he wished that federal judges could be given a stamp that read "stupid but constitutional."

States that have legalized marijuana have a certain view. The federal government has a different view. Yet these left-leaning states didn't roll over for the federal government. They didn't say, *"Well, I guess we have no choice but to concede to the feds and do what they tell us to do, despite the desires and beliefs of our citizens."* Indeed, they did exactly the opposite, essentially saying, *"Keep your federal drug laws. That's cool. But we're going in another direction. And remember, Mr. Federal Government, we states are not your slaves. We are your equals, not your inferiors, and we have certain rights, as well."*

Do we think it's a good idea to legalize recreational marijuana? Not at all. We think it's destructive to both individuals and societies.

But we do agree with an individual state telling the federal government to respect their rights.

And federal drug laws are not the only example of left-leaning states telling the federal government that they are going to exert their sovereign rights as states.

Nine liberal states have legalized physician-assisted suicide for the terminally ill. Again, we think this another terrible and morally destructive idea. But it appears to be within the prerogative of each state to decide.

Perhaps you are an environmental activist. If so, you should embrace the idea of federalism, for it allows states to enforce environmental standards that go beyond federal mandates. For example, California has asserted its right to enforce much more stringent auto emission standards than federal regulators do, this despite President Trump's efforts to roll back these state environmental laws.

Perhaps the best-known example of liberal federalism is the fact that many blue cities (and in some instances entire blues states) have declared themselves as "sanctuaries" from federal immigration law. Once again, California led the way when they enacted "sanctuary state" laws that imposed some restrictions on California law enforcement's ability to cooperate with federal immigration agencies. (It's important to note these state laws did not infringe on the federal government's ability to enforce its laws against illegal border crossings.) After being legally challenged, a federal court upheld the California law, citing principles of federalism in doing so, a legal finding that was then upheld by the appellate court.

Mark Joseph Stern is a legal analyst for the liberal website *Slate*. He has written about these court opinions supporting state laws over federal dictates, calling them "fantastic." He went on to say, "Its most immediate impact will be to remind Trump and [former attorney general Jeff] Sessions that they can't always boss blue states around."

Again, do we think sanctuary states are a good idea? We do not. But it's clear that the battles over sanctuary cities solidified the legal basis for states to press their own interest when they disagree with policies or laws implemented by the federal government.

Interestingly, many of these legal findings are rooted in precedents handed down by a conservative Supreme Court. Some think that is inconsistent, or at least ironic. But quite the opposite. A conservative Supreme Court should be one of the strongest defenders of states' rights. If you are a believer in "original intent" and a conservative reading of the Constitution, you must be a defender of states' rights.

A good example of this principle is the Supreme Court's 2011 decision in *Bond v. United States*, an important step toward protecting states' rights. In this case, Justice Anthony Kennedy said that federalism *"protects the liberty of all persons within a State by ensuring that laws enacted in excess of delegated governmental power cannot direct or control their actions…"* He also added that *"state sovereignty is not just an end in itself: Rather, federalism secures to citizens the liberties that derive from the diffusion of sovereign power."*

All nine members of the Court agreed.

We may disagree with some of the decisions that states make. We may think them foolish or counter-productive or against common sense and good morals. We may think some of them are simply stupid. But that's not the point. The point is that the states should be able to decide. States should be able to make decisions, good or bad, without the federal government menacing over them. States should be able to implement different policies, giving more choices and more voices to the people.

And remember, many on the other side of the political spectrum think that some of the decisions made by conservative states are foolish as well. That's what our Founders intended. Let the states have flexibility. Let them experiment. Let them reflect the will of the people who reside in that state.

Isn't that really what most of us are looking for? Conservatives. Moderates. Urban dwellers and rural cowboys.

Give us a little freedom to decide our own fate.

RED STATE FEDERALISM

If blue states are going to defy federal laws they don't agree with—and they certainly have—we would encourage red states to do the same thing.

Imagine what the conservative-leaning states could do if we unshackled them from the heavy hand of Washington, DC. Think of the freedoms we could protect if we allowed states to exercise the critical powers the Constitution intended them to have. States could, for example, protect their citizens against the overbearing and tyrannical power of Big Tech. And that's just one of the many things states could do, or have already done, to protect the freedom of their citizens.

Several red states have declared themselves "sanctuary states," immune from federal restrictions on the Second Amendment. These states have adopted laws or resolutions that oppose federal efforts to mandate universal background checks, ban assault weapons and high-capacity magazines, and implement supposed red flag laws that would inhibit gun ownership.

Despite the obvious objections from DC (and the nearly universal condemnation from the media), all fifty states have protected their citizens' ability to concealed carry a firearm for personal protection. This would not be true were it not for court precedents honoring states' rights.

Shortly after President Biden signed his executive order halting the deportation of illegal aliens, the Texas attorney general filed a lawsuit to stop the implementation of the executive order, claiming it violated existing law as well as a previous lawful agreement between Texas and the Department of Homeland Security. A federal judge agreed and blocked implementation of the executive order, affirming the idea of states' rights.

A South Dakota legislator gets the gold medal in the category of exercising states' rights, for introducing a bill that would enable the state attorney general to reject any presidential order that impinged upon any state citizen's Constitutional rights regarding the regulation of natural resources, land use, financial services, the agricultural industry, or the right to bear arms.

Texas denied Planned Parenthood any funding through the state Medicaid program.

States could also cement their power to protect the unborn, such as Texas has done when they defended their law outlawing second-trimester dismemberment abortions.

When President Biden eliminated some work requirements in order to qualify for SNAP assistance, various states decided to add their own work requirements to the federal welfare program.

Some states have chosen not to take federal funding for road and transit projects, thus allowing them to eliminate the onerous federal environmental mandates that come with transportation funding. On occasion, this has allowed them to complete projects in months instead of years, and, remarkably, to complete them at an overall lower cost to the state than if they had taken the federal funding.

The list of things that could be accomplished through empowering the states is long and exciting. Protecting free speech. Protecting LGBTQ and other minority rights while also protecting religious liberty (as Utah has done). Protecting the rule of law and due process. Individual states could sue Big Tech for monopoly violations while allowing their citizens to sue if they are muzzled for their political speech.

ECONOMICS, INNOVATION, COMMUNICATION

One issue that clearly illustrates the positive outcomes that come from allowing states to pick the solution best for them can be found in states' efforts to set their own economic policies.

For many years, twenty-nine states had minimum wage laws that were higher than the federally mandated minimum wage of $7.25 per hour. This worked for them. It was a decision each of these states made. And their citizens were clearly happy with this decision, as evidenced by the fact that they were never under any pressure to change it. But a federally mandated, one-size-fits-all minimum wage of $15.00 an hour is a very different thing in a high-cost state like New York than it is in a state that has a much lower cost of living, and thus a lower wage structure. For example, according to a recent study by the Kahler Financial Group, "a worker earning $15 an hour in Mississippi would have to earn $26.60 an hour in Washington, DC to have the same purchasing power. For a South Dakota worker, $15 an hour has the same purchasing power as $22.66 an hour in DC. Mandating that employers in Mississippi pay $15 an hour would be equal to forcing employers in DC to pay $26.60 an hour."

It's easy to imagine the negative impact on employment an equivalent $26.60 an hour minimum wage would have in some states. The number of lost jobs suffered under the federal mandate would be enormous.

Another important consideration is that when states make different decisions, they lead to different consequences. These consequences will then bear testimony to whether it was a good decision or not. Some things are self-critiquing, and, over time, the good or bad outcome of certain decisions become blazingly obvious. If California or Oregon or Washington want to welcome illegal aliens into their states, if they want to provide them with free health care, a college education, and other social benefits, and if they are willing to pay for it, then great, let them choose. If, on the other hand, other states want to enforce immigration laws and limit social benefits only to US citizens, great, then let them choose as well. Then let the natural consequences of these decisions create their own results. Because, over time, it will become obvious which was the best approach.

Our Founding Fathers were smart enough to imagine what the future would look like under the arrogance of a bloated and ineffective federal government lording over the states like the king of England they had just sacrificed their blood and treasure to be free of. But they also knew that states could become the incubators of ingenuity and innovation. States would take different approaches on how best to solve the same problems. The states would be willing to take risks the federal government might never take.

And finally, there is this: the states are much closer to the people, much more willing to listen, much more willing to respond. If our state leaders do something we don't agree with, we have a way to engage them, to let them know that we are angry. We know who to talk to. Even more important, we can actually talk to them. We can lobby our governor, our state legislators, our local leaders. Every citizen could sit down and talk with their state senator. Good luck meeting with their federal senator in Washington! Given the opportunity to meet with our state leaders, many times we can change their minds. And if we can't change their minds, then we can more easily vote them out of office.

Which is the thing that makes so many people angry about the federal government. We seem so powerless. We can't change anything. We feel ignored, and far too often, even mocked.

Millions of Americans want only one thing: to get the federal government out of seemingly every aspect of our lives. So let the states decide. Let the people have their voice.

CRITICAL RELIEF VALVE

Perhaps even more important than the various laws the states may implement is the emotional relief it creates in a society that is wracked by division. By embracing the values of federalism, we create space for those who disagree to coexist. We create a space for a little bit of peace. We create an emergency relief valve to some of the anger and frustration that so many people feel. Federalism can help keep the "loyal opposition" from turning bitter and disloyal. It would keep our nation from tearing itself apart. Republicans could take comfort knowing that during a Democrat presidency, red states could still pursue conservative goals, such as adding work requirements to welfare programs. Similarly, policy decisions in blue states could provide a similar outlet for liberals under a Republican president.

Federalism also could act as a powerful brake on federal orders that infringe on Constitutional rights. If legislators in DC faced the reality that states had the power to ignore laws that infringed on individual rights, their incentive for passing such laws would be reduced. Presidents would be forced to be much more judicious in issuing executive orders, knowing the states could ignore them, especially if they knew the courts would support the states in exerting their prerogatives under federalism.

Federalism also would allow Americans to "vote with their feet," something millions have already proven willing to do. Over the past generation, we've seen a significant migration from high-tax states to low-tax and more affordable locations. We've seen a significant migration from states that suffer under heavy government regulation and poor economic opportunities to those that offer greater economic freedom and opportunity. Federalism would create another opportunity for individuals to pursue their own interest and support their own values. If abortion on demand, a powerful state government, and generous social safety nets are important to you, you can choose to live in a state that provides the services you value. If, on the other hand, you think that school choice, the Second Amendment, religious freedom, and lower taxes are important to a growing economy and civil society, you could choose to live in a state that protects these priorities. Under federalism, you would have a choice. You could improve your position by simply making a move.

Blue states and red states, liberals and conservatives, moderates and independents—all could improve their lives by allowing states more autonomy and constraining federal power.

And it's our last shot!

It's the only way to reduce the rage and resentment that have overtaken our political discourse. It's the only way to offer people a way live in a society that doesn't seem always to belittle them, or cancel them, or malign them, or force them to support things that are deeply offensive to their values.

Perhaps even more important, it's the only way to keep our nation united enough that our enemies won't take advantage of our weakness. It's the only way we can keep our nation in a position where we can be an example of economic prosperity and freedom to the rest of the world. It's the only way to save our nation from our adversaries who are waiting for us to fail.

It gives us choice. It gives us freedom. It gives our children a future filled with hope.

It keeps our nation from fragmenting into tribes. It keeps our nation from breaking down to the point that we fall into chaos and even civil war.

If we don't do something, a catastrophe is coming. People are angry! They feel helpless, frustrated, and ignored. We simply cannot sustain this. The path we are on will lead to the destruction of our nation, the complete breakdown in our government and our society. If we don't create this relief valve by giving our citizens the sense that they are people, and not goats being herded by the elites, then many will join in the call for succession of the states. Old and young. Soccer moms and dads. Black and white, rich and poor, country folks and urban dwellers, everyone is fed up.

Though his own subjects thought that he was god, King Xerxes failed to control what they thought and said. No king or government can ever do that. It is impossible. Because men yearn to be free. Men fight to be free. And in the end, men *will* be free.

Federalism gives us the chance to claim that freedom. And it's the best chance we have to save the nation that we love.

Overcoming the Odds

But at the end of the day, even Federalism alone won't be enough to save us. It's imperfect. In some ways, it doesn't go far enough. Some worry that it may go too far. It leaves some questions unanswered and still other things to fight about. Yes, it would be an enormous step forward, but it won't bring about a utopia where all of our national problems are solved forever.

Or, as the brilliant Winston Churchill once put it, "Many forms of Government have been tried, and will be tried in this world of sin and woe. No one pretends that democracy is perfect or all-wise. Indeed, it has been said that democracy is the worst form of Government except for all those other forms that have been tried…"

And this is true. Freedom is messy. It's contentious. It takes an *enormous* amount of energy and commitment. It's difficult, and sometimes disappointing and as fragile as glass.

But it's also the greatest blessing ever given to man. With it, we *are* everything. We *have* everything. Our lives, our future, are children can be filled with hope. Without it, we have nothing. Which is the only explanation for the fact that, from the beginning of time, men have fought to be free.

COURAGE AND FAITH

But sometimes we're unsure, and maybe even frightened, that we may be unable to defend it. That's the way that so many people feel now.

Which is why we must show courage.

We have in our family a set of WWII US Army Air Corps pilot wings, which belonged to our father/grandfather, one of those incredibly brave young men who put everything on the line to fight tyranny and evil during WWII.

On one occasion, this old pilot was discussing the first couple years of the war, describing in intense detail the uncertainty and fear he felt. At some point, he was interrupted by a skeptical listener who said something to the effect that it must have helped, knowing that the Americans were certainly going to win the war.

The pilot stopped him short. "No, that's not true," he said, his voice filling with emotion. "Looking back on it now, it may seem certain that we would win, *but at the time, we didn't know!* Look what we had experienced. The loss of most of Europe. The humiliating withdrawal at Dunkirk. Pearl

Harbor. The Philippines. American soldiers without boots or rifles. Farm kids facing the most powerful military the world had ever seen. Huge losses in Northern Africa. Stuck in the cold mountains of Italy.

"So no, we didn't know if we could hold it all together. We didn't know if we would win."

To us, sitting here with the benefit of history, it may seem obvious that the Allies would defeat the great evil that had risen up in Europe. In hindsight, it seems apparent that the gods of war were on our side; that, plus the forces of economics, history, culture, industry, natural resources, leadership, and the moral courage that comes from defending home and freedom. Surely all of these would combine to make certain that the Allies would be victorious.

But at the time it wasn't obvious. In the middle of the crisis, many feared that we, as a nation, were probably dead.

That's one of the miraculous things about this country. The many times we have overcome the overwhelming odds.

So, if you think this time is hopeless, or that our nation is doomed, it helps to keep in mind that we've been through worse before. It helps to remember the examples of faith and courage that carried our nation through the darkest times. It helps to remember some stories such as these:

*　*　*　*　*

During the winter of 1609–1610, the settlers at Jamestown went through the Starving Time, a brutal winter when nearly 90 percent of them starved to death. Out of more than 500 settlers that occupied Jamestown in the fall of 1609, only 61 survivors were still alive come the spring. Through the bitter winter, the settlers were forced to eat worms, mice, leather from their shoes, anything they could find to fill their stomachs. Late the next spring, the few survivors who had made it through the winter found themselves on a rescue ship on their way back to England. When they happened on a supply ship at the mouth of the James River, they had a choice to make: continue on their ship back to England, or turn back to Jamestown and try again. In the face of overwhelming odds, and even while still suffering from hunger, the survivors had the courage to turn back and try once more.

How can we give up hope for our country when we remember the settlers who faced such suffering and fear?

*　　*　　*　　*　　*

There is a tragic story from the Battle of Malvern Hill during the Civil War. Attempting to take a prominent hill, a group of Northern soldiers were trapped by deadly shots coming from a small clump of trees. A young southern officer was expertly directing his soldiers' fire toward the Union men. Knowing it was critical for the Union army to take the hill, a Union sergeant bent a knee and raised his rifle. The moment the Southern officer exposed himself, he took his shot. The officer fell to the ground. The fallen soldier's men stood for a moment in confusion and then turned and scattered up the hill

Advancing to the clump of trees, the Union shooter walked to the wounded soldier and rolled him over. His face instantly turned white with unspeakable grief.

The dying man looked up. "Father," he whispered…then forever closed his eyes.

Recognizing his son who had gone south before the war, the father looked down in unimaginable pain.

In all of US history, there is no more powerful reminder of the pain and suffering our nation has gone through than the Civil War. A nation at war with itself. Brother against brother. Father fighting son. Friends and family torn asunder.

Seven days of fighting ended the Union Peninsula Campaign that took the young life of the Southern soldier. Twenty thousand Confederate soldiers were either missing, dead, or wounded upon the battlefield. Eleven thousand Union soldiers had met the same fate.

We used to think something like 540,000 soldiers died in the war, but recent research has revised that number upward, to a new estimate of 620,000—nearly equal to the 640,000 battlefield casualties in all other US wars combined. This from a nation of only 31 million people at that time.

For those who say that the times we live in are too hard, or that the nation is too fractured to keep together, or that the differences between us have grown to the point that they are irreconcilable now, a faithless marriage of two partners who have moved into their corners to scowl at and insult each other, we must say: *that cannot be true.* Even in the midst of the darkest storm, they found a way to keep the nation together. Surely, we can do it now.

And how could we justify our loss of faith to those who fought and bled during the Civil War? How could we justify our unwillingness to try *anything* to keep our nation together to those who fought for the sole purpose of keeping us unified as one!

*   *   *   *   *

The Great Depression was a cataclysmic event for our nation. Some of our major cities experienced 40 percent unemployment, 25 percent being the national average. Lawyers, teachers, accountants, and common laborers often found themselves sharing a campfire in one of the 6,000 hobo camps, or Hoovervilles as they called them, named after the sitting president. Young men often left home in their early teens to look for work, unwilling to be a burden on their families. Half of all banks failed. Housing prices plummeted. Savings were devastated. The economy shrunk by an astounding 50 percent in five years. Between 1929 and 1932, the stock market lost 90 percent of its value. International trade plummeted by 65 percent. In some rural counties, 90 percent of the citizens were on public assistance. In cities, lines for the soup kitchens extended for blocks.

Health deteriorated. Suicide rates spiked in 1933, before finally beginning to taper off. Homelessness became so common in the Midwest "dustbowl" that it almost became the norm. Families were broken, some men simply abandoning their children out of pure shame for not being able to provide for them.

The list of human suffering was painfully long.

But it did not last forever.

After WWII, economic opportunity, consumer demand, freedom of movement, and educational opportunities, along with unprecedented reductions in taxes, regulations, and spending, unleashed a ferocious economic machine, creating material wealth that would have been undreamed of just a few years before. By 1950, ten years after the end of the Great Depression, and only five years after the end of WWII, the United States had emerged as the world's richest country, with a GDP per capita that dwarfed almost every other nation.

As the second half of the twentieth century dawned, it was clear that the United States had risen to be the most powerful and wealthy nation the world had ever seen, a position we have held every year since.

Out of the ashes of the Great Depression came new hope and opportunity. We not only found the strength to work through the economic devastation, but we learned to thrive.

Because we were stronger as a nation than some people thought that we were.

*   *   *   *   *

On June 3, 1942, Torpedo Squadron Eight was flying over the vast expanse of ocean that separated the Japanese carrier fleet from Midway Island. For some of the young pilots inside the wallowing Devastator torpedo bombers, it was the first time they had ever taken off from an aircraft carrier. None of them had ever flown with an actual torpedo strapped to their airplane.

And the overwhelming majority would not live through the day.

It took an hour for the various fighter, torpedo, and dive bombers to take off from the carriers and form up. An hour wasted. An hour of circling the carriers, bobbing through the skies, burning fuel, and getting agitated, the pilots growing tired. By the time everyone was airborne, and the aircraft had turned toward the last known position of the Japanese fleet, the tropical heat had formed an overcast that covered the sky with a carpet of gray, making it impossible for the pilots to keep each other in sight. They struggled to stay in some type of combat formation, but it was impossible. Under strict orders to maintain radio silence, it wasn't long until the aircraft scattered for a hundred miles across the sky.

Which meant the plan for a coordinated attack was thrown out the window. Which meant that many of the pilots would be at the mercy of the onslaught of the Japanese defenses.

The Devastator aircrews understood that if they didn't link up with their fighter escorts, they were facing near certain death.

And yet they continued flying toward the target.

Eventually, the Devastators located the Japanese carriers. Enemy Zeros started swarming up to meet them. It was 9:18 in the morning.

Without waiting for their escorts, the Devastator pilots attacked.

The lead pilot rolled the aircraft and dipped toward the sea. A line of smoke screens started spewing from the carriers, filling the sky with trails of white and gray. It seemed there were a thousand Zero fighters coming at them, most of them screaming down from a higher altitude. Antiaircraft fire erupted from the escort ships, spewing black smoke and razor-sharp shrapnel. Unimaginable chaos followed. Aircraft crashing into the sea. Huge towers of spouting water blowing into the sky from the impact of other Devastators. Bursting, smoke-filled rounds of antiaircraft fire seemed to fill every foot of sky.

But the pilot continued flying toward the target.

On that fateful day, fourteen US Devastator torpedo bombers from VT-8 had taken off from the USS *Hornet*. Every one of them were shot down. Twenty-eight Americans were inside the Devastators. Twenty-seven of them died. Twenty-eight Devastators from two other squadrons attacked the Japanese carriers. Only six of them survived.

Not a single Devastator hit a target.

Every American fighter in the first wave of the attack either had to turn back or divert to Midway because they were running out of fuel. The entire VF-8 fighter squadron had to ditch in the ocean. Not a bomb or bullet was fired between them.

In wave after wave, these American pilots were shot down as they attacked the Japanese fleet. Yet, despite these incredible losses, despite the fact that most of the American pilots thought their attack had been futile, the Americans won the battle, one of the most decisive of the war.

Think about it for a moment—the fear and sense of hopelessness these pilots must have felt. They fought and bled and paid with their lives for this country. Dodging fire and heat and exploding shards of steel, they kept flying toward the Japanese carriers, even while knowing that most of them were doomed.

Which is exactly what we have to do today. Fight in the face of fear. Keep moving toward the target. Fight to keep our nation strong so that our adversaries don't pounce.

Because sometimes in life—as this history clearly shows—the outcome is uncertain. We may find that we can win, even when we think there is no hope.

And we can win this. We can save our nation.

But we have to keep faith. We have to show courage. And we have to stay in the fight.

SHERIDAN, WYOMING

A Few Years Later

"I swear, Peter, if you don't stop your whining, I'm going to let you stitch this wound up yourself," Victoria threatened as she moved the needle across the former soldier's jawline.

Peter had been out in the field working on a piece of broken pipe when it had busted, and a small piece of sharp metal had hit him in the jaw and opened up a wound nearly as long as his finger. He'd complained, but Victoria was insistent it needed sutures, and he was smart enough not to argue with his wife.

"I'm not whining," Peter protested and suppressed another grimace. A thought occurred to him, and although he knew he would pay a price for his humor, he couldn't resist. "I just want to make sure my face ends up looking better than yours did that time I gave you those dermal fillers."

Victoria glared and punched him playfully on the arm. After she finished sewing up the wound, she placed her tools back into the first aid kit. Peter moved to her side, grabbed her hand, and kissed her forehead. They stepped from the front door of their home and walked outside to enjoy the last few minutes of the sunset together.

The golden sun, the mountains, the rolling fields . . .

Maddie was in the yard, playing with her dog. She waved at them, and they waved back. Many times, Victoria and Peter had enjoyed the same sight together, but it never grew tiresome. Life was still difficult in many ways, but it was also simpler. Some things were worse, but some were better.

Peter's statement about the facial fillers had taken his thoughts back to the time when the world had seemed so much more complicated.

Peter and Victoria had always fought for freedom, for the right and the good. They had loved the United States because it had been a symbol of freedom, opportunity, and goodness. It had given its citizens the chance to succeed, to work, to provide for and protect their families, the freedom to say and do what they wanted, and worship how they may. Both of them had sacrificed for their country. Victoria's father had given his life for it. So had Peter's grandfather.

It was deep in their DNA, part of what made them who they were.

After the virus had decimated the population and the grid had collapsed, fear and darkness had hung over the nation like a shroud. Many thought the United States never would recover. But the will to survive was strong, the spirit of freedom too. The country was starting to heal now. Starting to rebuild.

Peter and Victoria had always known that freedom came at a cost; that each generation must want it, must fight for it. They knew who they were. They knew they would always fight to be free.

And they would teach their children to fight for freedom too.

ACKNOWLEDGMENTS

Special thanks for Congressman Rob Bishop for his contribution to the history of Federalism, Andrew House for providing the final security review, and Dr. Bob Sergott for his input and review on CRISPR technology.

ABOUT THE AUTHORS

Chris Stewart is a multiple *New York Times* bestselling and national award-winning author. He is a world-record-setting former Air Force pilot who now serves as a member of Congress on both the House Permanent Select Committee on Intelligence and the Appropriations Committee. He and his wife, Evie, are the parents of six children.

After twelve years of formal education in science and medicine, Dr. Dane Stewart is now a surgeon who currently practices in the field of ophthalmology. He is married with four children and lives in Colorado.